N. SCOTT MOMADAY

D1104878

N. Scott Momaday

N. SCOTT MOMADAY

The Cultural and Literary Background

BY MATTHIAS SCHUBNELL

UNIVERSITY OF OKLAHOMA PRESS : NORMAN AND LONDON

The paper in this book meets the guidelines for permanence and durability of the Committee on Production Guidelines for Book Longevity of the Council on Library Resources, Inc.

Library of Congress Cataloging-in-Publication Data

Schubnell, Matthias, 1953–
    N. Scott Momaday, man made of words.

    Bibliography: p. 299
    Includes index.
    1. Momaday, N. Scott, 1934– . 2. Authors,
American—20th century—Biography. 3. Kiowa Indians
in literature. 4. Indians of North America in
literature. I. Title.
PS3563.O47Z87   1985   818'.5409   85–40479
ISBN 0–8061–1951–9

Publication of this work has been made possible in part by a grant from the Andrew W. Mellon Foundation.

Contents

Acknowledgments

Many persons have contributed to this book by giving their time, advice, criticism, and support. To all of them I extend my sincere thanks.

I am particularly grateful to three teachers who educated and encouraged me at the University of Heidelberg: Josef Schwarz, who guided my first steps as a student of literature with the dedication of a learned mentor; Ronald Hindmarsh, whose rare talent to inspire and motivate led me to a deeper appreciation of literature and to invaluable experiences in England and America; and Herwig Friedl, whose loyal support sustained me in my research of American Indian literature.

At Bucknell University my critical perceptions were sharpened under the guidance of the late John Tilton, whose kindness I shall always remember. I owe much to Dennis Baumwoll, who helped me overcome some of the limitations of writing in a second language; and to Richard Drinnon, who introduced me to the work of N. Scott Momaday and made me sensitive to the problems of American Indian peoples.

I am indebted to Mike Weaver, who supervised my research at Oxford and whose sound judgment and confidence in my project helped me bring it to fruition. My special thanks go to N. Scott Momaday for his generous assistance in supplying information, unpublished material, and the illustrations to this book. I am indebted to Charles Lowell Woodard and Jack W. Marken, of South Dakota State University, who read part of my manuscript and offered excellent advice. I acknowledge my debt to the Cecil Rhodes Trust and the German Academic Exchange Service, which provided the funds for my research.

I am grateful to the following for permission to quote from the listed works:

Reprinted by permission from *The Way to Rainy Mountain*, © 1969, University of New Mexico Press.

Reprinted by permission of Harper & Row, Publishers, Inc.: *House Made of Dawn*, copyright © 1966, 1967, 1968 by N. Scott Momaday; *The Names*, copyright © 1976 by N. Scott Momaday; *The Gourd Dancer*, copyright © 1976 by N. Scott Momaday.

Reprinted by permission of Alfred A. Knopf, Inc., and Faber and Faber Publishers: *The Letters of Wallace Stevens*, edited by Holly Stevens, copyright © 1966; *The Collected Poems of Wallace Stevens*, copyright © 1954; *The Necessary Angel: Essays on Reality and the Imagination*, copyright © 1951.

Quoted by permission of the Bancroft Library: Correspondence and manuscripts by N. Scott Momaday deposited in the Bancroft Library.

From F. G. Tuckerman, *The Complete Poems of Frederick Goddard Tuckerman*, edited by N. Scott Momaday, copyright © 1965 by Oxford University Press, Inc. Reprinted by permission.

N. SCOTT MOMADAY

Introduction

N. Scott Momaday is an American Indian of Kiowa origin. He grew up among the Navajo and Jemez peoples of Arizona and New Mexico. Literary critics have directed their attention largely to his American Indian background and the ethnic elements in his work. This narrow critical perspective has failed to reveal the more complex literary and cultural influences which have shaped his writing. In an interview Ralph Ellison made this comment on the question of labeling writers according to their ethnic backgrounds:

> My approach is that I'm an American writer. . . . I write out of the larger literary tradition—which, by the way, is part Negro—from Twain to Melville to Faulkner. Another element I'm aware of is American folklore. And then all this is part of the great stream of literature.
>
> Americans didn't invent the novel. Negroes didn't invent poetry. Too much has been written about racial identity instead of what kind of literature is produced. Literature is color-blind, and it should be read and judged in a larger framework.[1]

This statement by a black writer addresses the very problem with which Indian and other minority writers are confronted: the ethnic label imposed on them by literary critics tends to draw attention to their "otherness," while their place in the larger context of society and the relation of their work to literature in general tends to be undervalued.

The temptation to examine Momaday's work only for its

"Indian" qualities has been considerable. Two examples of such approaches may suffice to show their shortcomings. A reviewer of Momaday's *The Names: A Memoir* suggested that the essence of the book is "undeniably Indian, with only an Indian's understanding of the beauty and value of life."[2] Margaret F. Nelson operated with similar racial criteria in her study of Momaday.[3] She claimed that one reason why Momaday "may be difficult to understand is that he 'thinks like an Indian'" and added that "Momaday is typically Indian in his refusal to explain."[4] She concluded that "Momaday's search for his identity is selective in typically Indian fashion."[5]

The use of the adjective "Indian" as a critical term is untenable because it is so vague as to be meaningless. More important, the suggestion that Momaday's work is reflective only of some kind of aboriginal mentality betrays an insufficient understanding of the context from which his writings emerge. Such a critical stance inevitably leads to an unbalanced and restricted view of his importance as a writer and may even give rise to racial stereotypes. Wallace Stegner made the point that Momaday should be recognized as the skilled and subtle writer he is, quite apart from the subject matter or his racial affiliation. He expressed his regret that "when a western American writer does get noticed, he may be noticed for the wrong reasons, and in Momaday's case, it is surely true that he is noticed to a considerable extent because he is Indian, and therefore bizarre."[6]

Racial identity is an important concern of many minority writers and thus demands the critic's attention. But since their identities are shaped in the tension between cultures, they embrace elements and patterns from different backgrounds. Moreover, these writers do not work in an artistic vacuum. They are free to incorporate elements from literature and art outside their immediate cultural spheres. Duane Niatum, a poet of Klallam descent, welcomed the use of English rather than tribal languages and the blending of components from diverse cultures in the works of indigenous writers. In an article significantly entitled "On Stereotype" he wrote:

. . . any Native American who takes the written arts seriously must train himself to become sensitive to the many facets of the English language, with the same devotion a shaman had for his healing songs a thousand years ago. Like the old shaman, he must gladly spend his life becoming more and more aware of the limitless ways in which he can discover how life shapes his language, and language, his life. Of course, as much as is humanly possible, the world's literature and arts ought to be made his own.[7]

The value of works by writers from minority groups lies not primarily in their depiction of traditions alien to the reader but in the way they bridge the gap between cultures and join literary and artistic traditions. Since the ethnic label distracts from these qualities, it is not surprising that many writers resent it.

Ellison, Saul Bellow, Duane Niatum, James Welch, and Momaday have all rejected categorization as black, Jewish, and Indian writers.[8] Momaday has made it plain that he does not consider himself an "Indian writer nor a spokesman for the Indian."[9] He stressed that "the contemporary Native American has himself determined, in good measure, the idea that we must have of him—that is to say that he must have of himself. . . . He stands now to realize himself *in the whole world*, having at last stepped out of the museum that we have made of his traditional world" (italics added).[10] Momaday's personal background and his academic interest in literature explain why his work is marked by cross-cultural fertilization. Yvor Winters, his Stanford University tutor, and writers like William Faulkner, Emily Dickinson, D. H. Lawrence, Isak Dinesen, Albert Camus, and Wallace Stevens, to name only a few, have left their mark on Momaday's writings. This crucial point would be missed entirely if one were to follow those critics who argue that "American Indian literature is something unique, and, as such, should be taught as something distinctive from American literature written by non-Indian authors."[11] It is against this critical stance that this study has been conducted.

The examination of the cultural and literary influences on Momaday's work in the following chapters requires some introductory remarks on the problem of stereotyping American Indians and on their contemporary situation. These two issues are crucial for an appreciation of literature by indigenous writers. Momaday made the point that "the Indian . . . , by virtue of his diversity, has been rather more difficult to identify than have other Americans. His ethnic definition, whatever it is, consists in an intricate complex of experience, and in numerous categories of language, philosophy, and society."[12] The recognition of these facts has been sadly missing in the history of Indian-white relations, and the resulting lack of understanding is one of the motivations for the self-portrayal of American Indian writers today. Momaday noted that "we have insisted in our fashion upon formulating a notion of 'the American Indian' and have therefore precluded at once the possibility of defining, let alone understanding his essential character and condition."[13]

The term "Indian" has indeed been a useful, if deceiving gloss for a highly complex and diverse set of cultures. It has been the cornerstone of a system of thought which enabled non-Indians to rationalize and account for the existence of native people with whom they came in contact. The fact that notions of "the American Indian" have been changing in the course of history indicates that they reflect more the character of the observers than that of those observed.

The aboriginal peoples of the Americas owe their name, of course, to Columbus's faulty geography in his search for a passage to India. The earliest depictions of "los indios" by him and, in 1504, by Amerigo Vespucci already contained the two extreme images of the Indian which were to remain dominant antipodes in the Western conception of American Indians in the centuries to come: the innocent, childlike, peace-loving, noble savage and the cunning, bloodthirsty, ignoble savage.[14] The dominance of one image over the other depended largely on whether the comparison of aboriginal life with European-American culture was intended to render proof of the superiority of Western civilization or to put forward a critique of civilized life. In both cases American Indians were viewed not in their own terms, as members of diverse and dynamic cultural groups, but as counter images against which Western societies could be interpreted.

It was the image of the ignoble savage which provided justification for the colonial pursuit and religious conversion of the indigenous tribes. Judged by the values of Christianity and European civilization, aboriginal cultures appeared to the vast majority of colonists to be inferior and in need of amelioration. Initially, the belief in a monogenetic origin for all mankind made the Indian at least potentially equal and explains the missionaries' sense of duty to "civilize" him. If the Indian could be educated, they believed, his soul might be rescued, and his land would become accessible to the settlers without the use of force. The idea of basic equality faded rapidly, however, when it became clear in the second half of the eighteenth century that the missionizing effort had generally been a failure. This realization led to a profound change in attitude toward Indians.

The idea of degeneration, a theory used since the late sixteenth century to explain cultural differences in terms of a departure from the Edenic ideal, was now applied to the Indian and suggested the irreversibility of his supposedly primitive status. His failure to embrace civilization was taken as proof that he represented a remnant of an age which had lost its right to continued existence. This conclusion also solved the moral question inherent in the young nation's demand for Indian land. Once it was established that the Indian was an obstacle to progress, the removal policy of the 1830s seemed a justified means to facilitate the westward expansion of the United States.

Scholarly "evidence" for the backwardness of American Indian cultures, provided by the new theory of evolution and the rise of scientific racism in the latter part of the nineteenth century, further legitimized, in the eyes of most white Americans, the concerted effort of dispossession and genocide which reduced the Indian population to pitiable condition by the end of the century.[15] By then the remaining native peoples were

vegetating on reservations which Momaday described as nothing less than "contagious colonies and concentration camps."[16]
The disruption of aboriginal life as the result of disease,
removal, and military defeat gave rise to the theory that the
Indian was doomed to extinction. This "vanishing-race"
theory, in which a sense of pity about the demise of the noble
savage, as he was now seen, conjoined with the interest in his
dwindling way of life, generated a host of activities to preserve
native cultures. If the actual people could not be saved, at least
their cultural remnants would remain accessible in museums
and libraries. This turn of events resulted in a projection of the
Indians into the past. Once their lives could be represented by
artifacts and museum pieces, their actual existence could be
ignored.

The projection of American Indians into the past is still a
prevalent attitude among non-Indians today. Robert Berkhofer's point that "modern Native Americans and their contemporary life-styles have largely disappeared from the White
imagination" is probably not exaggerated.[17] The new images
of the Indian in the public mind have emerged as a result of
primitivistic longings in a society whose trust in limitless technological advance and a purely scientific, materialistic view of
the natural environment is no longer secure. The Indian as
keeper of mystical knowledge or as natural ecologist is an up-
dated version of earlier images which reveals more about the
state of the dominant society than about contemporary Indians. Ironically, Momaday himself has come close to falling victim to the temptation of image making in his contributions to
the Indian-as-ecologist debate.[18] This shows that Indians are
not immune to adopting images created by mainstream American culture. On the whole, however, Momaday's work depicts
the worlds of American Indians objectively and without racial
bias.

Momaday has made clear his view on a contemporary self-
concept of Indians in many lectures, articles, and interviews.
He is an outspoken critic of the belief that a rigid adherence to
traditional ways of life is desirable for indigenous peoples, re-

gardless of whether this position is advocated by Indians or non-Indians. Momaday called the tradition-oriented Pueblos of the Rio Grande Valley "the most anachronistic clusters of humanity in this country, . . . islands of refuge in time and space, committed absolutely to the principles of independence and isolation."[19] He sees life on the reservation only as a stage of transition in the development toward a fusion of native and Anglo-American cultures in the framework of modern society. He noted that

it is imperative to consider that the Indian is, for the time being, better off in his own world than in another. His is the only world in which he has a fighting chance. Certainly the Indian cannot remain indefinitively isolated; that is neither possible nor desirable. When the Indian no longer needs the reservation, he will leave it of his own accord.[20]

Momaday witnessed the conflicts inherent in the interaction between native cultures and the dominant society. He knows that "there's a lot of violence in the Indian world—just now particularly. It's one of the manifestations of a loss of identity. The confrontation between the two worlds (the Indian and the rest of America) is essentially violent."[21] Momaday's call for a new definition of identity is essentially an attempt to resolve this conflict. He is concerned with a native identity which manifests a compromise between the extremes of traditionalism on the one hand and complete cultural assimilation, that is, the rejection of a tribal heritage, on the other. Momaday summed up the necessary steps toward a new and realistic conception of Indian existence in modern America:

The Indian, in order to discover who he is, must do that on a comparative basis. It does him no good to know who he is, so long as that knowledge isolates him . . . alienates and shuts him off from the possibilities that are available to him in the world. No. He must take advantage of the possibilities, recognizing the opportunities and taking advantage of them, retain his identity. We don't want to "freeze" the Indian in time, to cut him off at a certain point in his development. We don't want to end up with a 19th century man in the 20th century. He doesn't want that, and neither do any of us. It's just simply not among the available and desirable possibilities. He has to venture out, I think, beyond his traditional world, because there is another very real world. And there are more worlds coming, in rapid succession. But it is possible for him to make that adventure without sacrificing his being and identity.[22]

While this position is generally accepted by Indians, with the possible exception of an extremely conservative minority, it is still difficult for many Americans to reconcile it with their image of the Indian. After one of his public lectures Momaday was asked why he had "chosen the white man's way."[23] This question betrays the ethnocentric assumption that Western civilization is historical and dynamic while American Indian cultures are ahistorical and static. Berkhofer explained this common fallacy by saying that "if the Indian changed through the adoption of civilization as defined by Whites, then he was no longer truly Indian according to the image, because the Indian was judged by what Whites were not. Change toward what Whites were made him ipso facto less Indian."[24]

Confronted with such misconceptions, Indians today, according to Momaday, will "no longer allow their destiny to be determined by others or by their past. They are conceiving a new idea of themselves."[25] This idea is not a rejection of a tribal past. It is based on the belief in the necessity of cultural change and its compatibility with a continuing imaginative and emotional involvement in an indigenous heritage.

The achievement of a new self-concept is as difficult as it is necessary. The anthropologist Murray L. Wax made the point that "identity for a traditional Indian band was given and irrevocable." However, for most contemporary American Indians, who are "the product of mass society, the status of 'Indian' can only be maintained by a forceful act of will in the face of pressure and hostility, both from within and without the Indian world."[26] Momaday sees this act of will as an act of the imagination and places it at the center of his artistic work. "We are what we imagine," he says. "Our very existence consists in our imagination of ourselves."[27] In a modern world,

Indians can retain their tribal identities only through an intellectual and imaginative effort to keep alive their indigenous heritages.

For many, including Momaday, this means a conscious search for their racial origins and histories. Wallace Stegner, who has known Momaday since he was a student at Stanford, wrote about his personal and artistic growth: ". . . I have seen him gradually comprehending, accepting, even asserting his Indianness. Actually, of course, his Indianness is as much assumed as inborn."[28] This is not to say that Momaday is not a genuine Indian. Stegner's point is that with his mixed racial background Momaday has made a conscious decision to opt for and explore in depth his Indian heritage. Alfonso Ortiz, a leading Indian anthropologist and collector of oral traditions, remarked on the contemporary search for an indigenous identity that "the descendants of those tribes which were early overwhelmed by an advancing civilization have already begun to seek in archives for their identity."[29] Leslie Fiedler observed that "the Indian has begun to reinvent himself—in part out of what remains of his own tribal lore, in part out of the mythology and science created by White men to explain him to themselves."[30] Momaday has used his artistic talent to create an idea of himself out of his Kiowa heritage, his knowledge of other Indian cultures, his experience in modern American society, and his study of literature. All of these factors must be considered in an assessment of Momaday's work.

In drawing on historical, anthropological, literary, and biographical sources, this study of the cultural and literary background of Momaday's writings aims at a comprehensive and balanced evaluation of his art.

CHAPTER 1

A Biographical Sketch

N. Scott Momaday was born on 27 February 1934, in the Kiowa and Comanche Indian Hospital at Lawton, Oklahoma. His name was entered on the birth certificate as Navarro Scotte Mammedaty. Momaday had been written first but was subsequently crossed out.[1] In 1932 his father had officially changed his surname, Mammedaty, to Momaday.[2] Momaday's Indian status is documented in a notarized paper issued by the United States Department of the Interior, Office of Indian Affairs, Anadarko Area Office:

This is to certify that the records of this office show that Navarro Scotte Mammedaty was born February 27, 1934 at Lawton, Oklahoma and is of ⅞ degree Indian Blood, as shown on the Kiowa Indian Census role opposite Number 2035. The official Government agency records further show that his father is Alfred Mammedaty and his mother is Natachee Scott.

By Act of June 2, 1924 (43 Stat. 253), all Indians born within the territorial limits of the United States were declared to be citizens of the United States.[3]

Momaday belongs to a generation of American Indians born when most tribal communities had long ceased to exist as vital and supportive social organizations. His Kiowa ancestors shared with other Plains Indians the horrors of disease, military defeat, and cultural and religious deprivation in the course of the nineteenth century. Their only chance of survival was adaptation to new circumstances. Momaday's grandfather Mammedaty, for example, adjusted to changing conditions by taking up farming, a decision pressed upon him by the General Allotment Act of 1887. This legislation was designed to accelerate Indian assimilation by destroying the communally held land base and thus undermining tribal solidarity.[4] The decision must have been painful for him since the Kiowas had never had a farming tradition. But it allowed Mammedaty to establish the basis for his spiritual survival. He continued to pray in the Kiowa language and lived according to the old tribal ways, defying the law's ultimate goal of enforced assimilation.

In the following generation Momaday's father faced the challenge of change by acquiring a formal education, which allowed him to take advantage of modern American culture without relinquishing the essential features of his Kiowa identity. In his youth he listened to the ancient tales of his tribe and began his artistic career as a painter by sketching scenes from Kiowa oral tradition. He also painted and drew from memory the dances and costumes of the southern Plains tribes.[5] Among his particular strengths were "expansively conceived, boldly executed patterns associated with the virile color and strong action of Kiowa ceremony and design."[6]

Educated at Bacone College and the Universities of New Mexico and California, Al Momaday was a well-known artist and distinguished teacher, deeply committed to his native heritage. As the principal of the day school at Jemez Pueblo, he established an arts-and-craft program which brought international recognition to the school.[7] He died in 1981.

Momaday's father "was born in a tipi in a world from which it was both necessary and costly to succeed" in order to build a future in the larger context of American society.[8] His mother, Natachee Scott, on the other hand, was removed by three generations from the Cherokee woman whose first name became her own. She grew up in what may be called a middle-class family and was educated at Haskell Institute, Crescent Girls College, and the University of New Mexico. She studied art and journalism and is today a well-known painter and writer, the author of many short stories and three books, *Woodland Princess*, *Velvet Ribbons*, and *Owl in a Cedar Tree*.[9]

Natachee Scott had to rediscover her Indian heritage through an intellectual and imaginative effort. Momaday wrote about his mother:

. . . she began to see herself as an Indian. That dim native heritage became a fascination and a cause for her, inasmuch, perhaps, as it enabled her to assume an attitude of defiance, an attitude which she assumed with particular style and satisfaction; it became her. She imagined who she was. This act of the imagination was, I believe, among the most important events of my mother's early life, as later the same essential act was to be among the most important of my own.[10]

Natachee's decision to turn down offers from the Universities of Kentucky, Louisiana, and Wyoming and to choose Haskell Institute instead was a reaction against the disparaging attitude toward Indian culture which her white maternal grandmother and aunt expressed to her. Their prejudices fueled her desire to learn from her father as much about her native heritage as possible. Later she insisted on making contact with other Cherokees of her own age and experiencing different native cultures by studying at the Indian college in Kansas. She remembered her time there:

. . . for the first time in my life I felt that I was among my father's and grandfather's people. I learned their different tribal cultures, songs, music, dances. Indians have a terrific sense of humor, and I loved that. . . . I believe I learned a great deal of Indian culture while I lived two years among some seventy different tribes.[11]

Given his parents' academic background and their integration into Anglo-American culture, which did not sever their ties to their Kiowa and Cherokee ancestors, Momaday's prospect for a successful and truly bicultural education was better than it is for many young American Indians. His upbringing was less than tribal, and more than tribal. Unlike many Indians who find themselves trapped between two cultures, he could draw on the benefits of both. Momaday would model his own venturing out into the modern American world on the experiences of his parents and his grandfather Mammedaty.

The main event in Momaday's first year was a journey to Devil's Tower, in Wyoming. This trip to the Black Hills with his parents is of particular significance in that it constitutes a kind of initiation into the culture of his Kiowa ancestors. In one of their ancient stories the Kiowas had accounted for the creation of Devil's Tower (Tsoai), which they passed on their migration from Yellowstone to the southern plains.[12] Tsoai-talee, Momaday's Kiowa name, is derived from this story and translates to "Rock Tree Boy."[13] It was given to him by an old Kiowa man, Pohd-lohk, when he was six months old.

The purpose of the journey to one of the legendary places of Kiowa history lay in his parents' hope that "by means of the child the memory of Tsoai should be renewed in the blood of the coming-out people."[14] This example shows how from the very beginning of his life Momaday's development has been tied to his Kiowa heritage.

The friction between Momaday's mother and her husband's family, who considered her an outsider and treated her with contempt and cruelty, was a reason why the young couple and the two-year-old boy left Kiowa country and went west.[15] It was only during the summer months of later years that Momaday returned with his father to Oklahoma. These sporadic reunions with the Kiowa people were of lasting significance in creating his sense of belonging to a racial past. Although Momaday never learned the Kiowa language, he became familiar with the old tales and the history of his tribe. "There was great feasting," he remembered, "and people always came around to talk, to gossip, to laugh. It was then that I learned it was a privilege to be an Indian."[16]

Between 1936 and 1943, Momaday and his parents lived on the Navajo reservation at Shiprock, New Mexico, at Tuba City and Chinle, Arizona, and for several months on the San Carlos Reservation in southeastern Arizona. During this time, which was mainly spent in Dine Bikeyah, Navajo country, Momaday became familiar with Navajo culture and learned some of their language.

In 1943 the family moved to Hobbs, New Mexico, where Momaday's father found employment with an oil company and his mother worked for the U.S. Army at Hobbs Air Force Base. ˡThis "raw, undistinguished town on the flat hot apron of the Staked Plains," as Momaday remembered it, was to be his home for the next three years. [17] It was here, when he was nine, that he wrote his first poem, a tribute to a favorite dog. Somewhat later, under the impression of the battle preparations at Hobbs, he wrote a long epic poem about the men going to war. [18] Momaday's memories of this period show that his experiences and daydreams were not different from those of other boys growing up in World War II America. War heroes, football stars, and motion pictures figured prominently in his imagination, but there was also a growing awareness of his Kiowa heritage, which complemented his integration into mainstream American culture, and this set him apart from his non-Indian companions.ₗ

Momaday was proud of his "Indianness" without being able to define what it really was. His friends called him "chief," and he knew that he was different, but he was, as he later put it, "enough non-Indian to get along in either world." He added: "I never experienced the kind of segregation that a lot of Indian students do. I went to Indian schools, but my position in all of those schools was ambiguous. . . . I had the best of both worlds when I was growing up."ₗ[19]

During the war years at Hobbs, Momaday's parents felt a growing desire to return to the Indian world from which they had come. ˡWhen in 1946 they were offered teaching positions at a two-teacher day school at Jemez Pueblo, they welcomed the opportunity. Momaday remembered vividly his first awakening in the new home which was to become a definitive influence on both his personal and his artistic development:

One autumn morning in 1946 I woke up at Jemez Pueblo. I had arrived there in the middle of the night and gone to sleep. I had no idea of the landscape, no sense of where in the world I was. Now, in the bright New Mexican morning, I began to look around and settle in. It was the last, best home of my childhood.[20]

In the following years Momaday became closely acquainted with Pueblo Indian culture and the unique landscape of the Rio Grande valley:

Gradually and without effort I entered into the motion of life there. In the winter dusk I heard coyotes barking away by the river, the sound of the drums in the kiva, and the voice of the village crier, ringing at the roof tops. And on summer nights of the full moon I saw old men in their ceremonial garb, running after witches— sometimes I thought I saw the witches themselves in the forms of bats and cats and owls on fenceposts. I came to know the land by going out upon it in all seasons, getting into it until it became the very element in which I lived my daily life.[21]

Jemez Pueblo is a Towa-speaking village situated in the Canyon de San Diego on the east bank of the Jemez River, in Sandoval County, New Mexico.[22] During the years Momaday and his parents lived with the people of Jemez they became close friends with them. However, they lived in their community without being of it. They were excluded from the ceremonial practices to which only Jemez people were admitted. Momaday's parents worked in the small day school of the village but took up residence in Jemez Springs, a few miles up the narrow canyon. They settled in an old stone house called Stonehenge, once the rectory of the parish church, Our Lady of the Assumption. Momaday has described his family home as reminiscent of a castle or a haunted parsonage on the Yorkshire moors; its name reflects its druidic mystery, a sense of timelessness which informs the house and invites the mind to meditate and dream.[23] This sense of being removed from ordinary clock time was for Momaday reinforced by the spectacular sights of dawn and sunset, which created a dazzling composition of light, color, and shadow on the red-and-white sandstone walls of the canyon. From such experiences he acquired, as he put it, "the sense that you have lived through genesis and seen into the watch works of geologic time."[24]

While his involvement in the particular landscape around Jemez and his observations of the ceremonial calendar in the Pueblo village enabled him to develop a sensitivity for the ancient rhythms of tribal life, he was at the same time witness to fundamental changes which took place at Jemez after the war. When Momaday arrived at the village, its population numbered less than one thousand. Over the two decades from 1950 to 1970 this number more than doubled. The mode of life in the pueblo was increasingly influenced by the material culture of Anglo-America: cars and trucks replaced horse and cart; electricity allowed the use of artificial lighting, refrigeration, television, and radio; and a sewage system was introduced in the 1960s. Veterans returning from the war brought with them the experience of a different life-style in modern America and found it difficult to reclaim their places in the village community. Many of the most able members left Jemez to work off the reservation and were unavailable to fulfill their functions in the ceremonial life of the pueblo. Momaday has commented on these profound changes: "The forces of civilization and progress have moved across the pueblo like a glacier and, in their path, nothing can ever be the same again. Convenience has brought the old attendant ills. Alcoholism has become a menace of frightening proportion. Juvenile delinquency, unknown to Jemez in 1946, is now a cancerous problem."[25]

Momaday was allowed to join in the ancient practice of planting the cacique's field, a communal service to free the leader of the village from economic obligations. At the same time he met young people who eventually lost their sense of place, escaped into alcohol, and died in car crashes or fights or suicide. In Momaday's view, "Jemez is in a sense a late chapter in the history of white-Indian confrontation. . . . the age-old cultural conflict now centers upon the sedentary reservations of the southwestern United States."[26] The human misery growing out of such culture and identity conflicts he later epitomized in the figure of Abel, the protagonist of *House Made of Dawn.*

The firsthand experience of cultural and personal disintegration among his Jemez neighbors during the postwar years undoubtedly contributed to Momaday's conviction that only a sense of self which embraced both Indian and Anglo-American realities could lead to a worthwhile future. ⌊Education played a central role in Momaday's bicultural upbringing, and his mother was the driving force behind it⌋ She knew from her own experience how important an academic education is for Indians and that it need not jeopardize native identity. She saw to it that Momaday learned English as his first language. She was convinced that "if he were ever of a mind to learn the most difficult Kiowa dialect (or language) he could certainly come back and learn it."[27]

Momaday was thirteen when he moved to Jemez. Until the completion of seventh grade he was educated at the Franciscan Mission School in the village. He spent the eighth grade at the Indian school in Santa Fe, studying at Leah Harvey Junior High School. The next stations of his educational career were Our Lady of Sorrows School in Bernalillo, Saint Mary's in Albuquerque, and Bernalillo Public High School.[28]

One of the first indications that his mother's emphasis on a thorough education was bearing fruit was his superior performance during his final year of high school at Augustus Military Academy, in Fort Defiance, Virginia.[29] Momaday was impressed by the school's atmosphere of tradition and rigorous learning. He excelled as a member of the fencing team and was awarded a prize in declamation.[30]

Momaday's mother recalls that the English master at the academy was "surprised" and "appalled" that an Indian boy from the Southwest should have a command of English superior to that of any other student in his class.[31] This teacher would not remain the only incredulous observer who could not reconcile his image of the Indian with Momaday's great linguistic gifts. One reviewer of *The Names: A Memoir* felt it necessary to comment on "Momaday's extraordinary command of English," implying, if unintentionally, that Indians can be expected to have only a limited competence in English.[32]

After graduation in August 1952, Momaday began his studies as an undergraduate at the University of New Mexico in Albuquerque. Although he lacked a sense of direction in his academic work, he won several awards in rhetoric and declamation.[33] He majored in political science and minored in English and speech. Between 1956 and 1957 he went to the University of Virginia, where he enrolled in the law program.

It was there that Momaday met William Faulkner. The Jefferson Debating Society, of which Momaday was a member, invited Faulkner for a reading. Momaday remembered him as an inspiring man, impressive in his confidence and authority. This meeting had a lasting effect on Momaday, whose literary career was just about to begin. He noted later: "I like Faulkner, and I've read a lot of Faulkner, and I want to write like Faulkner; . . . I'm sure that I have tried to, but to what extent Faulkner is an influence on me, I really don't know."[34]

Eventually Momaday realized that law was not his vocation. He returned to Albuquerque more unsure of his goals than ever. It was at this point in his career that he became seriously interested in writing.[35] He graduated in 1958 with a B.A. in political science and accepted a teaching post at the Dulce Independent School on the Jicarilla Reservation, in the northeastern corner of New Mexico.

He worked in a newly established special program for speech training—proficient oral expression in English—which had been introduced in several New Mexico schools with majorities of Indian students. This is how Momaday judged the particular significance of this period:

In a sense the year that I spent at Dulce was critical for me. The course of my future life was determined there. I wrote in my spare time, of which there was a great deal, full of peace and quiet; and on the basis of my writing I was admitted to graduate school in California. It all happened so quickly! I was quite content at Dulce—in a rich, romantic way—and not until the very end did I have any intention of leaving. Had fate not intervened I should be there now, I believe.[36]

This fateful intervention was brought about by Yvor Winters, professor of English, literary critic, and creative-writing teacher at Stanford University. A friend, Bobby Jack Nelson, had urged Momaday to apply for the Wallace Stegner Creative Writing Scholarship in prose and poetry. This grant offered gifted writers a year of study at Stanford under the supervision of Wallace Stegner, who was responsible for prose, and Yvor Winters, who conducted the poetry class. Winters selected the candidates in poetry, and in a letter to Momaday announcing his election, Winters explained that he had "made the decision, and the matter is settled." Not surprisingly, Momaday was startled by this statement from a man he had never met, but, as he later remembered, the announcement "turned out to be exactly Winters; it was exactly his attitude in the way he spoke."[37] The fellowship, awarded him "in recognition of his respect for, control of, and enjoyment in using language," opened the door to an academic and artistic career and marked the beginning of a deep friendship between the two men which lasted until Winters's death in 1968.[38]

While Momaday was studying political science at the University of New Mexico, he was at the same time pursuing the interest in literature which his mother had cultivated early in his life. As the guardian of D. H. Lawrence's New Mexico writings, the English Department in the University of New Mexico put great emphasis on Lawrence's work and saw to it that Momaday got "a pretty strong dose of Lawrence," an influence which was to leave its mark on some of his later work.[39] Another writer who aroused Momaday's interest during that time was Hart Crane. Crane's attempt to fit the primitive, instinctual, mythic aspects of the New World and the modern, scientific, and artistic achievements of America into an organic whole caught Momaday's imagination. His discovery of Crane's poetry reinforced his own concern with the conflicts between pastoral and technological societies and between the aboriginal and the "civilized" Americas, both of which he knew so well. Crane's poem "The Bridge" influenced Momaday's first published poem, "Los Alamos," and many other pieces of this early period which Momaday did not preserve.[40]

Despite Momaday's avid reading and his experience as a young poet, such a prestigious institution as Stanford was somewhat intimidating, to say the least. This is how he re-called his early days on campus: "I was dazzled by the people around me, not only my professors, but the students as well, who had come from Harvard and Yale, Berkeley and Brandeis. They had all read Henry James; I had read Will James (not William, but Will)."[41] He was, of course, referring to the cowboy author and illustrator who gained popularity through his depictions of western life in such novels as *Cowboys, North and South*, *Smoky*, *Cow Country*, and *Sun-Up*.[42] By his own ad-mission Momaday "knew very little about poetry" and "could not tell a trochee from a iamb" before Winters took him under his wing.[43] Moreover, he had no intention of academic training beyond his fellowship period. He was intent on writing a long, narrative poem tentatively entitled "House Made of Dawn," and he planned to return to his teaching post with the Jicarilla Apaches at Dulce the following academic year. But encourage-ment to embark on an academic career was provided by Yvor Winters, who had identified Momaday's literary potential.

From the very start Momaday's encounter with Winters was fortunate. He had sent Winters a sample of his poetry, includ-ing "Earth and I Gave You Turquoise" and other pieces the-matically related to southwestern Indian life and the oral tra-dition. Momaday maintains that it was this subject matter which appealed to Winters. These early poems he submitted "were clearly Indian in character and I think he had an appre-ciation for what I was doing that very few other people would have had."[44] The reason for this becomes clear when one looks briefly at Winters's biography.

Winters entered the University of Chicago in 1917, where he joined the newly founded Poetry Club. As a member of this group he came in contact with Harriet Monroe, an editor of *Poetry: A Magazine of Verse*, who publicized the potential of American Indian verse to invigorate contemporary poetry.[45] As early as 1916 she published two experimental poems related to the Indian world by Constance Lindsay Skinner.[46] She had also been the driving force behind a special issue of *Poetry* dedicated to interpretations of tribal expressions by non-Indian poets.[47]

In this issue Carl Sandberg praised the work of Frances Densmore, one of the most accomplished translators of aboriginal oral expression, and stressed the importance of American Indian verse. In an ironic attack on those poets and critics who believed imagism in American poetry to be a modern phenomenon, he wrote, "Suspicion arises definitively that the Red Man and his children committed direct plagiarism on the modern imagists and vorticists."[48]

Young Winters became interested in this debate. He had received a complete set of *Poetry* from Harriet Monroe.[49] When in 1918 he left Chicago to be treated for tuberculosis in Santa Fe, he took his file of *Poetry* and other literary journals with him. These magazines and his books of poetry were his "chief source of education during a period of five years" in New Mexico.[50] Three of those years he spent in a sanatorium, and during the following two he worked as a schoolteacher in the mining camp at Madrid, twenty miles south of Santa Fe.

His geographical proximity to the Rio Grande Pueblos certainly increased his interest in American Indian cultures. In 1921 he spent some time at Ranchos de Taos, which had already become a colony of artists in search of the American aboriginal spirit in 1922. Winters's own artistic development during this early period was clearly affected by the close attention with which he followed the discussion of aboriginal verse and its incorporation into contemporary poetic production. He began to experiment with his own "Indian" poems.[51]

One event must have been particularly conducive to this development. During his stay at the Santa Fe sanatorium he met Alice Corbin Henderson, formerly the editor of *Poetry* and an active publicizer of the literary value of American Indian poetry. Winters had read her contributions to *Poetry*, such as her "Indian Songs"; an article entitled "A Note on Primitive Poetry," in which she had analyzed and praised aboriginal verse; and a review of George Cronyn's *The Path on the Rainbow*.[52] In the last piece she applauded Cronyn's anthology of Indian verse as "a genuine contribution to contemporary literature," drawing a connection between American Indian and non-Indian poetry:

Whether it is the spirit of the land reacting upon our poets to make them like the earliest owners of the soil and the sky, or whether it is due to some other cause, certain it is that these Indian poems are very similar in spirit and method to the poetry of our most modern American poets. Stephen Crane would have qualified as an Indian poet, and in the *Mid-American Chants* of Sherwood Anderson one finds almost precisely the mood of the songs accompanying the green corn dance of the Pueblo Indians.[53]

Winters borrowed Henderson's books and sought her advice on poetry.[54] One can safely assume that this relationship fed Winters's interest in American Indian literary production. He also read Frances Densmore's translations of Chippewa songs, which greatly impressed him: "These poems, so minute in appearance, shrill as the voice of a gnat dying out past the ear, are among the most endlessly fascinating poems of my experience."[55] With his characteristic strength of conviction he proclaimed that "the Wintu *Songs of Spirits*, translated by Jeremiah Curtin, are almost as tremendous as Blake."[56] He believed that other translations he had read, such as "the really great translations of Frances Densmore, Washington Matthews, Frank Russell, and Jeremiah Curtin . . . can take their place with no embarrassment beside the best Greek and Chinese versions of H. D. or Ezra Pound and which some day will do so."[57] Winters saw the spiritual value of American Indian verse manifested in two areas, namely

in a sense of the unity of the race and in a sense of the unity of both the race and the individual with the physical (which is also the spiritual, as there is only one) universe, which gives to all phenomena, personal or objective, an immediacy to the perceiver and a vastness of emotional implications, which our own culture, with all its ramifications of causes, explanations, and mystical dualisms, has lost, and which only the occasional artist—a Williams, for instance, or a Walsh—can regain for us. One feels in the unknown composer of the *Magpie Song* a consciousness of an entire race reacting to the freshness of all mornings on an everlasting prairie.[58]

Winters attempted to emulate these spiritual qualities in some of his own early poems, most notably in "The Magpie's Shadow," the title of which may have been inspired by the poem mentioned above. This cycle of one-line poems is based on American Indian verse forms.[59] Winters always retained an interest in Indian poetry. In the late 1940s he suggested that one of his doctoral students at Stanford, A. Grove Day, prepare a critical anthology of Indian verse. This dissertation, published in 1951 under the title *The Sky Clears: Poetry of the American Indian*, was dedicated to "Yvor Winters—Singer of Power."[60] Seven years later Winters received a sample of poetry from a Kiowa Indian, a descendant of the anonymous Kiowas whose poetry A. Grove Day had dealt with in her dissertation.

In the summer of 1959, Momaday met Winters in his home in Los Altos, California.[61] Winters became not only his guide into the world of English and American literature but, perhaps more important for Momaday at that time, a personal adviser who gave encouragement and built up the confidence necessary for the young poet to find his unique artistic expression. Momaday's respect and affection for Winters are apparent from the letters and articles in which he mentions him. On one occasion he wrote: "Yvor Winters . . . was one of the truly great men of his time, I believe. Until I met him, I had only vague, motion-picture ideas of greatness. Winters, more than any man I have ever known, had the strength of his convictions. I could not have imagined such moral and intellectual integrity."[62] While to Momaday Winters was something of a father figure, Winters saw in his student a promising literary talent.[63] During the first year of their cooperation Winters developed and formed this talent in his course "The Writing of Poetry," in which he instructed Momaday in traditional English verse forms, the postsymbolist method, and the art of syllabic poetry. One of the first successful products of this tutelage was "The Bear," a poetic re-creation of William Faulk-

ner's Old Ben in *Go Down, Moses*.[64] Winters expressed his satisfaction with it, saying that he wished he had written the
poem himself.[65] He repeated his praise later in his discussion
of the poem in *Forms of Discovery*.[66] However, the work at Stanford did not come easily to Momaday. His struggle against self-
doubt and insecurity is reflected in one of his early poems,
"Cocoon":

> I've come to know myself a chrysalis,
> Dehiscent, gorged, afraid the cockatrice
>
> Will turn his lethal stare summarily
> Upon my hope and insecurity.
>
> Where I foretold the days I've yet to live
> Thus, as I am, in doubt and tentative,
>
> Could I, without disdain or jealousy,
> Detect of my particularity
>
> Direction or degree of competence,
> Perception, knowledge, knack or excellence?
>
> My longest line's but half-encompassing.
> What judgment can of this defective thing
>
> Discern, delineate another state
> Than this, the poet inarticulate?
>
> The practiced mind translates adversity.
> I have to live with temporality
>
> Until, becoming merely old and ill,
> I pause for breath and am forever still.[67]

At the end of his first year at Stanford, Momaday submitted
for his M.A. degree "The Collected Poems of N. Scott Momaday," a collection of thirteen poems including "Earth and I
Gave You Turquoise," "The Bear," "Buteo Regalis," "Simile,"
and an early version of "Pit Viper," quite different from that
published in the *Angle of Geese* and *Gourd Dancer* collections.

During the following years Momaday's literary taste was
heavily influenced by Winters's lectures on major American
writers such as Nathaniel Hawthorne and Herman Melville

and major poets including Emily Dickinson, Hart Crane, and Wallace Stevens. Through Winters, Momaday became familiar with Jones Very and Frederick Goddard Tuckerman, two neglected nineteenth-century poets in the antitranscendental tradition, which Winters considered to be of the utmost importance. Momaday had intended to write his dissertation on Hart Crane, but Winters persuaded him to prepare a definitive edition of Frederick Goddard Tuckerman's poetry. This research led to a correspondence with Edmund Wilson, who had dealt with Tuckerman in *Patriotic Gore* and was one of the first literary critics to acknowledge the merit of this forgotten poet. Momaday suggested to Wilson some corrections in Wilson's discussion of historical and mythological allusions in Tuckerman's work. Wilson was impressed and offered his help in placing the complete edition with a publisher.[68] Momaday later acknowledged Wilson's generous support in the preface to the published edition.[69]

While working on his dissertation, Momaday continued to write poetry and discussed it in Winters's class with fellow poets Kenneth Fields, Phil Levine, and Robert Mezy. By the end of Momaday's studies at Stanford, Winters's rigorous instruction in the history of poetry and the techniques of writing verse had produced in Momaday a sense of saturation. He felt stifled, particularly by Winters's preoccupation with form, and his need for more elbow room led to the expansion of his creative work into prose.[70] He wrote "The Morality of Indian Hating," in which he blended expository prose with narrative, and a short story entitled "The Well."[71] During these first attempts at fiction he sought the advice of Wallace Stegner, who considered his writings "fragments, gropings" toward the new medium but also noted the rapid improvement of his prose toward "something solid and admirable."[72] "The Well" is an uneven, fragmentary story which is nevertheless interesting as a seminal piece foreshadowing the themes of conflict, violence, and witchcraft inherent in a tribal world, themes which were to be portrayed more fully in *House Made of Dawn*.[73]

After receiving his doctorate from Stanford in 1963, Momaday joined the faculty of the University of California at Santa Barbara, where he taught English and comparative literature until 1969. During this period he wrote what was to become his first great literary success, *House Made of Dawn*, a novel which he had started while working toward his degree at Stanford.[74] Yvor Winters remained his counselor in personal, artistic, and professional matters. Shortly after Momaday's graduation Winters wrote: "You are now a free man, but you will still have to study. This letter contains a little practical advice."[75] Over the next five years many such letters were to follow containing critical assessments of Momaday's progress as a writer, recommendations of literature which would prove influential to his work, and many words of encouragement reflecting Winters's deep conviction that his student was on the way to literary fame.

Winters saw Momaday primarily as a poet, and his expression of regret at the decline in poetic output after Momaday's departure from Stanford seemed to suggest a disapproval of his venture into prose.[76] That was not the case, however. To be sure, Winters believed that poetry was a much greater activity than the writing of prose, and this conviction provoked his statement of regret, but by the same token Winters was aware that Momaday showed great promise in prose as well. After a careful critical reading of "The Morality of Indian Hating," of which he warmly approved, he wrote to him: "Your talent for prose is probably equal to your talent for poetry. I see no reason why you should not be a famous man within ten years and perhaps a great one as well (they are not quite the same thing)."[77] He urged Momaday to try a combination of expository writing and fictitious, historical, or legendary narrative, advice which he was soon to follow in *The Way to Rainy Mountain.*

Winters closely monitored the genesis of *House Made of Dawn*, criticizing and praising its progress. After reading excerpts from it in the *Southern Review*, he wrote: "The chicken-pull section is one of the most brilliant things I have ever read. It ought to make your reputation right now, but it probably won't. If your novel, as such, is sufficiently solid to support this kind of writing, it will be a great novel and you will be very famous within a couple of years."[78] What at the time seemed like one of Winters's outrageous declarations, which earned him his controversial reputation in literary circles, turned out to have truly prophetic substance: less than two and a half years after this letter was written, Momaday was awarded the Pulitzer Prize for his first novel, which Winters never saw in its entirety. His death in 1968, only a few months before the book's publication, deprived him of sharing Momaday's triumph, in which he had such a great personal stake.

The English Department of the University of California at Santa Barbara asked Momaday to design a graduate-level course in American Indian studies which encompassed, among other things, the study of Indian oral tradition. This academic assignment coincided with a profoundly personal experience. Momaday had learned that the Tai-me bundle, a sacred object of veneration among the Kiowas, was extant and in the possession of a keeper in Oklahoma. His visit to this tribal shrine resulted in a strengthened sense of belonging to an ancient cultural heritage and in the realization that he had a responsibility in the fragile chain of Kiowa oral tradition.[79] The driving forces behind Momaday's search for Kiowa oral expressions and retracing of the migration route of his forefathers from the Yellowstone to the southern plains were his fear of the impending loss of much of Kiowa culture and his conviction that without a conscious exploration of his racial past he would foresake much of his human potential.[80]

The collection of Kiowa oral literature which Momaday subsequently compiled with the help of his father and Kiowa informers first appeared in a privately printed, limited edition entitled *The Journey of Tai-me*.[81] While much of his energy was focused on the Indian world during his work at Santa Barbara—apart from the Kiowa project he was continually working on *House Made of Dawn*—he did not neglect his scholarly interest in American poetry. In 1965 he published his dissertation, *The Complete Poems of Frederick Goddard Tuckerman*. On this occasion Winters highlighted the seeming incongruence between Momaday's Indian background and his literary and academic concerns in a letter to Orton Loring Clark, whose wife, Margaret, was Frederick Goddard Tuckerman's granddaughter and who had given his support to the compilation of Tuckerman's poems. Winters wrote: "Momaday is a Kiowa Indian. During Tuckerman's lifetime, the Kiowas were warring with the Cheyennes, the Comanches, and the Navahos, and were raiding Mexico and attacking white settlements this side of the border. . . . It might have amused Tuckerman if he had known that he would have a Kiowa for an editor a hundred years later."[82]

In 1964 Momaday had expressed his plan to probe more deeply into Tuckerman's poetry and his intellectual background and to place him alongside his fellow New England poets Very, Dickinson, and William Cullen Bryant. Winters advised him on this project and helped Momaday secure a Guggenheim Fellowship, which enabled him to take a leave of absence and move to Amherst, Massachusetts, in the fall of 1966.[83] The main objective of his research was to show the way in which Tuckerman and other writers remained outside the mainstream of nineteenth-century transcendental literature. Momaday's particular interest lay in the remarkable preoccupation with science which Tuckerman injected into his poetry. Unlike Emerson, who glossed over details in order to grasp wholes and comprehend cosmic unity, Tuckerman was scrupulously exact in his depiction of minute details and drew on a rich knowledge of astronomy, botany, and geology for his poetical renderings of the natural world. The connection between poetry and science emerged as the underlying theme of Momaday's study at Amherst, in which he included scientists such as Edward Tuckerman, the poet's brother and a noted scholar of botany at Amherst College, and Edward Hitchcock, an important geologist. In a letter to Winters, Momaday reported excitedly about his findings:

Everything has led me to the door of science. I am more and more impressed by the respect for science which such men as Edward Hitchcock and Edward Tuckerman instilled in this valley a hundred years ago. I was at Harvard yesterday, and I had a long and careful look at Emily Dickinson's herbarium; it is a remarkable thing. There was an introduction to astronomy in her father's library and, as you know, Frederick Goddard Tuckerman kept a notebook entitled "Journal of Astronomical and Meteorological Phenomena." If in the nineteenth century the Pioneer Valley was the last stronghold of orthodox piety, it was also the altar of science. The curious application of science to literature, the synthesis that Jonathan Edwards achieves for the first time in *Images and [sic] Shadows of Divine Things*, really comes of age in the third quarter of the nineteenth century at Amherst and Greenfield. In the same breath Hitchcock talks about permutations and poetry. He entitled one of his books "The Religion of Geology."[84]

In 1969, Momaday announced the forthcoming publication of his study under the tentative title *The Furrow and the Glow: Science and the Landscape in American Poetry, 1836–66*. He summarized it as dealing "with a particular quality of imagery— and a particular image—in American literature." He was "concerned primarily to investigate the way in which science informs the imagery and qualifies, to an important extent, a certain attitude toward the landscape in American intellectual history."[85] Despite this announcement and a preliminary contract with Oxford University Press, the work never reached publication.[86]

Momaday returned from Amherst to Santa Barbara, where he put the finishing touches to his first novel. *House Made of Dawn* was published in 1968, and a year later Momaday received the Pulitzer Prize for fiction.[87] While the literary establishment honored the first Indian with a major award, the American Indian community celebrated Momaday as its "Outstanding Indian of the Year." On 4 July 1969, he was formally initiated into the Gourd Dance, or Taimpe, Society, one of the ancient organizations of the Kiowa tribe. Momaday remembered the event thus: "Taft Hainta, the Taimpe Chief, gave me a beautiful red and blue robe, made of the finest German wool, which is the badge of the Taimpe Society, and my kinsman Marland Aitson made my trappings: a string of laurel beans, a sash, an eagle-feather fan, and a gourd rattle."[88]

In the summer of the same year the University of New Mexico Press published *The Way to Rainy Mountain*, which contains many of the stories from *The Journey of Tai-me* and additional historical, anthropological, and biographical material as commentary to the tales. In the fall of 1969, Momaday left Santa Barbara and moved to the University of California at Berkeley, where he was to stay for the next three years.

His literary output during this period was minimal, insofar as this can be assessed by the small number of publications, mostly reviews and short articles.[89] One of his published works is, however, of considerable significance. "An American Land Ethic" is an explicit statement in support of the conservationist movement, drawing public attention to the differences in attitude toward nature of aboriginal and non-Indian Americans.[90] With this article Momaday followed in the tradition of John Muir and Aldo Leopold, who campaigned vigorously for the preservation of the American wilderness and the extension of social ethics to include the relationship between man and his environment.

In the spring of 1972, Momaday began writing a weekly column for *Viva, Northern New Mexico's Sunday Magazine*. The eighty-six short essays which followed until December 1973 cover a wide range of topics and represent not only a wealth of information for the critic but a source on which Momaday was to draw later in writing his autobiographical work, *The Names*.

In the fall of 1972, Momaday joined the staff of Stanford University, but was immediately given leave to accept a post as the first Distinguished Visiting Professor of Humanities in New Mexico State University, at Las Cruces. His major project of the following year was a poetical sketchbook of Colorado, which Momaday produced in collaboration with David Muench, one of the most renowned photographers in the Southwest.[91] The combination of lyrical text and photography resulted in a magnificent celebration of the Colorado land-

scape, worthy of the tradition of joint ventures between pho-
tographers and writers which brought forth such classics as
Ansel Adams's and Mary Austin's *Taos Pueblo* and Adams's and
Nancy Newhall's *This Is the American Earth*.[92]

Momaday and Muench shared a belief in the spirit of place
and its bearing on individual human life, and it was this spiritual involvement in the natural world which stood at the center of their artistic expressions in *Colorado*. Muench explained
his stance:

I study under the tutorship of Nature. By being attuned to the
landscape—its natural rhythm and its pulse, the duration of time,
spatial forms, light, the mysterious—I am able, as a person, to
become involved in the presence of a place. . . . The underlying
ethos of my direction is to record the spirit of the land, a spirit of
place. . . . Hopefully, my work leads to the celebration of man and
the Earth and the mystical forces of nature which help shape our
destinies.[93]

While this statement is congruent with Momaday's approach
to the natural environment, Momaday also claims a racial stake
in his relationship to the Colorado landscape:

My mind has been involved in the landscape of Colorado for a long
time—from the moment I was old enough to conceive an idea of
my homeland (I have lived most of my life in view of the Rocky
Mountains); my blood even longer. For my ancestors were native to
the highlands of the continent. . . . A child who is born in the
mountains has them forever in his mind. They bear upon the mind
like a magnet. I have seen evidence of this in my own racial experience.[94]

Momaday masterfully employed the kind of prose poetry he
chose for the biographical commentaries in *The Way to Rainy
Mountain* to lend a voice to Muench's visual images, and his
precise descriptions of geological forms, plants, and the change
of seasons approach the intensity of his earlier nature poems.

Momaday returned to Stanford in the fall of 1973 to teach
his first term in the English Department. Again he dealt with
the art of storytelling and the oral tradition, but in the course

of the next eight years his seminars also included the western novel, the landscape in American literature, and nineteenth-century poetry. Afer only a few months in his new post he left again for the University of Moscow, where he taught a course on twentieth-century American literature during the spring semester of 1974. This experience had a crucial impact on his artistic activities.

Virtually all the poems collected in part three of *The Gourd Dancer* were written in Moscow, and in a number of unpublished pieces, among them "Bibi Khanym Mosque," "The Nickname of Nothing," and "Drawn in Lesions of Light," Momaday expressed his reaction to his new surroundings.[95] Russia not only demanded of him a direct poetical response, as in "Krasnopresnenskaya Station," but also focused his mind back to his origins in the United States. He noted: "One of the things about Russia that I could not have anticipated was the amount of time I would spend in my mind in the Southwest. My mind, at odd moments, when I was alone, harkened back to the Southwest. There seemed to be some kind of urgency to project myself back to my native landscape."[96] A poetical expression of this process of imaginative retrospection occurs in "Anywhere Is a Street into the Night":

> Desire will come of waiting
> Here at this window—I bring
> An old urgency to bear
> Upon me, and anywhere
> Is a street into the night,
> Deliverance and delight—
> And evenly it will pass
> Like this image on the glass.[97]

The stay in Moscow was a productive period for Momaday not merely as a poet. It was under the influence of Russia that he ventured into a new medium of artistic expression, drawing. As a boy Momaday had witnessed his father's creative work and his teaching of painting and drawing to the students at the Jemez day school. He had met other artists who visited

Al Momaday, among them the late Quincy Tahoma, who became a highly regarded American Indian painter.[98] Nevertheless, the sudden urgency to express himself in the new medium came as something of a surprise. "I have an idea," Momaday said, "that all the while I was growing up and watching my father at work at his easel or his drafting board, I was learning something about art, but I didn't put that together at first. When I went to Russia, something clicked inside me, and I began sketching and drawing. It became very important to me from that moment."[99] His fascination with the unlimited potentiality which informs drawing found expression in a poem of the same period. In "For the Old Man Mad for Drawing, Dead at Eighty-nine," Momaday wrote, "In this and that and another stroke / there is something like possibility / succeeding to infinity."[100] Two years later he returned to the same subject in *The Names*, investigating the relationship between language and visual representation in a drawing.[101]

Since 1974 painting and sketching have become for Momaday important forms of creative expression. In 1976, during a "great burst of energy," he audited a drawing class at Stanford. He also met the artist Leonard Baskin at his summer home in Maine, where he received some instruction in drawing.[102] Momaday's talent developed rapidly. From sketching and drawing in ink—three examples are included in *The Gourd Dancer*[103]—he moved on to acrylics and oil on canvas and, most recently, to etching. Often he has combined his artistic and literary talents, adding a drawing to a commemorative article for Yvor Winters and illustrating a limited edition of his poem "The Colors of Night."[104] Two sketches of his ancestors, Natachee Galyen and Anne Ellis, and a drawing of Devil's Tower, in Wyoming, are included in *The Names*.[105] Five illustrations complement his essay "The Pear-Shaped Legend: A Figment of the American Imagination,"[106] and a drawing of an aged Indian and his horse illustrates his poem "Plainview: 2."[107] A self-portrait of Momaday accompanied a published interview with University of Arizona students.[108] In March 1979, Momaday had a one-man show of drawings and paintings at the University of North Dakota, which was subsequently exhibited at galleries in Minneapolis and in Norman, Oklahoma. A large number of his works have been shown in Santa Fe and Phoenix.

The reception of his paintings, drawings, and etchings has been more than favorable. In 1980 he received an honorary doctorate of fine arts from Morningside College, and in 1981 in the Fifth Annual Exhibition of "Art from the Earth" in Norman, Oklahoma, he won the award in the contemporary art section. One of his projects has been a series of etchings depicting Plains Indian shields. In American Indian cultures shields, like names, represent the essence of a man. Like the drawings in the calendar histories of the Kiowas, the designs on the shields tell a story. In his six etchings Momaday brings together visual representation and oral tradition by blending design with calligraphy. He commented on this technique: "I've been interested in calligraphy as a visual element for its own sake, and it doesn't matter if people can read the text on these prints. Their actual meaning is far less important than the overall visual impression."[109] Momaday adapted the designs for his etchings from five shields in the Museum of the American Indian of the Heye Foundation, in New York, and from an Apache shield in his private collection. They have been reprinted as complements to six stories Momaday published under the title "Tsoai and the Shield Maker," Tsoai being, of course, one of his Indian names.[110] These stories are in the vein of those in *The Way to Rainy Mountain*, echoing the history of his Kiowa ancestors.

That since 1974 Momaday has concentrated on his development as a painter may be one reason why his literary output has been scarce in recent years. However, he has always heeded Yvor Winters's advice "Write little, do it well."[111] Winters once wrote to him that "any poet with a critical conscience will publish a small body of work."[112] Mindful of these words, Momaday collected only forty-three poems in *The Gourd Dancer*, the production of almost twenty years of poetry writing.

Momaday's latest book-length work appeared in 1976. *The Names: A Memoir* is a logical progression in the definition of his Indian identity. If *House Made of Dawn* illustrated the tragic consequences of an Indian's confusion over his place and self, and *The Way to Rainy Mountain* reflected Momaday's own exploration of his racial heritage, so *The Names* illustrates his personal quest for an American Indian identity. It has rightly been called an Indian *Roots*.[113] Together with his article "I Am Alive," it gives a full account of Momaday's tribal heritage.[114]

In 1981, Momaday moved to Tucson, where at this writing he teaches at the University of Arizona. In recent years he has lectured and given readings from his work on four continents; taught at Stanford, Princeton, and Columbia; and received the Pulitzer Prize and a score of other literary awards as well as eight honorary doctorates. His work has been translated into Russian, Polish, German, Italian, Norwegian, and Japanese. And yet, as important to Momaday as all these honors is the acceptance of his work by other American Indians, and not only by his Kiowa kinsmen. In a conversation Momaday mentioned a Navajo woman to whom he had given one of his books. She had read from it to an old man on the reservation, who said when she had ended: "The man who wrote this is a Navajo." Momaday takes great pride in the Navajo's compliment.[115]

N. Scott Momaday has no difficulties in reconciling his work at prestigious academic institutions with visits to the Navajo ceremony of the Yeibichai at Lukachukai or the Kiowa Gourd Dance at Carnegie, Oklahoma. No one has characterized him better than his friend Yvor Winters, who wrote to him: "You are an Indian in a white man's world and are doubly isolated, but the fact gives you a remarkable point of view. But . . . you are isolated by something else, and far more isolated: you are what the biologists call a mutation. You cannot account for such people by their pedigrees."[116]

The following two chapters examine what Winters may have meant by the word "mutation." Both chapters focus on the manner in which influences of different cultural and artistic traditions have crystallized in Momaday's work. Chapter 2 discusses his theory of language and the imagination in light of the oral tradition and his reading of Western literature. Chapter 3 attempts to show how Momaday's depiction of nature and the American landscape blends American Indian perceptions of the universe with the tradition of nature writing in American literature and other non-Indian influences.

The Man Made of Words: N. Scott Momaday's Theory of Language and the Imagination

Central to this chapter is Momaday's essay "The Man Made of Words," in which he discusses the nature of the oral tradition and, in general terms, his conception of language and the imagination.[1] His considerations are rooted in the belief that man's existence and reality find their fullest manifestation in language. The notion that "we don't really begin . . . to exist until we convert ourselves into language" is an underlying theme in Momaday's work.[2]

In *The Names*, Momaday describes his growing awareness of himself in terms of a discovery of language. In *The Way to Rainy Mountain* the Kiowas' emergence from the hollow log into the world is completely realized only through a transformation into language when they name themselves "Kwuda, the Coming Out People." In *House Made of Dawn* and in section six of "The Colors of Night," Momaday shows the consequences of failure in this process of articulation. One of the main causes of Abel's dilemma in *House Made of Dawn* is his inability to take possession of himself in relation to his social context and his natural environment through language. He is "inarticulate," and "he has not got the right words."[3] Significantly, it is not until his prayer, "Restore my voice for me," has been answered that he acquires a sense of belonging and identity. The parable of the child who appears in an Indian camp speaking an unintelligible language suggests that the ultimate reality of existence is not physical but linguistic and is shared by a community. The child, though well enough perceived, fails to become part of the community because it has given the people "not one word of sense to hold on to."[4]

The following statement is a key to the understanding of N. Scott Momaday as a writer and of the connection between his art and his personal identity: "It seems to me," he declares, "that in a certain sense we are all made of words; that our most essential being consists in language. It is the element in which we think and dream and act, in which we live our daily lives. There is no way in which we can exist apart from the morality of a verbal dimension."[5] Momaday's definition of an American Indian is also a self-definition: ". . . an Indian is an idea which a given man has of himself. And it is a moral idea, for it accounts for the way in which he reacts to other men and the world in general. And that idea, *in order to be realized completely, has to be expressed*" (italics added).[6] Momaday's writings are, to use one of Yvor Winters's phrases, "forms of discovery" as well as reflections of his being.[7] They are the medium by which he takes possession of himself in the realm of ideas. They allow him to explore, understand, and formulate his identity and the forces which have shaped it.

Before the determining factors which have contributed to his views on language and literature can be traced, it is necessary to understand Momaday's general theory of language. He suggests that language represents a dimension of reality which exists before and independent of individual existence. Human reality and consciousness are realized to the extent that man appropriates himself to this verbal dimension. Momaday explains:

You grow up into an understanding of language and through that to an understanding of yourself. That's how it has to happen. We are determined by our language; it holds the limits of our development. We cannot supercede it. We can exist within the development of language and not without. The more deeply we can become involved in language, the more fully we can exist.[8]

The Way to Rainy Mountain and *The Names* are two stages in Momaday's search for self-realization in language. In these two works in particular he tells the story of himself, an act which he describes as "a cumulative process, a chain of becoming, at last of being."[9] His lack of consciousness in childhood he attributes to the fact that he had not yet affirmed his existence in language: "Had I known it, even then language bore all the names of my being."[10] Self-realization, then, is a central motif in Momaday's creative work, and language the medium through which it is achieved.

It was not coincidence that Momaday's interest in assessing his exact position in relation to his Kiowa heritage and modern American culture and his preoccupation with the possibilities of language originated at approximately the same time. Momaday was nearly thirty years old and at the end of his academic training at Stanford when these concerns set in motion the creative ventures which produced, parallel to each other, *House Made of Dawn*, *The Journey of Tai-me*, and *The Way to Rainy Mountain*. He had, of course, been writing before and during his studies in California, but the work which emerged after 1963 is clearly of a different order. The creative process had become an act of conscious self-exploration. The largely philosophical, metaphysical themes of the poetry he wrote under Winters's supervision now gave way to more immediate personal concerns: the meaning of tradition for American Indians in a modern world, the question of reconciliation between a tribal past and contemporary American society—in short, the problem of "who am I?"

From the outset Momaday's upbringing and education were geared to a successful performance in the "white man's world." From very early on he was aware of his peculiar position on both sides of the dividing line between two cultures. His ability to move easily from one to the other constituted a valuable asset, although it could also be an obstacle. It was essential for him to be alert at all times to the advantages and limitations of his existence in two worlds. When he was a boy, his competence in English facilitated his progress at school, but it distanced him from a number of his peers whose language created a natural barrier. This distance deepened into isolation on the occasions of religious ceremonies from which he was excluded as a member of a different tribe. His claim to being a Kiowa, however, could not be disputed, and he was proud of it. At high school and at the military academy his background inevitably aroused interest and made him more self-conscious about his "Indianness." It may well be that the cultural and geographical distance from his home which he must have felt during the four years at Stanford gave rise to Momaday's need for an assessment of who he was. Winters's later statement testifies to that possibility: "You are an Indian in a white man's world and are doubly isolated, but the fact gives you a remarkable point of view."[11] The creative surge which followed the Stanford period seems to have been a logical response to this isolation.

Momaday, by his own admission, had always taken his native heritage for granted. Now he realized a need and a responsibility to spell it out. His encounter with the Tai-me bundle, the extant manifestation of the powerful Kiowa medicine, must have had a strong impact on his search for his racial past.[12] His research of Kiowa oral tradition, which was simultaneously an exploration into the meaning of language, and his journey along the migration route of his ancestors resulted from a desire to put himself into a racial context. The following statement, perhaps better than any other, reveals the kind of awareness Momaday had reached when he set out on his personal and artistic quests:

If the Indian is to be defined in terms of his tradition, then it becomes a matter of asserting one's self and preserving one's identity. . . .
. . . everybody is required at some point in his life to manifest his spirit, to express his spirit as he understands it. And for the Indian, I think that's one thing, as opposed to what it is for other people. He does that by keeping alive his traditions, by returning to them, by continually expressing them over and over again. *He works within the verbal dimension.* [Italics added][13]

This verbal dimension is, of course, the oral tradition. In the formulation of his spirit, however, Momaday draws on his knowledge of literature in general. He has made it clear that he has nourished his "imaginative life from both those sources."[14] Given his cultural and academic background, his views on the relations among language, reality, and the imagination grew out of his involvement in Kiowa oral tradition as well as out of his literary studies.

The basic compatibility between these two areas is grounded in the fact that the storyteller, whose only medium is the human voice, and the poet and novelist, who have recourse to writing, ultimately work toward the same goal, toward understanding existence and reality in language. Momaday's place in the oral as well as in the written tradition testifies to the universality of the human need to define existence through words.

Momaday once confessed that Emily Dickinson had taught him "a good deal about language—and in the process a good deal about the art of intellectual survival." He praised her for the "truly remarkable life of the mind" she lived.[15] Studying her poems gave him insight into "the mystery and miracle of language," and he realized the meaning of her writing to her personal existence: "Her survival was largely intellectual, . . . I don't suppose we know exactly what her life was, but it must have been painful to her in many ways, and I suspect she wrote in order to make it endurable."[16]

Momaday, too, sees the use of language in his creative work as a way of accommodating himself to life and achieving a greater awareness of his own being: "I don't want to make pronouncements, but I believe that I fashion my own life out of words and images, and that's how I get by. . . . Writing, giving expression to my spirit and to my mind, that's a way of surviving, of ordering one's life, . . . that's a way of making life acceptable to oneself."[17] This statement is relevant, to a greater or lesser degree, to all writers. There are, however, a number of poets and novelists in whose work Momaday found specific confirmation of the power of language and its role in the growth of human self-awareness.

One of them is the American poet Wallace Stevens, whose work Momaday greatly admires. One clue to Momaday's sym-

pathy for Stevens's nominalist poetry is the title of the essay
"The Man Made of Words," which focuses on the notion that
reality and human existence are constructs of the imagination.
Stevens argues this very point in a poem entitled "Men Made
out of Words." He suggests that reality consists of ideas in the
mind, that man creates his own life out of words in myths,
dreams, philosophical propositions, and, of course, in poetry:

> What should we be without the sexual myth,
> The human revery or poem of death?
>
> Castratos of moon-mash—Life consists
> Of propositions about life. The human
>
> Revery is a solitude in which
> We compose these propositions, torn by dreams,
>
> By the terrible incantations of defeats
> And by the fear that defeats and dreams are one.
>
> The whole race is a poet that writes down
> The eccentric propositions of its fate.[18]

In "The Idea of Order at Key West" Stevens gives an even
clearer example of the way man creates his own world in his
imagination:

> She was the single artificer of the world
> In which she sang. And when she sang, the sea,
> Whatever self it had, became the self
> That was her song, for she was the maker. Then we,
> As we beheld her striding there alone,
> Knew that there never was a world for her
> Except the one she sang and, singing, made.[19]

Reality has existence only in the mind of the perceiver. Stevens comments on this idealist position in two of his letters.
His statements show a striking similarity to some of Momaday's pronouncements on the same issues:

If poetry introduces order, and every competent poem introduces
order, and if order means peace, even though that particular peace
is an illusion, is it any less an illusion than a good many other things

that everyone high and low now-a-days concedes to be no longer of any account? . . .

In *The Idea of Order at Key West* life has ceased to be a matter of chance. It may be that every man introduces his own order into the life about him and that the idea of order in general is simply what Bishop Berkeley might have called a fortuitous concourse of personal orders. But still there is order. [20]

Momaday echoes Stevens's belief in the poet's task of creating order—"writing . . . is a way of ordering one's life," he said—and he shares the notion that man's view of his world is a product of the imagination, and thus illusory. [21] Like Stevens, Momaday invokes Bishop Berkeley's idealist position as a model for man's relation to the external world:

. . . There are modes and modes of existence. If a tree falls in the desert, and I am not there to see that it falls, it falls nevertheless. So I am told. But the event has to be perceived, I contend, or else it cannot be said to take place in fact. A thing is realized by means of perception, and not otherwise. Existence itself is illusory; we inhabit a dream in the mind of God. [22]

In subscribing to Berkeley's tenet of "esse est percipi," Momaday indicates that for him reality exists ultimately in the mind. "Life . . . ," he wrote in his autobiography, "is simply the construction of an idea, an idea of having existence, place in the scheme of things." [23] And the construction of this idea is the responsibility of the human imagination: "We are what we imagine. Our very existence consists of our imagination of ourselves. Our best destiny is to imagine, at least, completely, who and what, and *that* we are. The greatest tragedy that can befall us is to go unimagined." [24] This much-quoted statement is at the center of "The Man Made of Words" essay, in which Momaday elaborates on "the relationship between what a man is and what he says—or between what he is, and what he thinks he is." Momaday contends that "man has consummate being in language, and there only. The state of human *being* is an idea, an idea which man has of himself. Only when he is embodied in an idea, and the idea is realized in language, can man take possession of himself."[25] The imagination as the generating force of human reality is of the utmost importance for Momaday, as it is for Stevens. Momaday emphatically·expressed his belief "in the supremacy of the imagination."[26] Stevens, in his poem "Another Weeping Woman," addressed the imagination as "The magnificent cause of being, / . . . the one reality in this imagined world."[27] For Stevens, reality is a kind of fiction founded on sense perception and constructed by the human imagination. Momaday shares this position. He has confessed: "I believe that fiction is a superior kind of reality. What we imagine . . . that's the best of us."[28]

Momaday's nominalist position can be traced throughout his writings, often in the context of the oral tradition. Perhaps the most revealing statements of his belief in the creation of reality through language are the sermon of Tosamah in *House Made of Dawn* and the story of Momaday's encounter with Ko-sahn.[29] In the first instance Momaday compares the biblical and Indian creation stories. Creation through the Word is an idea common to many religions.[30] Momaday renders the moment of origin as an event in sound:

Something happened! There was a single sound. . . . Nothing made it, but it was there; . . . It was almost nothing in itself, a single sound, a word—a word broken off at the darkest center of the night and let go in the awful void, forever and forever. And it was almost nothing in itself. It scarcely was; but it *was*, and everything began.[31]

While in many American Indian religions the Word as the creative agent is the only truth and a mystery sufficient in itself, the biblical account of Genesis by John links the Word to a personal God. Momaday comments:

[John] was desperate and confused, and in his confusion he stumbled and went on. "In the beginning was the Word, and the Word was with God, and the Word was God." . . . He tried to make it bigger and better than it was, but instead he only demeaned and encumbered it. . . . He imposed his idea of God upon the everlasting Truth. "In the beginning was the Word. . . ." And that is all there was, and it was enough.[32]

This different attitude toward the original power of language represents a crucial contrast between native and non-Indian cultures in America. Tosamah serves as Momaday's mouthpiece when he says:

The white man takes such things as words and literature for granted, as indeed he must, for nothing in his world is so commonplace. . . . He has diluted and multiplied the Word, and words have begun to close in upon him. He is sated and insensitive; his regard for language—for the Word itself—as an instrument of creation has diminished nearly to the point of no return. It may be that he will perish by the Word.[33]

In contrast, the old Kiowa woman referred to in *House Made of Dawn* is fully aware of the fragility of the Word in an oral tradition: ". . . her regard for words was always keen in proportion as she depended upon them. You see, for her words were medicine; they were magic and invisible. They came from nothing into sound and meaning. They were beyond price; they could neither be bought nor sold. And she never threw words away."[34] Momaday's regard for language, then, derives from an idealist philosophy and a nominalist view of reality, but it is equally rooted in Indian thought, particularly, as the following example illustrates, in the Navajo view of the universe, with which Momaday is closely familiar.

Gary Witherspoon, in his study of the Navajo world view, pointed out that for the Navajos "mental and physical phenomena are inseparable" and that "thought and speech can have a powerful impact on the world of matter and energy."[35] This contradicts the dominant Western concept of separation of mind and matter, idea and entity, subject and object, which is responsible for the belief that thought or spoken words cannot affect the structure and operation of reality. According to the Navajo creation myth, the world was thought into existence by the Diyin Dine'é, the gods and supernaturals. The same concept is common to other peoples of the Southwest and is personified in the figure of Thought Woman.[36]

Navajos perceive the world as the external manifestation of primordial knowledge. All natural phenomena and beings are believed to have inner forms which are the product of thought and which can be influenced by speech. First Man and First Woman thought these inner forms into existence and assigned them their places and functions. Their final manifestation was then realized through words in prayer and song. The holiness of words is based on their creative power in thought, which gave rise to the universe in its present form, and on their trans-formative and regenerative power in speech, which allows man to control and manipulate the external world. Witherspoon summarized this complex conception of reality thus:

This world was transformed from knowledge, organized in thought, patterned in language, and realized in speech (symbolic action). The symbol was not created as a means of representing reality; on the contrary, reality was created or transformed as a manifestation of symbolic form. *In the Navajo view of the world, language is not a mirror of reality; reality is a mirror of language.*[37]

It is against this background that Momaday's description of Navajo and Pueblo singers at Jemez becomes meaningful: "It seemed to me that the singers—and especially the old men among them—bore everything up on the strength of their voices, the valley, the mountains, and the gray November sky; that if suddenly they should fall silent, the whole of Creation would collapse in a moment."[38]

The realization of existence through language and the crea-tion of reality through words are recurrent themes in Moma-day's work. The man made of words is a symbol of Momaday himself, his world, and the world of his characters. The first thing his Kiowa forebears did after their mythical emergence from the underworld was to give themselves a name, without which their emergence would have been unfinished and their existence incomplete. About himself Momaday says at the be-ginning of *The Names*: "My name is Tsoai-talee. I am, there-fore, Tsoai-talee; therefore I am."[39] He insists that to be is to have a name, to have existence in language:

I believe that a man is his name. The name and the existence are indivisible. One has to live up to his name. I think names are ter-ribly important. Somewhere in the Indian mentality there is that

idea that when someone is given a name—and, by the way, it transcends Indian cultures certainly—when a man is given a name, existence is given to him, too. And what could be worse than not
having a name.[40]

In one of his newspaper columns Momaday takes this idea out
of its American Indian context and presents it in an imaginary
dialogue between Isak Dinesen and Billy the Kid, thus indicating his belief in its universal significance:

> BILLY: . . . Once upon a time there was a man.
>
> ISAK: What was his name, pray tell?
>
> BILLY: That's just it; he had no name.
>
> ISAK (Delighted): No name! What an extraordinary tale! A
> tragic tale, I believe.
>
> BILLY: Yes, but . . .
>
> ISAK: But inasmuch as the man had no name . . .
>
> BILLY: Then he could not be said to exist, don't you see?
>
> ISAK: And therefore the tragedy is a minor one at best, since
> it involves no one.[41]

Perhaps the single most eloquent example of what Momaday
has called the "verbal dimension of reality" and the role of the
imagination in its creation is the story about his encounter
with the old woman Ko-sahn. When putting the finishing
touches to the manuscript of *The Way to Rainy Mountain*,
Momaday was struck by a sudden sense of doubt about the
reality and meaning of the words on the page in front of him.
In this moment of crisis a visionary experience restored his
belief in the magic of language:

> My eyes fell upon the name Ko-sahn. And all at once everything
> seemed suddenly to refer to that name. The name seemed to human-
> ize the whole complexity of language. All at once, absolutely, I had
> the sense of the magic of words and of names. Ko-sahn, I said, and
> I said again Ko-sahn!
> Then it was that that ancient, one-eyed woman Ko-sahn stepped
> out of the language and stood before me on the page.[42]

In the following dialogue Momaday suggests that his vision of the woman is only a figment of his imagination and questions the reality of her existence. Ko-sahn's reply encompasses Momaday's ideas of reality, language, and the imagination:

You have imagined me well, and so I am. You have imagined that I dream, and so I do. . . .
You imagine that I am here in this room, do you not? That is worth something. You see, I have existence, whole being, in your imagination. It is but one kind of being, to be sure, but it is perhaps the best of all kinds. If I am not here in this room, grandson, then surely neither are you.[43]

The conclusion of this mysterious encounter highlights Momaday's idealist position; not only the figure of Ko-sahn but Momaday's own being are constructs of his imagination: "Then she turned slowly around, nodding once, and receded into the language I had made. And then I imagined I was alone in the room."[44] Referring to the impact of this experience, Momaday later said: "I think that existence is illusory. I don't know what it is to be, and I sometimes think that being and existence are simply a dream that we have, as in this case."[45]

The verbal dimension of reality illustrated by Momaday's visionary experience is the definitive feature of an oral tradition. The meaning of living in an oral culture is difficult to understand. Native peoples have relied on songs, prayers, myths, and legends for their self-definition and imaginative needs. The oral tradition has provided them with a common bond and a sense of belonging to a chain connecting them with their tribal past and future. The cultures have depended on the memories of individuals for continuation and have always been but one generation removed from extinction.[46]

A verbal universe is, of course, not only the home of ancient storytellers but also the concern of modern writers. Language and the artistic imagination have acquired an independence of their own in the works, for example, of James Joyce and Marcel Proust. Their worlds lie wholly within the framework of memory. Not surprisingly, Momaday's *The Names* shows signs of

influence by Joyce's *A Portrait of the Artist as a Young Man*. Like
Joyce, Momaday sees human development as a growing up to
an awareness of language. Self-awareness is proportionate to an
awareness of names. The artist constructs reality through his
command of words. Language is no longer a mirror of reality
but reality itself. Momaday's encounter with Ko-sahn bears all
the characteristics of a Joycean epiphany, the sudden transformation of a word into corporeal existence.

The similarities with Proust are equally striking: the emphasis on the subjectivity of experience, the profound belief in the
power of language, the concern with names.[47] Names, for
Proust, are carriers of the past which recreate experience outside the dimension of chronological time. He calls these forms
of epiphanies "resurrections, . . . fragments of existence with-
drawn from Time."[48] Such experiences, set in motion by words
or through sense perceptions like sound and smell, are not
replicas of past sensations but those past sensations themselves.[49] Proust's beliefs are very close to Momaday's conviction
that man's essential being consists in language: "Real life
. . .,—the only life in consequence which can be said to be
really lived—is literature."[50]

Like Momaday's crisis of confidence in the reality of language, which was resolved by the appearance of Ko-sahn,
Proust's famous example of involuntary memory, when events
from the past come back to life triggered by the sound of a
spoon or the sensation of tripping against a cobblestone—the
sensation which accompanied the original experience in the
past—is preceded by his suspicion that "literature was less
charged with reality" than he had believed.[51] The extraordinary experience of the past in the present suggests to him not
only that an extratemporal being exists within man but also
that it is language which, as the performative, dynamic force
in memory and the imagination, can conquer time. Through
language life can be fully realized, illumined, and restored
within the confines of a book.[52] Ideas can be preserved from
annihilation and oblivion in the safety of the written word.[53]

Momaday's belief in language as the true dimension of existence has been confirmed by experiences which are of the same nature as Proust's resurrections. The old woman Ko-sahn, who stepped out of her name in Momaday's manuscript, proved to him the existential reality of names. Another intimation of the past which impressed itself on Momaday with such lifelike quality as to be virtually indistinguishable from the original event is recorded in one of the *Viva* columns. Momaday relates the sensation he experienced when reading a letter about an excursion at Dulce, fifteen years after it was written:

> . . . in this simple description, this evocation of an afternoon that was scarcely remembered, if remembered at all, I was transported in my mind. It was a strange thing for me, a returning, a doubling back in time, and it seemed to involve not only my memory but my whole being. I could see what was there in the landscape, could see it in extraordinary detail. I was conscious of the light in the trees, how it slanted down upon the road. I could feel the motion of the car; I caught the scent of smoke in the air, and of cedar and pine, and I heard the shouting and the laughter of the boys and girls. How strange! After fifteen years I am there, looking on, as if I had never left that road, and the slim boy on the black horse is going round and round.
>
> Language, even so incidental as this passage in an old letter, can be powerful beyond belief. In language you can even deflect the force of time.[54]

It is an essential characteristic of Momaday's belief that the experience of the past in the present is not restricted to an individual's personal past. By connecting extratemporal experience with the oral tradition, Momaday finds a sense of being which transcends individual existence and encompasses the historical, racial, and mythical past. This is significant not only because the knowledge of one's ancestry provides a sense of belonging in the continuum of time but also because the memory which has been created by oral transmission can be activated and brought to life in the imagination. In this way it becomes part of the present, a realm in which contemporary man can actively participate in his heritage.

One of the charges against Momaday's writings is that he

deals in nostalgia.[55] Nostalgia is a wistful or excessively senti-
mental yearning for a return to or a return of some real or
romanticized past. It is obvious from Momaday's career and his
statements on the place of Indians in the modern world that he
has no desire for such a return. What he does stress, however,
is his need to acknowledge his investment in the tradition of
his people and his need to fulfill his responsibility of living in
the presence of the past.

Momaday uses several terms to describe the extension of individual memory into anteriority: "blood memory" or "blood
recollection," "whole memory," "memory of the blood," and
"racial memory." They all describe a verbal dimension of reality
which perpetuates cultural identity. Again, one must remember Momaday's definition of an Indian as an idea a man has of
himself. He points out that "the imaginative experience and
the historical express equally the traditions of man's reality."
They are brought together in the racial memory.[56]

One Indian speaker, T. E. Sawyer, declared that it is the
historical experience of a people which precludes cultural assimilation. He added:

It is this same historical experience of a people which gives rise to
the identity of a people. And it is a common misunderstanding to
think that group identity is the sum of cultural traits. Identity is a
conception of and feelings about the events which a people have
lived. It is the meaning of events in which one's ancestors took part,
in ways that make one proud, which differentiate people into ethnic
groups.[57]

Momaday's re-creation of the Kiowa migration, a journey
which "continues to be made anew each time the miracle comes
to mind," is one case in point.[58] His imagining of a day in the
life of Pohd-lohk, whom he knew as a child, is another. Particularly significant is his preoccupation with Mammedaty, his
paternal grandfather, who died two years before Momaday was
born.

When Momaday began to contemplate the meaning of his
racial past, he realized the loss which the lack of a personal

link to his grandfather represented. The painful recognition of being severed from this link in the chain of generations found expression in the poem "Rainy Mountain Cemetery."[59] A remark Momaday made in a letter to Yvor Winters, who had read an early draft of the poem, plainly illustrates his sense of loss and isolation: "The dark stone . . . is the tombstone of my forefather, whom I never knew and whose name represents nothing to me so much as the lifeless stone in which it is cut."[60] This was written at a point when his search for his Kiowa past was already well advanced. It seems, however, that he had not yet found the belief in the oral tradition and his artistic imagination to bridge the gap which his grandfather's death had opened up. His growing insight into the verbal dimension of reality over the following years enabled him to fashion an idea of Mammedaty which has a truth of its own, as if the two men had actually met. In one instance Momaday projects himself into a giveaway ceremony in which his grandfather was honored by his people. This is how he describes the nature and significance of his vision:

This blood recollection, which is an intricate image indeed, composed of innumerable details, is especially vivid and immediate to me, a whole and irrevocable act of the imagination. I have the sense always that the event, the dramatic action, is just now, in a moment, taking place in the real world. I have held on to this vision for many years, keeping it within my reach, bringing it into focus in moments of peace and quiet. I have walked about in this vision, taken it into account from many different angles, across many distances, in many different lights. And I have thought about it; I have tried to understand it in its own terms; I have tried to perceive myself in it.[61]

His vision is the product of the stories Momaday heard about Mammedaty. It is marked by two crucial implications which illustrate the growth of his understanding of the vitality of Kiowa oral tradition: he has discovered the performative, ritualistic power of language, language not as reflection of experience but as experience itself; and, second, he has realized that this aspect of language holds the key to a dimension of reality outside the continuum of clock time and thus to a form of immortality. Since these two notions are at the heart of Momaday's work, they need to be considered carefully.

One of the essential characteristics of the oral tradition is the assumption that what is orally performed is not a reproduction of the event related but the event itself. The social setting of the performance, the gathering of the audience around the singer or storyteller, and the introductory formula frequently used indicate that what follows lies outside the continuum of ordinary time. The past comes alive in the story or the song through the immediacy of the spoken word.[62] The experiential quality of language creates the event's own dimension of reality.

In the religious context he examined, Mircea Eliade distinguished between the sacred and the profane, which he classified as "two modes of being in the world, two existential situations assumed by man in the course of his history."[63] The concept of sacred time, he suggested, is a useful analogy to the nature of the oral tradition. He pointed out that *sacred time is reversible* in the sense that . . . it is a primordial mythical time made present."[64] Through ritual religious man steps out of ordinary temporal duration and enters into mythical time. This act is infinitely repeatable. Eliade concluded that religious man "refuses to live solely in what, in modern terms, is called the historical present; he attempts to regain a sacred time that, from one point of view, can be homologized to eternity."[65] These considerations are directly applicable to Indian oral traditions, which, to a great extent, are concerned with myths and religious stories, such as the account of creation or of the emergence of the tribe. One of the most important purposes of these stories is to bring the members of the tribe into contact with the creative powers which brought the universe and the people into being. The reentering of mythical time restores and rejuvenates the community and eases the toils of the present.

The breaking down of the barrier between present and past equally applies to those stories which deal with secular historical events. It is the magic of the storyteller which moves the listener across time and place, bringing him in touch with his ancestors and the places the people once inhabited. In this verbal dimension Momaday has found a clearer understanding of his racial identity, and he emulates the storyteller's attitude toward the word in his writings. He is well aware of the problems involved in this process: "When you translate the spoken to the written word, you freeze it, paralyze it. It loses something of its vitality and flexibility."[66] Momaday's recital of his poems and parts of *House Made of Dawn* is informed by a vitality which the reading experience cannot generate to the same degree.[67] Nevertheless, if the reader conceives of words as events, he can share in the actuality of experience inherent in language.

The dramatic consequences of Momaday's discovery of the potential in language for his relation to his racial past can best be shown in the development from the poem "Rainy Mountain Cemetery" to the evocation of the giveaway ceremony in "The Gourd Dancer." In the line from Momaday's letter quoted above—"[Mammedaty's] name represents nothing to me so much as the lifeless stone in which it is cut"—the memory of his ancestor seems forever lost. By way of the oral tradition, however, Momaday later succeeded in creating a link to his forebear. In the last section of "The Gourd Dancer," entitled "The Giveaway," Momaday's belief in the power of language echoes in these lines: "Someone spoke his name, Mammedaty, in which his essence was and is. . . . And all of this was for Mammedaty, in his honor, as even now it is in the telling, and will be, as long as there are those who imagine him in his name."[68] This idea suggests not only that the living can experience the past but that the dead continue to live in the present. The oral tradition, in its verbal dimension, constitutes a form of immortality.

Momaday's conviction that language manifests both a dimension in which man takes possession of his being and a realm in which he continues to exist when his physical life has come to an end is contained in this sentence: "The name was that of the seed from which the man issued into the world as

well as that of the memory into which the man dissolved."[69]
The second part of this proposition contends that in the shift
from a physical to a verbal dimension man's being prevails
indefinitely. He lives on in his name or in the stories which are
remembered about him by successive generations. Momaday
went so far as to suggest that the distinction between existence
in a physical and a verbal sense is more apparent than real. He
said that ". . . in some real sense, we are the principle characters in the stories of our lives—the most important stories that
we shall ever tell or hear told."[70] Elsewhere, he wrote about
one of his characters: "The old man's real existence was at last
invested in his talk; there he lived, and not elsewhere. He was
nothing so much as the story of himself."[71] The clearest illustration in Momaday's writings of the idea of language as a form
of spiritual perpetuation is the story of the arrowmaker:

If an arrow is well made, it will have tooth marks upon it. That is
how you know. The Kiowas made fine arrows and straightened them
in their teeth. Then they drew them to the bow to see if they were
straight. Once there was a man and his wife. They were alone at
night in their tipi. By the light of the fire the man was making
arrows. After a while he caught sight of something. There was a
small opening in the tipi where the two hides were sewn together.
Someone was there on the outside, looking in. The man went on
with his work, but he said to his wife: "Someone is standing outside. Do not be afraid. Let us talk easily, as of ordinary things." He
took up an arrow and straightened it in his teeth; then, as it was
right for him to do, he drew it to the bow and took aim, first in
this direction and then in that. And all the while he was talking as
if to his wife. But this is how he spoke: "I know that you are there
on the outside, for I can feel your eyes upon me. If you are a Kiowa,
you will understand what I am saying, and you will speak your
name." But there was no answer, and the man went on in the same
way, pointing the arrow all around. At last his aim fell upon the
place where his enemy stood, and he let go of the string. The arrow
went straight into the enemy's heart.[72]

The story of the arrowmaker is about a moment of crisis in
which life is secured through language. More significantly, not

only is life saved by words in the particular situation of danger but existence is eternalized because the event has been considered important enough to be preserved in a story and handed down from generation to generation. In this aspect of the story Momaday sees the "link between language and literature."[73]

The story of the arrowmaker is a parable illustrating the essential function of language in a man's life. Through language man orders, controls, and preserves his existence. It is the element in which he lives. Momaday concludes his own interpretation of the story:

The arrowmaker is preeminently the man made of words. He has consummate being in language; it is the world of his origin and of his posterity, and there is no other. But it is a world of definite reality and of infinite possibility. I have come to believe that there is a sense in which the arrowmaker has more nearly perfect being than have other men, by and large, as he imagines himself, whole and vital, going on into the unknown darkness and beyond. And this last aspect of his being is primordial and profound.[74]

This statement reveals the fundamental aspects of language as it is conceived in the oral tradition: its creativity and originality, its indestructibility, and its power to preserve human existence through space and time. As such this idea is central to an understanding of Momaday's work, in which the dividing lines between reality and imagination, between past, present, and future, and between individual and racial experience are blurred.

Momaday has stressed that his views on language and the imagination have been shaped by both the oral tradition and literature. He sees oral and written traditions not as antipodes but as complements. Literature, he contends, is "the end product of an evolutionary process, and the so-called 'oral tradition' is primarily a stage within that process, a stage which is indispensable and perhaps original as well."[75] This view is shared by many literary critics as well as scholars of oral expression.

René Wellek and Austin Warren made the point that every student of literature should have a sound knowledge of the oral tradition for an understanding of the processes involved in literary development. [76] Walter Ong drew attention to the fact that "our concept of oral performance has long been derived from our concept of literature despite the fact that in actuality it is literature which grows out of oral performance." [77] Ruth Finnegan, too, stressed the continuity of oral and written literatures:

There is no deep gulf between the two: they shade into each other both in the present and over many centuries of historical development, and there are innumerable cases of poetry which has both 'oral' and 'written' elements. The idea of pure and uncontaminated 'oral culture' as the primary reference point for the discussion of oral poetry is a myth. [78]

Momaday's belief in the compatibility of oral and written traditions and his preoccupation with blending the two find eloquent expression in this statement:

I think you see in what we customarily think of as our best literature precisely those things which characterize oral tradition. I look at the people whose writing I admire most—people like Herman Melville and Emily Dickinson and Isak Dinesen, who is one of my favorite writers; and it seems to me that their attitude toward language is virtually the attitude which informs the oral tradition. It is the storyteller's attitude. Too few writers have developed that understanding of literature, but it's possible that the things which separate oral tradition and written tradition are more apparent than real, and that they can be virtually one and the same thing. That is, they can be informed by the same principles, and they should be. I hope that's one of the things that will happen in time. We should be working to bring those traditions closer together than they are. [79]

Of the writers mentioned above the work of Isak Dinesen has probably most affected Momaday's perception of language. Her writings were recommended to him by Yvor Winters, who wrote: "Another book you should read is *Out of Africa* by Izaak [*sic*] Dinesen. . . . It is one of the finest books of our time." [80] Momaday's reading of Dinesen coincided with his exploration into Kiowa oral tradition, which explains the profound impact of the book.

Isak Dinesen is the pen name of the Danish Baroness Karen Blixen, who spent the years between 1914 and 1931 in Kenya, where she managed a coffee plantation. In *Out of Africa* and *Shadows on the Grass* she recounts her experiences with the native people and the African landscape. She found the natives' ties to their past and the land eloquently reflected in their stories.[81] She realized how far removed she was from this oral culture: "The Europeans have lost the faculty for building up myths and dogma, and for what we want of these we are dependent upon the supplies of our past. But the mind of the African moves naturally and easily upon such deep and shadowy paths. This gift of theirs comes out strongly in their relations with white people."[82] The mystery of language revealed itself to her in the naming practices of the aborigines:

When natives name white men after animals . . . their minds run along the lines of the old fables, and these white men, I believe, in their dark consciousness figure as both men and beast. And there is magic in words: a person who has for many years been known to all his surroundings by the name of an animal in the end comes to feel familiar with and related to the animal, he recognises himself in it.[83]

Dinesen, like Momaday, saw that man in an oral culture becomes his name and finds his fullest manifestation in language. The process of storytelling is for both writers a process of creating a sense of self. Momaday maintained that "the possibilities of storytelling are precisely those of understanding the human experience."[84] He quoted in this context Dinesen's aphorism that "all sorrows can be borne if you put them into a story or tell a story about them."[85]

This position led both writers to a perception of reality as a verbal dimension. The dividing line between physical reality and existence in language becomes fluid. This point has been amply documented in Momaday's work. A good example from

Dinesen's writings is the opening of her story *Ehrengard*, in which she illustrates the identity of life and story:

An old lady told this story.
A hundred and twenty years ago, she began, my story told itself, at greater length of time than you or I can give to it, and with a throng of details and particulars which we can never hope to know. The men and women who did then gradually build it up, and to whom it was a matter of life and death, are all long gone. . . . To them a name was a sacred thing, and with both pride and humility each of them held his or her name to be the noblest and most important—and the lasting—part of his or her person and existence.[86]

Life as a story, stories as real experience, a name as the concentration and preserver of personal being, and the imagination as the ultimate form of existence—all these notions Momaday discovered in the exploration of the oral tradition and the work of Isak Dinesen. The idea of the world as a creation of the artist's imagination he found in the works of Joyce and Stevens and Proust. The experience of the past in the present, such as the encounters with Ko-sahn and Mammedaty, proved not to be a peculiarity of oral cultures. Proust's resurrections and Vladimir Nabokov's confession, "I do not believe in time," which Momaday likes to quote, are equivalents in modern fiction.[87] They bear witness to the universality of imaginative power and of the magic of language in the artist's search for self-realization. It is against this background that Momaday comes to his final conclusion on the role of literature, oral or written: ". . . man achieves the fullest realization of his humanity in such an art and product of the imagination as literature—and here I use the term 'literature' in its broadest sense. This is admittedly a moral view of the question, but literature is itself a moral view, and it is a view of morality."[88] N. Scott Momaday is a man made of words, an artist who discovered in his oral heritage and in the literary works he studied that he could find, express, and preserve his being through the power of the word.

CHAPTER 3

The American Earth

Nature and the American landscape are central features of Momaday's writings. The desert and canyons of the Southwest, where he grew up, and the Great Plains, where the culture of his Kiowa ancestors blossomed and declined, are more than mere settings for his works. They have deep cultural meaning for his understanding of an indigenous identity. Attachment to their homelands has been a powerful source of strength among American Indian peoples. They see their existences shaped and sustained physically and spiritually by the land. Their awareness of spiritual power in the natural world is acute, and their perception is colored by mythological and historical dimensions attached to their tribal territories. This peculiarly native attitude is reflected in much of Momaday's work.

The opening passages of *House Made of Dawn* generate a sense of the aboriginal conception of the land. Many of the lyrical pieces in *Colorado: Summer, Fall, Winter, Spring* portray the land in terms of ancient myths and archetypal legends. Momaday described "The Garden of Gods," a rock configuration in Colorado, as "the work of the old, obscure deities which persist only in the moaning winds of Mesa Verde, the makers of form and substance in the earth, of music and motion, light and delight, those for whom Creation was an idea of stone monoliths in the sand, mountains in the continent, planets in the void."[1] And he referred to the legend which explains that "the mountains were conjured up from the depths of a dark, primordial sea. Water touches a holiness to the mind and sight. Indeed it is appropriate to believe in the legend; such beliefs are integral to the soul. Only water, in its pure, persistent life, is equal to the mountain."[2] Perhaps the most explicit example of Momaday's Indian view of the North American continent is a little-known early poem entitled "Eve My Mother, No." It contains the characteristic notions that the earth is alive, that it creates and sustains cultures, and that it is everlasting:

> Eve my mother, no.
> I am come from another.
> She lies in the peneplanes
> Of the Medicine Wheel and
> In the red sediment of the Llano,
> Older by planets than Eve.
> I have walked with silent steps
> Over her granite breast
> And heard her breathe sorrow
> From the throat of a lonely loon.
> I have heard her chanting
> To the Kayenta moon, mournfully.
> I have seen her smile beneath
> A harvest of rain-scented corn.
> I have seen her writhe in coition
> With a frenzied sky, desperately.
> I have heard, too, the urgent lowing
> In pine, cedar, juniper birth.
> Above all, I have seen her patient,
> As no other thing is patient,
> Waiting wise and loving
> While her dancing sons defile.[3]

Momaday is particularly interested in the ways individuals or groups are shaped by the physical world and the spiritual forces they believe to be inherent in it and how in turn these individuals or groups relate to the environment.[4] In his many statements on the relationship between the aboriginal peoples of North America and their continent he has pointed to the sacred character of this bond between man and earth.[5] Indian tribes have managed to survive largely because of their close ties to their land. These ties ensure a sense of rootedness and continuity which has become a rare feature in a rapidly expanding and highly mobile American society. The land, from a tribal point of view, is the common denominator of a community's mythical and historical past as well as its present and future. The oral traditions of Indian peoples teach that the land is the place of tribal origin.[6] And the respective geographical features—mountains, caves, or lakes—are worshiped as sacred shrines. The awareness of the presence of previous generations in the soil has also been a strong motive behind the resistance to relinquishing homelands. Chief Curley of the Crows declared:

The soil you see is not ordinary soil—it is the dust of the blood, the flesh and the bones of our ancestors. . . . You will have to dig down through the surface before you can find nature's earth, as the upper portion is Crow. The land as it is, is my blood and my dead; it is consecrated; and I do not want to give up any portion of it.[7]

For traditional American Indian communities the spiritual implications of the natural world stood at the very center of their world views. The inner world of the spirits were more significant and "real" than the outer, material world. Virtually all tribal philosophies maintain a fluid line between what is natural and supernatural, material and spiritual, conscious and unconscious. They do not posit a dualistic division between spirit and matter, for, according to Paula Allan, "the two are seen to be two expressions of the same reality—as though life had twin manifestations that are mutually interchangeable and, in many instances, virtually identical aspects of a reality that is, essentially, more spirit than matter, or that more correctly manifests its spiritness in a tangible way."[8]

Since traditional American Indians considered every aspect of creation a manifestation of an impersonal spirit, they conceived of themselves as interrelated with the whole of the universe in a complex system of kinship. Their interaction with the environment aimed at achieving a state of balance and harmony rather than domination. Their means were ritual and prayer and an intimate knowledge of the natural world. They humbled themselves in their mindfulness of the common source of life which they shared with the rest of creation. The land, then, was a spiritual entity, the place of origin, source of subsistence, home of gods, culture heroes, and ancestors, and the place of existence for future generations. Today the land is still treated with the same esteem by many indigenous peoples whose values have remained traditional.

Momaday characterized the Indian perception of the world as focusing on the infinite details of their immediate surroundings, while the eye of the mind brings past and future, origin and destiny into a unified field of vision.[9] He described this complex mode of perception:

The native vision, this gift of seeing truly, with wonder and delight, into the natural world, is informed by a certain attitude of reverence and self-respect. It is a matter of extra-sensory as well as sensory perception, I believe. In addition to the eye, it involves the intelligence, the instinct, and the imagination. It is the perception not only of objects and forms, but also of essences and ideals.[10]

He referred to the Indian relationship to the land as "a matter of reciprocal appropriation" in which, through a moral act of the imagination entailing both ethical imperatives and historical responsibilities, man's rightful place and deeds in the physical world are determined.[11] This conception, according to Momaday, has been the result of an evolutionary process:

. . . the Indian has determined himself in his imagination over a period of untold generations. His racial memory is an essential part of his understanding. He understands himself more clearly than perhaps other people, given his situation in space and time. His heritage has always been rather closely focused, centered upon the landscape in a particular reality.[12]

In contrast, the idea of a personal investment in and responsibility for the land has been alien to most Anglo-Americans. The seemingly inexhaustible geographical expanse and natural resources needed no particular respect or care. Their beliefs in the benefit of progress and the divine gift of dominion along with an impersonal, unemotional relationship to the natural world left little room to question the legitimacy and desirability of the pioneer effort. Yet since the early nineteenth century there have been dissenting voices who, bewildered and alarmed by the rapidly changing conditions of the landscape as well as plant and animal life, expressed doubts about the adequacy of the price which had to be paid for the benefits of progress.[13]

Momaday is, of course, aware of this dissenting Anglo-American tradition to which his own work belongs. In an interview he stressed that a sense of place is by no means exclusive to aboriginal people in America,[14] and in *Colorado* he attributed a sense of tenure in the land to the people in that state's small towns.[15] He also wrote in the idiom of Faulkner of his tobacco-growing Kentucky forebears that they understood "in their blood that [the tobacco's value] consists not only in the cash for which it is given up in trade, but also in the remembered wilderness that was given up for it."[16] He found a sense of place not only in his neighbor Joe Tosa, a native of Jemez, but also in Fray Angelico Chavez, the priest at Jemez, and in his artist friend Georgia O'Keeffe.[17]

Momaday himself is partly to blame for the obscurity of the non-Indian elements in his treatment of the man-land relationship. His contributions to the "Indian-as-ecologist" debate tended to polarize Indians as attuned to the land and non-Indians as estranged from it, and these political rather than literary statements concealed the significant influences of sources outside his Indian background on his vision of the natural world.[18]

A careful reading of Momaday's work reveals that a discussion of his treatment of the American landscape simply in terms of aboriginal perceptions cannot account for the numerous references to ideas which belong firmly to the nature tradition in American literature. Indeed, it is in Momaday's nature writings that his ability to draw on both his Indian heritage and his knowledge of Anglo-American literature becomes particularly apparent. To arrive at a balanced picture of Momaday's sources, it is important to isolate the elements

which place him in a tradition of writers who gave literary
expression to the value and significance of the American wilderness.

Given Momaday's academic background it is hardly surprising that his writings contain long-established perceptions of
nature in American literature. In an interview Momaday expressed his deep personal and academic concern for the American landscape:

I like to teach that course [Landscape in American literature] more
than any other. I am very much in tune with the landscape. I've
always been interested in how man relates to the land. I use that as
a focus and how it is reflected in principal American writers. If there
is anything that distinguishes American literature from European
literature, it is that [American emphasis upon land].[19]

Among the writers Momaday discusses in this course are Jonathan Edwards, Henry David Thoreau, Ralph Waldo Emerson,
Walt Whitman, Willa Cather, and, most significant, the naturalist John Muir.

There is ample evidence that William Faulkner, Isak Dinesen, and D. H. Lawrence have influenced Momaday's view of
the American earth. A number of passages must be read
against the background of the deistic and transcendental traditions in American literature. The influence of Yvor Winters
and the work of Frederick Goddard Tuckerman also appear in
Momaday's writings. Most important, however, Momaday belongs to a group of writers who are concerned with the spirit
of the American continent.

Momaday's indebtedness to Faulkner is reflected in some of
the technical aspects of his writings, particularly in *House Made
of Dawn*: the fragmented narrative perspective, the disjointed
time scheme, the connection of surface meaning to underlying
symbolic patterns, the use of different styles for different characters.[20] Thematically the two writers resemble each other in
the way they stress the importance of a functioning tradition
for individual human existence. They see the acceptance of
responsibility in the historical continuum as a prerequisite for

survival. Faulkner's remark that "no man is himself, he's the sum of his past, and in a way . . . of his future, too"[21] and Momaday's contention that "notions of the past and future are essentially notions of the present"[22] are crucial for an understanding of their works. Faulkner's Joe Christmas and Abel, the central figure in *House Made of Dawn*, are characters who suffer because they have lost control over their pasts and, without the support of viable traditions, have lost their sense of self.

The kinship between Faulkner and Momaday is perhaps most conspicuous in their views of modern urban America. Faulkner's work presents, in the words of one scholar, "a criticism of the prevailing commercial and urban culture, a criticism made from the standpoint of a provincial and traditional culture."[23] If one thinks of the treatment of the city in *House Made of Dawn*, the above statement seems equally appropriate for Momaday's work. Faulkner exposes the rapacity of Anglo-American pioneers who desecrated the wilderness for utilitarian purposes. In one of his stories he wrote, ". . . then came the Anglo-Saxon, the pioneer, . . . turning the earth into a howling waste from which he would be the first to vanish . . . because . . . only the wilderness could feed and nourish him."[24]

Faulkner contrasted this insensitivity toward the physical environment with a sense of place which grows out of man's rootedness in the land. Central to this idea is the belief that individuals and cultures are molded by their homelands and that they must maintain a close relationship to them. One of Faulkner's characters spells out this notion of geographical determinism: "That's the trouble with this country: everything, weather, all, hangs on too long. Like our rivers, our land: opaque, slow, violent; shaping and creating the life of man in its implacable and brooding image."[25] The idea reappears in *Light in August*, where Faulkner wrote about the fleeing Joe Christmas that "it is as though he desires to see his native earth in all its phases for the first and last time. He had grown to manhood in the country, where like the unswimming sailor his

physical shape and his thought had been moulded by its com-
pulsions without his learning anything about its actual shape
and feel."[26] Among the characters who are attuned to the land
are Ike McCaslin and Sam Fathers, the descendant of a Chick-
asaw chief, in Faulkner's "The Bear" and old man Francisco in
House Made of Dawn. The episode of Francisco's pursuit of the
bear and subsequent initiation as a hunter owes much to Faulkner's story, as one critic has argued convincingly.[27]

For Faulkner nature was where man could learn the lesson of
the wilderness and cultivate a code of honor. Through an appropriate relation to the natural world man could improve
himself ethically and achieve the fullest realization of his humanity. Momaday's appeal for a return to a greater consciousness of and respect for man's physical environment not only
suggests a similar land ethic but reflects a hope which Faulkner
had lost. For him the wilderness was doomed and with it human integrity, which was severed from its source of nourish-
ment.

Isak Dinesen's *Out of Africa* is another influence which has
left a mark on Momaday's evocation of the American landscape.[28] This account of the author's life on a coffee plantation
in Kenya stands, in Momaday's view, as "one of the great books
of our time."[29] Momaday referred to the personal importance
of this work, saying: "I think more of that book than I do of
anything else in recent English literature. I read it over and
over."[30] A close look at *Out of Africa* reveals that it has affected
not only Momaday's conception of language, as shown in the
previous chapter, but also his view on the man-land relation.

In the most general terms Dinesen and Momaday have created powerful evocations of their respective geographical environments. Momaday noted with respect to Dinesen's grasp of
the sense of place that "she entered so completely into the
landscape of the place that it became at last the landscape of
the mind. This is not an easy transformation to make, and it
is not easy to understand. It is as if the very soil itself has never
really existed, until it came to exist in the writer's particular
sense of it."[31] Momaday aspired to do the same in his literary

re-creation of the southwestern landscape. He noted in an interview:

I think that you can create a landscape that doesn't have its likeness in the actual world and you can make that a very exciting thing in itself. Dinesen in *Out of Africa* describes the Masai reserve and its hills: while I don't believe those hills exist, they are hills which "belonged." That, to me, is an exciting thing that happens only in language and the kind of writing challenge which I find interesting.[32]

While Dinesen's close association with the tribesmen of East Africa gave her an understanding of an aboriginal conception of the land, Momaday gained similar insights through his closeness to the Navajo and Jemez peoples. Both writers are profoundly interested in the reciprocal relationship between geography and human life. Some examples from their works show a common concern with the question of man's lasting impact on the landscape and the land's impact on the human mind.

Dinesen and Momaday both believe that man is ultimately a manifestation of the soil. Dinesen declares that "the Natives were Africa in flesh and blood. . . . We ourselves, in boots, and in our constant hurry, often jar with the landscape. The Natives are in accordance with it." She sees both the native people and the animals as "weighty with such impressions of the world around them as have been slowly gathered and heaped up in their dim minds; they are themselves features of the land." She describes geographical formations, plants, trees, and the indigenous people as "different expressions of one idea, variations upon the same theme."[33] Momaday, too, sees man and land as inseparable. According to him, ". . . the Indian conceives of himself in terms of the land. His imagination of himself is also and at once an imagination of the physical world from which he proceeds and to which he returns in the journey of his life. The landscape is his natural element; it is the only dimension in which his life is possible."[34]

The assumption that man partakes of the spirit of a given place and becomes a human embodiment of it leads both writers to the question whether man's existence leaves a lasting spiritual imprint on his or her environment. After her return to Denmark, Dinesen speculated on whether her presence was still alive in Africa:

If I know a song of Africa,—I thought,—of the Giraffe, and the African new moon lying on her back, of the ploughs in the fields, and the sweaty faces of the coffee pickers, does Africa know a song of me? Would the air over the plain quiver with a color that I had on, or the children invent a game in which my name was, or the full moon throw a shadow over the gravel of the drive that was like me, or would the eagles of Ngong look out for me?[35]

Momaday similarly speculated about the reciprocity of influence between man and other forms of life. His metaphysical thought is triggered by the observation of an octopus:

I like to think that it might have been dealing with me, that in its alien, ocean mind it was struggling to take my presence into account, that I had touched its deep, essential life, and it should never lose the impression that I had made upon it. . . . And now I wonder, what does it mean that, after these years, I should write of the octopus? . . . Only just now, as a strange loneliness, it occurs to me that this creature has, for some years now, been of some small consequence in the life of my mind. And I wonder if, in the dark night of the sea, there, deep within its own sphere of instinct, the octopus dreams of me.[36]

Momaday and Dinesen also share the belief that the unity between a landscape and its inhabitants prevails beyond death, when the land receives man and makes him part of itself. Dinesen's description of the burial of her friend Denys in the hills of Kenya and Momaday's story of the unmarked grave of an Indian woman are expressions of their mindfulness of the presence of the dead in the soil.[37]

The eighteenth- and nineteenth-century concept of sublimity and transcendental ideas of American nature writing form another background to Momaday's prose. In one of his essays

Momaday described a trip with a friend into the high desert of the Joranda range:

> We were here a long time—as the sun descended the light softened, and the whole landscape seemed absorbent, informed with radiance, great with light—and we were reluctant to leave. But we felt very good about the afternoon. In it we had been restored. We had touched the sacred earth, had reassured ourselves that it was there still, beyond the wrappings of our civilization.[38]

This passage reflects particularly well Momaday's awareness of the transcendental tradition, specifically the works of John Muir and Henry David Thoreau.

The description of the land in terms of radiance and light echoes Muir's portrayal of the Californian Sierra as "the luminous wall of the mountains."[39] Muir, who founded the Sierra Club in 1892, was probably the foremost proponent of wilderness preservation in the second half of the nineteenth century. In an ideal way he combined a scientific interest in ecology with a transcendental perception of nature. Despite the hardships of his boyhood on the central Wisconsin frontier, which led many other pioneers to hate the wilderness, Muir derived intense delight from it and soon began to construct a mystical philosophy of nature which drew heavily on the transcendental ideas of his day.[40] This philosophy grew out of a deep personal struggle against Calvinist thought, which rejected nature religion as pagan and insisted on the Bible as the only proof of God's majesty.

John Muir's reading of Emerson, whom he later met in Yosemite, and his academic training in botany, geology, and the new theory of evolution laid the groundwork on which he built his nature writings.[41] Muir traveled widely across the continent, from Florida to Alaska, keeping his journal and publishing travel accounts. The place of his deepest involvement both in scientific study and in the metaphysics of nature became the Yosemite Valley in California. On his solitary hikes into the mountains he collected evidence for the glacial theory, studied plant and animal life, and wrote long meditations on the divine spirit which he apprehended in the minutest facet of the land-scape. Yosemite was to him a laboratory and a church, a place of research and worship. Almost every page of his writings on California reflects this approach to the natural world: a detailed description of the environment, followed by an analysis of the ecological processes at work, and a metaphysical conclusion. His greatest achievements as a naturalist were the propagation of wilderness conservation and the demonstration that scientific investigation of nature and religious and aesthetic appreciation of it need not be mutually exclusive.

The notion of a necessary polarity between civilization and unspoiled nature, another issue in Momaday's passage above, follows in the tradition of Thoreau. A finely balanced relationship between city and wilderness was seen by Thoreau as the prerequisite for physical and spiritual health.[42] The following quotation amounts to a transcendental creed: "I believe that there is a subtle magnetism in Nature, which, if we unconsciously yield to it, will direct us aright. . . . In Wilderness is the preservation of the world. . . . I believe in the forest, and in the meadow, and in the night in which the corn grows."[43] Thoreau believed that an individual or a society cut off from the invigorating forces of nature was doomed. The best choice for man, he held, was an existence which oscillated between unspoiled nature and the achievements of civilization.

In numerous depictions of the natural world Momaday echoes Jonathan Edwards and employs the standard rhetoric of Emersonian transcendentalism. He describes a strong wind sweeping across from the sea as "the hand of God" taking hold of him.[44] A violent thunderstorm he renders in these terms: ". . . the earth and sky are at odds, and God shudders."[45] In the peculiar angle with which the Washita River and Rainy Mountain Creek cut through the southern plains, Momaday perceives "an idea of geometry in the mind of God."[46] This imagery rings not only of Edwards's assumption that the phenomenal world is "but a type of the infinite magnificence" of God[47] but also of Muir's description of the divine design in the mountains of Yosemite.[48] Momaday renders a mystical experi-

ence by one of his relatives in deistic rhetoric: his uncle James
heard beyond the magnificence of a desert night "the laughter
of God" and marveled at the beauty with which "God had
drawn the sky with light."[49]

These examples clearly reflect Momaday's reading of eigh-
teenth- and nineteenth-century writings on the American wilderness. The Puritan belief in the sinfulness of human existence
and the fear of the corrupting forces of wilderness for civilized
life had created a deep cleavage between man and nature. The
"wilderness temptation" was proof for the colonists of satanic
forces drawing them into the dark forest to a state of bestiality
and savagery.[50] However, the growing stability of colonial and
postrevolutionary America with its growing cities and the retreat of wilderness areas favored the rise of the concept of sublimity and led to a reversal in the judgment of the relationship
between man and his natural environment.

The concept of sublimity suggests the association of God
and nature. It was proposed by Deists, who believed in God as
the prime cause of the cosmos and secured their faith through
a rational examination of nature.[51] If the work of God on earth
was the proof of his beauty and majesty, it could best be studied
in the realm of wild nature, where God's creation still remained
untouched by human interference. It was this course of reason-
ing which bestowed intrinsic religious and aesthetic value onto
an area which the Puritans had feared and detested.

Jonathan Edwards was the last and perhaps greatest of the
Calvinist writers. A look at his work reveals a deistic perception of nature as the medium through which man could approach the glory of God. In *The Images or Shadows of Divine
Things*, Edwards wrote, ". . . the works of God are but a kind
of voice or language of God to instruct the intelligent beings
in things pertaining to Himself."[52] The contemplation of nature becomes significant as an exercise not only in the appreciation of its physical beauty but also of the spiritual beauty it
foreshadows. The natural beauty of creation is only a faint
reflection of the infinitely greater divine beauty. Edwards looks
through nature toward heavenly worlds: "The immense mag-

nificence of the visible world in inconceivable vastness, the incomprehensible height of the heavens, etc., is but a type of the infinite magnificence, height and glory of God's work in the spiritual world."[53] The terminology with which he describes the dualistic character of nature encompasses such terms as "image," "shadow," "language," and "type," the key term being "resemblances." This system of thought and the language employed in its expression anticipate the content and terminology of the transcendental writings of Emerson and Thoreau.

As the central figures of the American romantic movement, Emerson and Thoreau adopted the notion of sublimity and proclaimed their trust in the goodness of man, who was, like the rest of creation, endowed with a spark of divinity. This confidence in man and nature was the result of a growing discontent with a society on the verge of industrial transformation. The appeal of primitivism created an attitude of defiance against civilized society and led to the celebration of the wilderness as the only remaining place of refuge from a corrupting civilization.

The transcendentalists, like the Deists, postulated a dualism between the physical universe and a higher, transcendental, spiritual realm. Through his involvement in the natural world the transcendentalist hoped to catch a glimpse of the divine. In contrast to the Deists, who based their faith in the existence of a higher order on a rational analysis of nature, the transcendentalists relied on the power of intuition for their mystical experiences. Nature was not only a window through which man, thanks to the divine nature of his soul, could reach what Emerson called the "Oversoul"; it was also the realm in which man could reach moral and creative perfection. Emerson expressed the belief in the ultimate benevolence of nature in these much-quoted sentences: ". . . in the woods we return to reason and faith. . . .in the wilderness, I find something more dear and connate than in the street or villages."[54]

While both Emerson and Thoreau had a keen interest in the physical properties of the natural world, they were more concerned with nature's spiritual implications. Thoreau pointed out that "man cannot afford to be a naturalist to look at Nature directly. . . . He must look through and beyond her."[55] In another context he explained that he was not concerned with nature per se but with nature transformed by and perceived through the power of the imagination:

The most stupendous scenery ceases to be sublime when it becomes distinct, or in other words limited, and the imagination is no longer encouraged to exaggerate it. The actual height and breadth of a mountain or a water-fall are always ridiculously small; they are the imagined only that content us. Nature is not made after such a fashion as we would have her. We piously exaggerate her wonders as the scenery around our home.[56]

Emerson expressed a similar opinion in his "Nature" essay: "When I behold a rich landscape, it is less to my purpose to recite correctly the order and superposition of the strata than to know why all thought of multitude is lost in a tranquil sense of unity."[57] For both men nature's importance lay first and foremost in the fact that it manifested a cipher for a higher spiritual order and only second in its physical, aesthetic appeal.

This was the dominant position in the literary circles of transcendental New England, and there were few writers at the time who did not share the tenets of Emersonian romanticism in their contemplation of nature. One who remained detached from the transcendental interpretation of the universe was a Massachusetts poet, Frederick Goddard Tuckerman, whose work was the subject of Momaday's doctoral dissertation.

In the introduction to his edition of Tuckerman's poetical work Momaday spelled out the basic differences between Tuckerman's ideas and the predominant transcendental thought of his time. Acknowledging that "Tuckerman's departure from Emersonian intuitive tradition is neither total nor unique," Momaday nevertheless saw the rational and scientific approach with which Tuckerman confronted nature as the central distinguishing element.[58] While the transcendentalists focused on the symbolic and moral implications of the material world,

Tuckerman studied its physical aspects; while their confidence in the possibility of mystical transcendence blunted their sensitivity to the minute details of creation, Tuckerman looked at nature with the eyes of a scientist, scrutinizing it in the deep conviction that nature would ultimately resist his attempts to comprehend it. His poems reflect a wide knowledge of botany, astronomy, and geology as well as a distrust of pantheistic thought and mystical experience.

Momaday concluded his observations on Tuckerman's special position in nineteenth-century American poetry:

Superficially, he preserved the stage properties of contemporary Romantic literature: the spirit of isolation, a dissociation of emotional cause and effect, a preoccupation with nature. But Tuckerman's sense of isolation is defined in terms of intellectual honesty rather than self-reliance; his taste is measured in the fact rather than the celebration of sentiment; his attention is trained upon the surfaces rather than the symbols of his world.[59]

The extent of Tuckerman's influence on Momaday's nature writings is difficult to assess. Three similarities, however, cannot easily be overlooked. Like Tuckerman, Momaday is something of an amateur naturalist, capable of describing and naming minute details in the natural world.[60] Second, Momaday, like Tuckerman, exerts the power of his imagination on the landscape in order to re-create its past and repopulate it with its vanished inhabitants.[61] And third, some of Momaday's work reflects a view of nature not dissimilar from Tuckerman's in that it suggests the ultimate inscrutability and potential evil of the physical world.

The last similarity characterizes a number of poems Momaday wrote at Stanford under the supervision of Yvor Winters, among them "Before an Old Painting of the Crucifixion" and "Comparatives." The existential position of human life in an indifferent universe which Momaday assumes in these poems may have resulted from his reading of Tuckerman's ode "The Cricket." Winters's philosophical convictions were an additional influence. A detailed examination of the relationship between Momaday and Winters and their work on Tuckerman can be found in chapter 7.

The coexistence of deistic, transcendental, and existential ideas in Momaday's writings indicates that his depiction of nature is not consistent. These differing intellectual positions are a reflection of his wide literary background. There is, however, one assumption which occurs consistently throughout his work: that the inhabitants of a particular geographical region fall under the influence of a spirit of place. This assumption places Momaday into an intellectual tradition of considerable importance.

The idea that spiritual beings inhabit the physical world is a universal feature of primitive religions. One of the declared aims of Christianity has been to destroy this concept in an effort to loosen the ties between man and his native soil. The estrangement of man and earth was later accelerated by the rise of science and technology.[62] Many critics of modern civilization have seen the rational, scientific, and mechanical mode of being as potentially fatal for humanity and have proposed a reorientation to an intuitive, organic perception of the universe. They maintain that modern man's spiritual homelessness and sense of fragmentation can be remedied only through a reattunement to the natural cycles and rhythms of the physical world. This idea is, of course, central to Momaday's work.

In his youth Momaday was part of a small cultural group whose mystical and religious values sustained its connection to the natural world. Without advocating a return to traditional Indian practices, Momaday believes that many of their conceptions of the world can be adopted and incorporated into modern life. He stated emphatically:

Now more than ever, we might do well to enter upon a vision quest of our own, that is, a quest after vision itself. And in this the Indian stands to lead by his example. For with respect to such things as a sense of heritage, of a vital continuity in terms of origin and of destiny, a profound investment of the mind and spirit in the oral tradition of literature, philosophy, and religion—those things, in short, which constitute his vision of the world—the Indian is perhaps the most culturally secure of all Americans.[63]

This quest for vision must above all lead to a new awareness of the spirit of the American continent.

While it would be beyond the scope of this book to give a comprehensive account of the development of the "spirit of place" concept, it may suffice to point to some of its main proponents. In the first third of the twentieth century the idea was discussed by historians, psychologists, and writers, most notably by Oswald Spengler, C. G. Jung, and D. H. Lawrence. They diagnosed the dissociation from the natural world as the cause of modern civilization's impoverishment.

Spengler wrote in his introduction to *The Decline of the West: Form and Actuality* about cultures, "each springing with primitive strength from the soil of a mother-region to which it remains firmly bound throughout its whole life-cycle."[64] He described the final stage of cultural development in his theory of the rise and decline of civilization:

There, separated from the power of the land—cut off from it, even, by the pavement underfoot—Being becomes more and more languid, sensation and reason more and more powerful. Man becomes intellect, "free" like the nomads, whom he comes to resemble, but narrower and colder than they. "Intellect," "Geist," "esprit," is the specific urban form of the understanding waking-consciousness. All art, all religion and science, becomes slowly intellectualized, alien to the land, incomprehensible to the peasant of the soil. With the Civilization sets in the climacteric. The immemorially old roots of Being are dried up in the stone masses of its cities. And the free intellect—fateful word!—appears like a flame, mounts splendid into the air, and pitiably dies.[65]

D. H. Lawrence saw the problem in much the same way. In "A Propos Lady Chatterley's Lover," he wrote:

Oh, what a catastrophe for a man when he cut himself off from the rhythm of the year, from his unison with the sun and the earth. Oh, what a catastrophe, what a maiming of love when it was made a personal, merely personal feeling, taken away from the rising and the setting of the sun, and cut off from the magic connection of the solstice and the equinox! This is what is the matter with us. We are bleeding at the roots, because we are cut off from the earth and sun and stars, and love is a grinning mockery, because, poor blossom, we plucked it off from its stem on the tree of Life, and expected it to keep blooming in our civilized vase on the table.[66]

Lawrence's essay "The Spirit of Place," in which he postulates "some subtle magnetic and vital influence . . . which keeps the inhabitants stable," first appeared in November 1918, the year Spengler published *The Decline of the West*.[67] Lawrence was probably familiar with Spengler's ideas, although it is uncertain whether he knew them as early as 1918, when he suggested the influence of geography on the growth of civilizations.[68]

There can be no doubt, however, that Lawrence was aware of how significant the psychological thesis in his essays on American literature was for contemporary psychological research. A letter to his American publisher, B. W. Huebsch, reveals Lawrence's secretiveness and suspicion that his findings might be exploited by others, particularly the Freudian circle in Vienna.[69]

It may just be a curious coincidence that C. G. Jung addressed what he called "the mystery of the earth" in his study "The Role of the Unconscious," also published in 1918. This essay discussed in distinctly Lawrencean terms the impact of the American continent on the physical and psychological state of the immigrants:

One only needs to see how, in America, the skull and pelvis measurements of all the European races begin to indianize themselves in the second generation of immigrants. That is the mystery of the American earth.

The soil of every country holds some such mystery. We have an unconscious reflection of this in the psyche: just as there is a relationship of mind to body, so there is a relationship of body to earth.[70]

Jung, who developed a keen interest in America and its aboriginal inhabitants, visited Taos in 1924, the time of Lawrence's residence there. He remained concerned with the phenomenon of geographical determinism and developed his thoughts in two further articles, "Mind and Earth" and "Complications of American Psychology," published in 1928 and 1930. In "Mind and Earth" he reiterated his theory of the mind's conditioning by a geographical environment. America served as the modern example of the remolding of a race under the impact of a new continent. The psychological and physical changes he believed to have discovered in the immigrant population of the New World he described as the "mysterious Indianization of the American people."[71] In "The Complications of American Psychology" he made the same point by stressing that "man can be assimilated by a country" and that in the New World "the spirit of the Indian gets at the American from within and without."[72] Lawrence's "spirit of place" becomes in Jung's terminology the "*genius* or spiritus loci."[73]

The extent to which Lawrence and Jung agreed in their observations on the man-land relationship and the need to incorporate repressed or unconscious influences into human life as a way to psychic balance becomes overt in the similarity of the following two passages. Jung wrote:

. . . the American presents a strange picture: a European with Negro behaviour and an Indian soul. He shares the fate of all usurpers of foreign soil. Certain Australian primitives assert that one cannot conquer foreign soil, because in it there dwell strange ancestor-spirits who reincarnate themselves in the newborn. There is a great psychological truth in this. The foreign land assimilates its conqueror. But unlike the Latin conquerors of Central and South America, the North Americans preserved their European standards with the most rigid puritanism, though they could not prevent the souls of their Indian foes from becoming theirs. Everywhere the virgin earth causes at least the unconscious of the conqueror to sink to the level of its indigenous inhabitants. Thus, in the American, there is a discrepancy between conscious and unconscious that is not found in the European, a tension between an extremely high conscious level of culture and an unconscious primitivity. . . . Alienation from the unconscious and from its historical conditions spells rootlessness. That is the danger that lies in wait for the conqueror of foreign lands, and for every individual who . . . loses touch with the dark, maternal, earthy ground of his being.[74]

Lawrence noted in *The Symbolic Meaning*:

It is plain that the American is not one with the Red Man whom he has perforce lodged in his own soul. It is a dangerous thing to destroy any vital existence out of life. For then the destroyer becomes responsible, in his own living body, for the destroyed. Upon the destroyer devolves the necessity of continuing the nature and being of the destroyed. . . . the Red Indian lives unappeased and inwardly destructive in the American.[75]

Despite the apparent similarities there is no conclusive evidence of direct influence of Lawrence on Jung or vice versa.

Two other writers addressed the "spirit of place" idea in 1923 and 1927. One of them, William Carlos Williams, wrote without doubt under the influence of Lawrence and, like Mary Austin, argued for a reorientation of the American artist to the New World.[76] Austin postulated the existence of an American rhythm which affects the artist on an unconscious level. She deduced this theory from her study of American Indian poetry and went as far as to claim that she could identify a "landscape line" in aboriginal poems which reflected the artist's rootedness in a specific locality.[77] The spirit of place, she argued, influenced the Indian poet through rhythmic impulses. And, she believed, non-Indian artists, exposed to the same impulses, would have to react as the natives did, thus creating a truly American art: "I . . . became convinced as early as the first years of the present century, that American poetry must inevitably take, at some period of its history, the mold of Amerind verse, which is the mold of the American experience shaped by the American environment."[78]

William Carlos Williams, too, saw the need for an openness

to the influence of the American continent. Having declared that "our resistance to the wilderness has been too strong," he suggested that Americans, and American artists in particular, "must sink first" and touch what he called the "genius of the place" or the "spirit lost in the soil" before they could grow and produce truly American culture. He echoed both Lawrence and Jung when he exclaimed: "No, we are not Indians but we are men of their world. The blood means nothing; the spirit, the ghost of the land moves in the blood, moves the blood."[79] Like Lawrence, Williams believed that American civilization must adopt an aboriginal element in order to find roots in the New World. In his reassessment of Daniel Boone, Williams wrote:

There must be a new wedding. . . . To Boone the Indian was his greatest master. Not for himself surely to be an Indian, though they eagerly sought to adopt him into their tribes, but the reverse: to be *himself* in a new world, Indianlike. If the land were to be possessed it must be as the Indian possessed it. Boone saw the truth of the Red Man, not an aberrant type, treacherous and anti-white to be feared and exterminated, but as a natural expression of the place, the Indian himself as "right", the flower of his world.[80]

Finally, one other voice deserves mention in this context. In 1929, Waldo Frank discovered at the core of such men as Emerson, Thoreau, Whitman, and Poe "the neo-primitive American soul, essentially theirs and yet the sperm-seed of a tradition older than Europe."[81] Frank was above all interested in the utilization of America's "peculiar energy" for the creation of a national identity:

Upon the side of our hope, there is first and last the peculiar energy of the American world—the forming life of our land which makes us all, nordic or Negro, American; and which relates us more essentially with the Indian and the Peruvian, than with our blood-brothers of Europe.
. . . there is in us all the dark conscience of our murder of the primeval forests—of something in their depth which is a depth in us; of our refusal of their value, of our disdain of the red man who was the spirit of those forests and who is yet, beneath the layers of law and memory, the spirit of ourselves. For our root is the red man;

our true building must rise from recognition of his base in our heart: and our denial of this is a disease within us.[82]

Momaday's treatment of the "spirit of place" theme comes closest to the ideas of D. H. Lawrence. Momaday believes in "a deep, aboriginal intelligence in the soil" which creates and shapes cultures.[83] The major characters in *House Made of Dawn* undergo changes and reach new insights under the influence of the spirit of place. In the novel the land manifests an active agent which exerts its power on the consciousness of both Indians and whites. In *The Way to Rainy Mountain*, Momaday recaptures the relationship of his Kiowa ancestors to the landscapes which left their impressions on the tribe during its migration from the Yellowstone to the southern plains. It is a reconstruction of the changes in the tribal psyche brought about by exposure to different physical environments. *Colorado*, *The Names*, and many of Momaday's poems reflect his belief in an organic and creative interdependence between himself and the places he has lived in. These works are affirmations of the communion between man and the land which can be achieved through reverence, respect, and the awareness that only a deeply rooted connection to the land can sustain individual and communal life.

With respect to the link between landscape and art Momaday shares Lawrence's tenet that "all art partakes of the Spirit of Place in which it is produced."[84] In a book review entitled "The Land Inspired the Artist," Momaday wrote:

The land itself seems to inspire artistic expression. In every season it is touched with clear and brilliant light; there are natural formations of every shape, color, and size—and these very dimensions seem to change with the time of day. So deeply involved with this landscape are those who live within it that it may be said to determine human thought and expression.[85]

Momaday would also agree with Lawrence's statement that "race is ultimately as much a question of place as of heredity."[86] Their close affinity on the issue of a landscape's power over human existence is best illustrated by comparing two statements which are remarkably similar in content and style. Momaday wrote:

The bristlecones are the thorns of the ancient earth. And they are vital. It is that, the impulse of life in them, that sets them apart from other wonders, I believe. There have been moments, a few, in which, by means of some extraordinary act of the imagination, I came suddenly upon a full awareness of the life force within me, intensely conscious of my being alive, of sharing in the irresistible continuum of life itself. And those moments have been as much of immortality as I can comprehend. Such moments are concentrated in these trees, and they have neither a beginning nor an end in time.[87]

This is how Lawrence interprets a pine tree, probably the one next to his Kiowa Ranch near Taos, which was later painted by Georgia O'Keeffe:[88]

It gives out life, as I give out life. Our two lives meet and cross one another, unknowingly: the tree's life penetrates my life, and my life the tree's. We cannot live near one another, as we do, without affecting one another.

The tree gathers up earth-power from the dark bowels of the earth, and a roaming sky-glitter from above. And all unto itself, which is a tree, woody, enormous, slow but unyielding with life, bristling with acquisitive energy, obscurely radiating some of its great strength.

It vibrates its presence into my soul, and I am with Pan. . . .

I have become conscious of the tree, and of its interpenetration into my life. Long ago, the Indians must have been even more acutely conscious of it, when they blazed it to leave their mark on it.[89]

These similarities are perhaps not coincidental. Momaday is closely familiar with Lawrence's work, particularly with his New Mexico writings, and both have written out of the same sense of place.[90]

During his stay at Kiowa Ranch, Lawrence wrote a number of short stories in which he examined the reaction of female protagonists to the southwestern landscape. A comparison of "The Princess," "St. Mawr," "The Woman Who Rode Away," and "Sun," a story set in Greece which Lawrence wrote after his return from America, with Momaday's treatment of his female protagonist in *House Made of Dawn*, Angela, reinforces the impression that Lawrence and Momaday are kindred spirits in their fictional treatment of the genius loci of the American Southwest.[91]

The three women of Lawrence's New Mexico stories and the heroine of "Sun" are all, in one way or another, refugees from unsatisfactory existences. They escape from deadening environments and enchaining relationships and follow the promise of more fulfilling lives in the stark, threatening landscape of southwestern America and the Greek countryside.

The unnamed protagonist of "The Woman Who Rode Away" breaks out of her paralyzing marriage to a materialist husband, a caricature of industrial man. She turns her back on his world of business, enters the mystical world of an ancient Indian civilization, gives herself up to it, and through ritual death experiences a unification with the cosmos.

In "The Princess," Dollie Urquhart's personal and sexual development has been stifled by her domineering father. Her upbringing as the last representative of an aristocratic family has resulted in an abnormal mental state. It precludes a normal relationship to men, whom she can comprehend only in the abstract. She is sexless, decadent, and, after the death of her father, intensely isolated. Lawrence describes her as "not quite human."[92] When she meets a Mexican guide, Domingo Romero, on her visit to New Mexico, she feels attracted to his maleness. She accepts his "daemon" as compatible with her royal standing. And yet, as it turns out, she ultimately cannot break out of her isolation and enter into a meaningful relationship with Romero: "She wanted warmth, protection, she wanted to be taken away from herself. And at the same time, perhaps more deeply than anything, she wanted to keep herself intact, intact, untouched, that no one should have any power over her, or rights to her."[93] On a trip into the mountains with her guide she is frightened of the inhuman wilderness and repelled by Romero's animality. She wills herself to submit to him sexually, and the Mexican is triumphant in his conquest. The subsequent battle of wills, during which he abuses and holds her against her will, ends tragically with the shooting of Romero by a forest ranger and leaves her "slightly crazy."[94]

Lou, the heroine of "St. Mawr," retreats from a sterile, disappointing relationship with her husband into a state of intense admiration of the vital force of her horse, St. Mawr, which Lawrence draws as a powerful sexual symbol. Like Dollie in "The Princess" she is yearning for life, but she conceives of it as an abstraction rather than as being attached to a man. She is frightened by the deadness she perceives in men and in herself, and she reaches out for an impersonal source of vitality: ". . . if we could get our lives from the source, as the animals do, and still be ourselves."[95]

She eventually leaves her husband and travels from England to New Mexico, taking St. Mawr with her. Lawrence spells out the antipodes between which Lou searches for a remedy to her anxieties: "The marvellous beauty and fascination of natural wild things! The horror of man's unnatural life, his heaped-up civilization!"[96] She leaves the horse on a Texan ranch and travels on the Southwest. By now she is fully aware of her needs: "She wanted relief from the nervous tension and irritation of her life, she wanted to escape from the friction which is the whole stimulus in modern social life. She wanted to be still: only that, to be very, very still, and recover her own soul."[97] And as far as sexual attachment to a man is concerned, she notes: ". . . sex, mere sex, is repellent to me. I will never prostitute myself again. Unless something touches my very spirit, the very quick of me. I will stay alone, just alone. Alone, and give myself only to the unseen presences, serve only the other, unseen presences."[98] In the spirit of place of the vast and living and frightening landscape she finally finds the impersonal vitality she has been looking for. Her retreat from sexual interaction finds its final stage in self-imposed chastity, fueled by a sense of mission "to keep herself for the spirit that is wild."[99] The story concludes with Lou, now in a state of complete isolation, cherishing her immersion in the wild spirit of an awesome place.

All these stories have in common female protagonists whose sexual lives have been deadened in one way or another. The underlying cause is, in Lawrence's terms, a decadent and sterile modern civilization. None of the three characters achieves a satisfactory revitalization, but Lawrence had no doubt that the potential for rejuvenation lies in the spirit of aboriginal America. While these summaries are overly simplified and reductive, they disclose the central patterns of the stories: civilization versus wild nature; self-conscious, willful females versus dark, aboriginal, dominating males; deadness versus vitality; the foreign versus the indigenous.

Momaday's treatment of Angela in *House Made of Dawn* can be seen as part of a similar pattern, especially when one compares it with Lawrence's short story "Sun." Both Angela St. John and Juliet in "Sun" leave the city to find remedy for ill health. Juliet removes herself from a lifeless husband, while Angela's neurotic shame of physicality hints at a problematic relationship in her marriage. Both women undergo transformations through the impulse of "the vivid wildness of the old places of civilisation," as Lawrence put it, Juliet among the peasants of Greece and Angela among the Rio Grande Pueblos.[100] Most significantly, they are restored, if only temporarily, by the natural healing powers of the sun and the magnetism of the desert landscape. They are both attracted to indigenous men whom they perceive as figures of vital sexual potency, and neither of them can avoid a return to their old restrictive backgrounds in "the fatal chain of continuity."[101]

Angela is the product of an environment and a society which have led her to doubt her instincts and natural worth. Her state of mind is marked by an intense feeling of shame which is the result of her inability to accept, let alone enjoy, the physical aspects of human existence. She is torn between a strong desire to follow her instincts and the controlling force of her conscience which suppresses these impulses. This tension leads to

a deep split in Angela's personality. The symptom of her inner
conflict is the rejection of her body:

She thought of her body and could not understand that it was beautiful. She could think of nothing more vile and obscene than the
raw flesh and blood of her body, the raveled veins and the gore upon
her bones. And now the monstrous fetal form, the blue, blind, great
headed thing growing within and feeding upon her. [102]

She not only disclaims her own body but, in rejecting the
growing child in her womb, she rejects, in a sense, life itself.
Her stay in the Indian town and particularly her relationship
with Abel create a strength which helps her to overcome her
feelings of guilt. With great economy and skill Momaday
shows the struggle between instinct and conscience which
threatens to tear Angela apart. The following scenes are central
in the development of the conflict which is finally resolved
through Angela's new awareness of human nature and the nature of her environment.

The passage quoted above which reveals Angela's estrangement from her own body is followed by a highly symbolic
scene. Angela has watched Abel cutting wood, and the sight
of his strong body arouses her sexually. Despite her attraction,
Angela is unable to accept her desire. The following image,
however, makes it clear how the instinctual forces operate in
Angela's subconscious:

She went out into the soft yellow light that fell from the windows
and that lay upon the ground and the pile of wood. She knelt down
and picked up the cold, hard lengths of wood and laid them in the
crook of her arm. They were sharp and seamed at the ends where
the axe had shaped them like pencil points, and they smelled of
resin. When again she stood, she inadvertently touched the handle
of the axe; it was stiff and immovable in the block, and cold. [103]

This scene with its phallic symbolism reveals both Angela's
sexual desire and frustration.

Momaday uses still another image to describe Angela's fascination for the animal powers she senses within herself and in
nature:

Once she had seen an animal slap at the water, a badger or a bear. She would have liked to touch the soft muzzle of a bear, the thin black lips, the great flat head. She would have liked to cup her hand to the wet black snout, to hold for a moment the hot blowing of the bear's life.[104]

In her sexual relationship with Abel, Angela's instinctual self is restored. Their encounter is, in much the same way as that between Dollie and Romero in "The Princess," a battle of wills, and Angela submits only unwillingly. But unlike Dollie she finds fulfillment. In the ensuing love scene Abel is portrayed as a Pan figure who revitalizes Angela. In this sexual communion the young woman again has the vision of the bear and the badger, the symbols of animal life: "He was dark and massive above her, poised and tinged with pale blue light. And in a split second she thought again of the badger at the water, and the great bear, blue-black and blowing."[105] Even though the relationship between Angela and Abel is ultimately unsuccessful, her life enters a new state of balance. She grows aware of sounds, shapes, and colors around her, enters the circle of natural life, absorbs the beauty of the land, and re-creates it in her imagination.[106]

The wilderness which attracts Angela and threatens Dollie in "The Princess" is portrayed in strikingly similar images. As Dollie and Romero climb into the mountains, the wind comes "rustling from the west, up the funnel of the canyon, from the desert. And there was the desert, like a vast mirage tilting slowly upwards towards the west, immense and pallid, away beyond the funnel of the canyon. . . .the wind blew like some vast machine."[107] In the following passage Angela receives her symbolic baptism:

Thunder cracked in the sky and rolled upon the mountains. It grew deep and filled the funnel of the canyon and reverberated endlessly upon the cliffs. Lightning flashed, rending the dark wall of rain, casting an awful glare upon it, and the rain moved into the canyon, almost slowly, upon the warm and waning gusts of drought, and the golden margin of receding light grew pale in the mist. And there behind the squall of still-invisible torrents coming on, like the sound of a great turbine, the roar of the wind and the rain.[108]

Finally, through the elemental forces of nature Angela is purged of her fears of civilization. It seems as if the life-bringing rain washes away Angela's anxieties. Her growing awareness of nature and her sensibility to her environment have a therapeutic effect:

And in the cold and denser dark, with the sound and sight of the fury all around, Angela stood transfixed in the open door and breathed deep into her lungs the purest electric scent of the air. She closed her eyes, and the clear aftervision of the rain, which she could still hear and feel so perfectly as to conceive of nothing else, obliterated all the mean and myriad fears that had laid hold of her in the past. Sharpest angles of light played on the lids of her eyes, and the great avalanche of sound fell about her.[109]

The above examination shows some of the common ground held by Lawrence and Momaday with respect to the tension between civilization and a seemingly less advanced but more organic and integrated form of social organization. They are kindred spirits in their perceptions of a necessary harmony between man and the land, in their beliefs in the molding influence of a spirit of place, and in their convictions that man must respond to this unconscious impulse.

This discussion of Momaday's treatment of the American earth against the background of historical conceptions of the wilderness in American literature and the comparison of his work to individual writers who shared his interest in the relationship of man and earth does not suggest any direct borrowing. It seeks to throw light on a wider intellectual and literary framework in which Momaday's writings share. The discovery of this common ground shows that he cannot simply be labeled as an "Indian" writer, unless this term is wide enough to acknowledge that he is an artist who knows his place in the tradition of American literature and, through his truly original imagination, creates a blend of this tradition with his personal attachment to American Indian cultures.

CHAPTER 4

The Crisis of Identity:
House Made of Dawn

The Novel's Genesis, Early Reception, and Autobiographical Background

When the Pulitzer Prize jury for fiction, consisting of the writer and critic Edmund Fuller; Raymond Walter, Jr., of the *New York Times*; and P. Albert Duhamel, of Boston University, selected *House Made of Dawn* for their award, they took the reading public as well as the author by surprise. Momaday at first refused to believe the news, and some of the senior editors at Harper and Row could not even remember the novel.[1] The jury explained their decision:

Our first choice is N. Scott Momaday's *House Made of Dawn* because of its, in the words of one of the members of the jury, "eloquence and intensity of feeling, its freshness of vision and subject, its immediacy of theme," and because an award to its author might be considered as a recognition of "the arrival on the American literary scene of a matured, sophisticated literary artist from the original Americans."[2]

The quality and success of Momaday's first novel are the result of a long-ripening process from the conception of the work in the early 1960s to its publication in 1968. *House Made of Dawn* was originally intended as a book of poems. When Momaday was a student at Stanford, he changed his plan and began to write early sections of it in prose. Wallace Stegner, to whom Momaday entrusted some of his early stories, gave him valuable advice. But none of these pieces was mature enough to be included in Stegner's collection *Twenty Years of Stanford Short Stories*.[3] Only one of these stories, "The Well," was published, in the literary magazine *Ramparts*.[4] Despite its fragmentary character the story is interesting as an example of Momaday's attempt to give literary expression to his experience of an Indian world eroding under the stress of culture clash.

Written more than five years before the publication of *House Made of Dawn*, "The Well" contains a number of the themes and prototypes of some of the characters which were to reappear in the novel. Hobson, the story's protagonist, later replaced by Abel, returns after twelve years, "in which he had become a man," to the Jicarilla Apache Reservation in New Mexico.[5] The setting is the area of Dulce where Momaday worked during 1958. In the novel he changed the scene to Jemez Pueblo, with which he was more intimately familiar. Like Abel, Hobson is out of tune with the world he had left, drowning his confusion in alcohol yet striving nonetheless to recover his roots: "He no longer knew anything of these people. For a time he had fixed his eyes on the landscape, but it too had changed. His homeland lay dim and dark in his memory, and there only."[6] A similar scene appears in the first chapter of *House Made of Dawn*, when Abel searches for some sign of recognition in the landscape.[7]

Hobson meets an old woman, Muñoz, who is not only an early version of the witch Nicolás but in her changelessness resembles the old man Francisco and functions as a foil for Hobson's own transformed state of being. A brief flashback, revealing Hobson's first encounter with Muñoz as a child, is reproduced almost verbatim in the novel as the passage describing Abel's terrifying experience with the old witch Nicolás (pp. 15–16). Hobson is deeply alienated; he has nothing to talk about when he meets an old friend, Josie, who plays an important role in *House Made of Dawn* (p. 106). He no longer knows her.

He attempts to reintegrate himself into the ceremonials of the tribe. But like Abel he remains ultimately isolated: "He wedged himself into one of the rings and *tried* to take up the chant. . . . He closed his eyes, and shapes *almost* familiar to him took form against the lids" (italics added).[8] The subsequent events in the short story portray the symptoms of disintegration in the Indian world, particularly those of alcoholism and violence. But they also suggest a continuing belief in the validity of witchcraft. Hobson witnesses how the old woman Muñoz is tortured by three drunk Indians. The men have fooled the woman by making her believe in the existence of a whisky well, pouring whisky over her as she is lying helplessly on the ground, struggling against the men's boots. But suddenly, after one of them showers her with dirt, events take a dramatic turn. Using her power of witchcraft, Muñoz sends the culprit flying through the air, and he crashes heavily to the ground. Hobson's intervention at this point brings the confrontation to a close.

During the following hours which Hobson and Muñoz spend together, a degree of compassion and understanding between the two emerges. He cares for her, while she, ignoring previous events and relying on her supernatural powers, offers to show him the whisky well. As they walk along the corrals, the man who suffered at the hands of the old woman suddenly confronts them and stabs Muñoz. This scene anticipates Abel's slaying of the albino in *House Made of Dawn*.

As in the novel, in "The Well" the themes of violence, witchcraft, and cultural and personal disintegration are set against the backdrop of a mysterious, beautiful, yet indifferent universe. The story was a nucleus from which Momaday, over the following five years, would fashion *House Made of Dawn*, bringing to bear on the text rapidly growing abilities of lyrical description and the handling of intricate technical devices and complex themes.

In February 1966, an editor at Harper and Row, Frances McCullough, once Momaday's fellow student and editor of Stanford's literary magazine, *Sequoia*, invited him to submit a manuscript for possible publication in a new poetry program.[9] She knew of his poetic talent, having published some of his poems in *Sequoia*, and assumed that he had enough material for

a collection. Momaday replied that he could not offer a sufficient number of poems to fill a volume, explaining that he had
neglected poetry in favor of prose during the three years since
his graduation from Stanford. He offered to send part of a novel
in progress instead.[10]

McCullough urged Momaday to submit his manuscript for
the Harper Prize Novel contest.[11] She subsequently played a
significant role in the process of editing and rewriting the novel
and was instrumental in contracting it with Harper and Row
and placing Momaday's excerpt from *The Way to Rainy Mountain* with *The Reporter*.[12] Perhaps her most valuable contribution to *House Made of Dawn* was her advice to Momaday not to
rush the unrevised manuscript into the Harper contest and
subsequent publication but first to rework it thoroughly. She
was particularly critical of the fragmentary structure and lack
of cohesion of the early drafts. It was her suggestion to concentrate the narrative perspective in the figure of Ben Benally, a
device which Momaday employed only in chapter 3, "The
Night Chanter." She also advised Momaday to incorporate the
excerpt from *The Way to Rainy Mountain*, the Kiowa migration
story, into the novel. Moreover, McCullough must be given
credit for urging Momaday to drop or modify some of the less
convincing characters of the first draft.[13] It was also her idea
to date the four chapters of *House Made of Dawn* to aid the
reader in keeping track of the novel's complicated time
scheme.[14]

No sooner was the manuscript in its final form than Momaday came to realize the problems which were to arise from his
novel's cultural background. McCullough had already hinted
at some of the difficulties the reader might have with Pueblo
ceremonials, the figure of the albino, and the witchcraft
theme.[15] The publisher's "Brief Description" of the novel, dis-
tributed to reviewers and salesmen before publication, must
have confirmed her worst fears:

In this strongly lyrical first novel, N. Scott Momaday traces the
disintegration of a young "longhair" American Indian who cannot

accommodate the contradictions between the ancient ways of the reservation where he grew up and the "outside" world. For Abel, the first sign of trouble shows up during his service in World War II, when one day he goes berserk, attacks a tank, and dances wildly around it yelling war whoops; later, back on the reservation, it is a wholly different kind of madness that leads him to cold blooded murder of a white man. From that point on, Abel is running— away from himself and from the best efforts of those who try to save him: his friend Benally (who sees the problem perfectly but cannot solve it for Abel), a well-meaning social worker in Los Angeles, Abel's heartbroken grandfather.[16]

This first paragraph of the summary alone contains so many misunderstandings that Momaday felt a need to put some of them right. He noted that "the term 'longhair' . . . belongs more truly to the old man [Francisco]" than to Abel. Juan Reyes, the man killed by Abel, is not a "white man" but an "albino Indian and a witch." Momaday elaborated on this point: "He is a white man, or rather 'white man' in quotes, in appearance, but in fact he is neither white nor a man in the usual sense of those words. He is an embodiment of evil like Moby Dick, an intelligent malignity."[17] Momaday chose to ignore other misconceptions. Abel's first signs of trouble, for instance, occur long before he enters the army; he is running, to be sure, away from the forces which threaten to annihilate him, but, more important, he is running, symbolically and ritualistically, back to the source of his strength, which lies in his native culture. Benally and the grandfather are far from being helpless onlookers; Ben's performance of the Night Chant ceremony and Francisco's hallucinatory recollections of his past are significant contributions to the restoration of Abel's sense of self. These points will be discussed in detail below from the perspective of the Indian identity crisis and the use of ritual patterns in *House Made of Dawn*.

Many of the reviews of the novel were favorable and well informed.[18] Others, although positive in their final analysis, betrayed the critics' difficulties in understanding the work's cultural implications. One reviewer, acknowledging the author's Kiowa heritage, assumed his home to be in "Arizona or thereabouts" and without much regard for detail summed up the novel as depicting "the inner life of a Kiowa Indian."[19] P. L. Adams fell into the same trap: "Mr. Momaday is a Kiowa, and the portion (about two thirds) of his first novel which deals with Kiowa tradition . . . is unusual and good."[20] *House Made of Dawn* is, of course, mainly concerned with Navajo and Jemez Pueblo cultures; only Tosamah's evocation of his tribal ancestry introduces Kiowa culture into the text.

Joseph Illick, in a positive evaluation, mistakenly assumed that "a house made of dawn is a day" rather than the Navajo image of the cosmos. Ignoring Abel's incantation of the creation hymn at the conclusion of the novel, Illick saw him as "unreconstructed" and "inarticulate," suggesting that the drift toward final disintegration is continuing.[21] This view of the novel's ending, resulting from an unawareness of the symbolic and ritualistic patterns in *House Made of Dawn*, reappeared in a number of later interpretations.[22]

Some of the less favorable reviews were marred by their writers' lack of understanding, racial bias, or inability to see the novel as something more than a social statement. William James Smith obviously failed to see not only the meaning of the novel's title, complaining that there was "something broken-backed about the title to begin with," but also the cause of Abel's distress and the implications of the central witchcraft theme.[23] He simply glossed over these crucial issues by saying that "Abel is a moody sort and gets off to a bad start by murdering a mysterious albino who seems to personify evil in Abel's befuddled brain." He concluded his disparaging criticism with the patronizing remark that "it is slightly un-American to criticize an American Indian's novel."[24] Mary Borg found little to commend in the novel, which according to her is marred by "sentimentality and a mixture of turgid stylizing and transparent intent."[25] She falsely assumed that the Kiowa hero ends in destruction, and, after acknowledging with surprise the novel's Pulitzer award, saw "its social conscience" as the only possible explanation for this honor.[26] An anonymous review in the *Times (London) Literary Supplement* was in a similar vein.[27] Finally, John Leonard suggested that the Pulitzer Prize was awarded to Momaday's novel because it was a "safe" choice, "a pet instead of a work of art."[28] Fortunately a growing number of critical evaluations have rectified many false assumptions about *House Made of Dawn* and illuminated the great complexity of its content and structure.

A reading of *House Made of Dawn* against the background of Momaday's life reveals the novel's richness of autobiographical detail. The exploration of Kiowa history in Tosamah's speech is only the most obvious example of Momaday's own search for his racial antecedents, a search which he continued and amplified in later works. But while the "blood memory" of his forebears is largely a product of Momaday's historical imagination, the portrayals of Jemez and Navajo cultures grow out of immediate personal experiences.

The southwestern landscape and Jemez and Navajo life are central to Momaday's world. The notion of witchcraft which permeates the novel had been very much a part of his consciousness while he was growing up among the Jemez people. Momaday suggested that "witchcraft is a natural thing, not logical as much as natural. It is something that exists, it is part of the world we live in. . . . It is taken as a matter of course, for granted. . . . Everybody has a deep conviction that it exists. It is an expectation, and it is an expectation that is not disappointed among Indian people."[29] As a boy Momaday witnessed the "runners after evil" who guard the Jemez Pueblo against witches.[30]

The figure of Tosamah is largely autobiographical, not only because of his involvement in Kiowa history but also because of his regard for language and the oral tradition. This makes him, to a certain degree, Momaday's mouthpiece, even though Momaday pointed out that "Tosamah is more articulate" than he is and that he "speaks more glibly."[31] It is particularly in the way the fictional character manipulates language that he reflects Momaday's own fascination with words. Momaday's preoccupation with Navajo culture is reflected not only in the novel's title and the symbolic healing act, the Night Chant, but also in the figure of Benally. Benally relates much of what Momaday saw during his boyhood in Navajo country. Momaday once noted: "I feel closer to the Navajo than to other peoples. I also identify with Benally for that reason."[32]

While *House Made of Dawn* reflects in many ways its author's background, it is also a detached portrayal of the tragic consequences when identity cannot be formed or begins to disintegrate as a result of conflicts in the Indian world. Abel, the novel's protagonist, epitomizes the Indian identity crisis, a phenomenon particularly prevalent after World War II, when many veterans failed to find a way back into their native communities.[33] Abel's tragedy lies in his inability to determine his place and define himself. His crisis is intensely personal, and yet it represents a latent crisis of American Indian cultures in general. A key message of *House Made of Dawn* is that the survival of American Indians depends on the continual reassessment of their identities. This reassessment must be achieved by each successive generation. It is in this context that one can understand Momaday's central statement on the search for selfhood: "We are what we imagine. Our very existence consists in our imagination of ourselves. Our best destiny is to imagine, at least, completely, who and what, and *that* we are. The greatest tragedy that can befall us is to go unimagined."[34]

Abel's suffering results from a sense of loss which he cannot comprehend. It is his existence between two cultures which threatens to destroy him, and redemption comes only when he renews his attachment to his tribal heritage. Momaday sees Abel's plight thus: "He tries desperately to live in the present; yet he is hopelessly determined by the past. He is a tragic figure in the sense that his disintegration is brought about by circumstances which he can neither prevent nor understand."[35] Comparing himself to the generation of American Indians of which Abel is a representative, Momaday points to the fact

that he never suffered a sense of loss as Abel does.[36] The Kiowa
Reservation was dissolved as a result of the Dawes Act of 1887;
this led to the decline of the Kiowas as a unified people and
required from the individual member of the tribe a new affirmation of identity. Momaday's father and grandfather showed
him how this affirmation could be achieved.

Abel has no such support. He grows up in a traditional
society which is functioning and whole yet at the same time
"something of an anachronism."[37] There are pressures within
this community and outside of it for which he is entirely un-
prepared. The resulting crises and sense of loss are, as Momaday put it, characteristic of

the people one generation back, particularly those who were taken
forcefully, as it were, conscripted, and taken from a traditional
world that is characterized by harmony and peace and order, and set
down in a world that was characterized at that time by chaos, World
War II. There is no way, I think, that you can imagine what sort of
adjustment that requires. And the people to whom it happened were
a particularly tragic generation.[38]

If Momaday's *The Way to Rainy Mountain* and *The Names* are
expressions of his own search for an Indian identity, then *House
Made of Dawn* must be read as a powerful plea for such a search
and a realistic portrayal of the forces against which it must be
accomplished.

Abel's Boyhood: Harmony and Conflict

My reading of *House Made of Dawn* focuses on the novel's thematic center: the problem of identity. First I deal with Abel's
early years of harmony and the gradual emergence of conflicts
which lead to his departure from the community. Next I examine Abel's attempts to resolve his confusion after his return
from a war which has further undermined his sense of belonging. In fact, Abel has become a man between two cultures,
unable to cope with either. In the last section of this reading I
argue that Abel's eventual return to his native culture takes the

course of a rite of passage. The interpretation is based on a close analysis of the novel's symbolism against the background of Mircea Eliade's studies of initiation ceremonies and religious patterns.

By way of introduction to the tragic effects of identity conflicts among American Indians as Momaday witnessed them at Jemez, it may be best to quote from one of his letters. I have deleted the names of the victims to protect their privacy and that of their families:

Abel is a composite of the boys I knew at Jemez. I wanted to say something about them. An appalling number of them are dead; they died young, and they died violent deaths. One of them was drunk and run over. Another was drunk and froze to death. (He was the best runner I ever knew). One man was murdered, butchered by a kinsman under a telegraph pole just east of San Ysidro. And yet another committed suicide. A good many who have survived this long are living under the Relocation Program in Los Angeles, Chicago, Detroit, etc. They're a sad lot of people.[39]

This statement spells out the disastrous violence, suffering, and despair which frequently accompanies cultural change. While Abel's conflicts are aggravated by a particularly unsettling historical period, his difficulties in reconciling his tribal origin with the presence of a modern world are a latent and potentially disruptive problem for every generation of American Indians.

Abel is struggling to find an identity within his own tribe long before he comes into direct contact with the culture of modern America. From a developmental point of view his experience is universal: it is the struggle of a young man to establish a stable position in his community. From a historical perspective his crisis reflects a crisis of his culture which denies its young tribal members accommodation to changing conditions.

Abel's problem grows out of a generation conflict within a tribal community in which the ancient traditions tend to lose their meanings for young Indians in their confrontation with the cultural tradition of modern America. The old generation of traditionalists tends to exert pressure on young tribal members in order to assure the perpetuation of the old ways. This can lead to a conflict between communal obligations and the search for a new Indian identity which must include the benefits of modern society.

Abel cannot simply adopt the traditional customs of his tribe as would have been natural in a community unaffected by the encroachment of an alien culture. He turns his back on the Indian world and enters modern America. Here, under the influence of an unsympathetic environment, Abel's conflict is aggravated. He shows all the symptoms of identity confusion: estrangement from both the tribal and the Anglo-American cultures, sexual and emotional disturbance in his personal relationships, and an inability to channel his aggression appropriately.

His return to the native community suggests that Indian cultures are capable of overcoming such crises, not by isolating themselves but through an adherence to basic traditional values and by the selective acceptance of new elements from other cultures. This strategy, which has been a strength of American Indian societies throughout the period of contact with other cultural groups, must be continued. In giving an account of the developmental crisis in the protagonist's life history Momaday makes a statement about Indian life in a period of increasing cultural and economic pressures. *House Made of Dawn*, then, is a novel about an individual and a communal search for identity.

The Indian community in which Abel grows up belongs to the Rio Grande Pueblo villages in New Mexico. Momaday opens the first chapter with the place name "Walatowa, Canyon de San Diego." Walatowa literally means "the people in the canyon."[40] It is the native name of Jemez. As a result of their geographical isolation and their cultural conservatism the Rio Grande Pueblos have succeeded in keeping their languages, religions, and traditional customs relatively intact despite the pressures of Spanish and Anglo-American cultural encroachment. This is how Momaday portrays life in the village:

The people of the town have little need. They do not hanker after progress and have never changed their essential way of life. Their invaders were a long time in conquering them; and now, after four centuries of Christianity, they still pray in Tanoan to the old deities of the earth and sky and make their living from the things that are and have always been within their reach; while in the discrimination of pride they acquire from their conquerors only the luxury of example. They have assumed the names and gestures of their enemies, but have held on to their own, secret souls; and in this there is a resistance and an overcoming, a long outwaiting. [P. 56]

Abel grows up in a world where the preservation of old values counts more than progress. Even today Pueblo life revolves around a complex system of religious ceremonials based on a solar calendar, whose keeper is the cacique, the Pueblo medicine man. According to his observation of the course of the sun, the cacique determines all the essential events of tribal life, the planting, harvesting, and the religious ceremonies.

In *House Made of Dawn* the old man Francisco functions as the teacher and guardian of the traditional Pueblo way of life. He represents the old generation of the tribe which possesses the cultural heritage and strives to preserve it by handing it down to the next generation. Francisco teaches his grandsons, Abel and Vidal, to observe the sun. He tells them that "they must know the long journey of the sun on the black mesa, how it rode in the seasons and the years, and they must live according to the sun appearing, for only then could they reckon where they were, where all things were, in time" (p. 177). In revealing the connection between the sun, the landscape, and the rhythms of Indian life, Francisco roots the two boys in the old ways of the tribe. Francisco's teachings are central to their development as well as the perpetuation of Jemez tradition.

Under the guidance of old man Francisco, Abel is raised according to the tribal patterns of his people and acquires a deep feeling for his environment. Typical of Abel's consciousness is his natural attitude toward death: ". . . he knew somehow that his mother was soon going to die of her illness. It was nothing he was told, but he knew it anyway and without understanding, as he knew already the motion of the sun and the seasons" (p. 15). Abel is at the center of Indian life. He herds sheep, takes part in a deer hunt, and participates in the ceremonial activities of his tribe.

Despite this seeming harmony with the tribal world, however, Abel somehow remains a stranger within his community. Not only during his time away from the reservation but also while growing up among his own people, he lives in a state of isolation. He was born into his position as an outsider: "He did not know who his father was. His father was a Navajo, they said, or a Sia, or an Isleta, an outsider anyway, which made him and his mother and Vidal somehow foreign and strange" (p. 15). Tribal communities are not necessarily homogenous entities as they are often perceived by outsiders; within the tribe subgroups may exist which do not meet the full acceptance of the majority. The early deaths of his mother and brother increase Abel's isolation. He is left with his grandfather, Francisco, as his only other relation.

Preoccupied with Abel's conforming to the tribal tradition, Francisco monopolizes his education. He forbids him to find a substitute mother in Josie, one of the women in the village (p. 106). The lack of family ties prevents Abel's full integration into the native community. As Abel approaches adolescence he finds it increasingly difficult to accept tribal patterns and the domineering authority of his grandfather.

It is common for young people at this stage of personal development to question the way of life which adults in their families or communities expect them to adopt. Momaday shows in his novel the severity of the conflict between a budding individual and a rigid tribal pattern which depends for its perpetuation on the absence of individual awareness. He reveals how the crisis in Abel's personal development reflects a crisis in Pueblo culture.

Pueblo traditionalists maintain that in an age of growing pressure from outside the tribal culture can only survive in isolation. Even though technical attainments of Anglo-American culture have been adopted for their obvious usefulness, Pueblo communities are very reluctant to allow any interference that could dilute traditional tribal life. This inevitably leads to tremendous pressures in the educational processes of young Indians. A culture which depends for its survival on the adoption of age-old patterns by the next generation not only shelters against influences from the outside but also ignores or even suppresses the individual needs of its members. Thus a generation conflict is almost unavoidable.[41]

The pressure exerted upon young Indians by the older generation of traditionalists often leads to the opposite of what was intended: young Indians, feeling deprived of the choice between the traditional and a more individual way of life, turn their backs on the native community. Robert F. Spencer saw one reason for the Indians' migration to the large cities today in "a wish to evade the responsibilities of what they had come to feel as the constricting burdens of tribal and kinship ties, or to escape from what they felt was the stifling pressure to conform to traditional behavior and values, which was exerted by the older generations of reservation Indians."[42] This view is supported by Thomas Weaver and Ruth H. Gartell, who noted that it is not only the desire for adventure and economic advancement which makes young Indians leave the reservation but also the search "for easement of their responsibilities to tradition and for a more general identity with other Indians instead of just their own tribe."[43]

Abel's decision to leave the Pueblo community grows out of the realization that he cannot find an identity simply by adopting the teachings of his grandfather. Momaday shows by means of a few central events that Abel has no choice but to step out of the limiting realm of his native village in order to remain true to himself.

A most significant experience during Abel's adolescence is his vision of an eagle which carries a snake in its talons: "He had seen a strange thing, an eagle overhead with its talons closed upon a snake. It was an awful, holy sight, full of magic and meaning" (p. 18). Both eagle and snake have deeply religious meanings for the Indians of the Southwest. The snake is associated with the coming of water and is worshiped in ceremonies such as the famous snake dance of the Hopis.[44] The eagle is believed to attain supernatural powers on its flights and is revered in the eagle dance.[45] The appearance of the eagle and snake together is of particular religious importance, just as the plumed serpent is a major mythological figure.[46]

For Abel the eagle is a symbol of freedom, beauty, and life: "They were golden eagles, a male and a female, in their mating flight. They were cavorting, spinning and spiraling on the cold, clear columns of air, and they were beautiful" (p. 20). When Abel first sees the two birds, he is "on the rim of the Valle Grande, a great volcanic crater that lay high up on the western slope of the range. It was the right eye of the earth, held open to the sun. Of all places that he knew, this valley alone could reflect the great spatial majesty of the sky" (p. 19). Standing high above the plateau he has a view of the whole extent of his world and observes the eagles as they fly across and beyond the land, disappearing in the endless sky. Perhaps it is in this vision that Abel realizes the limitations of his life under the rules of his tribal community.

His observation of the eagles and the snake gains him the permission of the Eagle Watcher Society to take part in an eagle hunt. Again he sees the two eagles and eventually succeeds in catching the female bird. He returns to the other hunters in the plain who celebrate him in much the same way as Francisco was celebrated after his successful bear hunt. Abel, however, cannot enjoy this honor. He does not understand or cannot accept that his respect for the animal can be reconciled with his act of depriving it of its freedom for the benefit of the community. Eagle feathers are highly valued as indispensable requisites for ceremonials.[47] The closeness of the captive eagle's spirit to the village is regarded as a beneficial influence on the life at Jemez.[48]

When his peers allow the less attractive male eagle to return to the sky, Abel is overcome by a feeling of longing, as if he wanted to follow the bird:

It leveled off and sailed. Then it was gone from sight, but he looked after it for a time. He could see it still in the mind's eye and hear in his memory the awful whisper of its flight on the wind. It filled him with longing. He felt the great weight of the bird which he held in the sack. The dusk was fading quickly into night, and the others could not see that his eyes were filled with tears. [P. 24]

Instead of feeling victorious about the hunt, in keeping with tribal tradition, Abel is sad and disgusted. He decides to kill the bird rather than allow it to live in captivity in the village. This killing is not a ritual act, as one critic assumed, but an act of rebellion against a tribal custom Abel cannot comprehend.[49] This interpretation is corroborated by the absence of any ritual preparation and by Abel's psychological state when he acts.

There are a number of other scenes in the novel which show Abel in similar emotional states in response to animal life. After the rabbit hunt he feels "something like remorse or disappointment" about the killing of animals (p. 22). Similarly, he shows a strange affection for the small fish along the coast of California: ". . . small silversided fishes spawned mindlessly in correlation to the phase of the moon and the rise and fall of the tides. The thought of it made him sad, filled him with sad, unnamable longing and wonder" (p. 91).

These emotional reactions reflect a deep respect for the well-being of other life forms, an attitude common among American Indian peoples.[50] However, Abel fails to see the wider implications of the man-animal relationship in his tribal religion. The hunting and killing of animals does not constitute a breach of the spiritual bond between man and animal if it is performed in the appropriate traditional way. According to John Witthoft, ". . . game animals were gifts of the Creator and of the lesser supernaturals to the hunter, provided the hunter did his work properly and well and conducted his affairs in a precisely correct fashion. This involved matters of conservation, ritual, and taboo."[51]

Momaday dramatized this concept in Francisco's bear hunt. Francisco proceeds strictly according to the code of honor which regulates the hunt:

And he did not want to break the stillness of the night, for it was holy and profound; it was rest and restoration, the hunter's offering of death and the sad watch of the hunted, waiting somewhere away in the cold darkness and breathing easily of its life, brooding around at last to forgiveness and consent; the silence was essential to them both, and it lay out like a bond between them, ancient and inviolable. [P. 180–81]

The bear's knowledge of Francisco's approach, the absence of fear and hurry, and Francisco's following "in the bear's tracks" suggest an old intimacy between the hunter and the hunted. The ritual blessing of the bear with pollen is an expression of gratitude and respect, a plea for propitiation.

Without the knowledge of these ancient practices Abel reacts emotionally rather than ritualistically. His shame and disgust are inappropriate responses within the framework of traditional Indian thought and reflective of his estrangement from his tribal heritage. Abel's failure to perceive or accept the intricacies of tribal tradition is also at the center of his conflict with Francisco. The young Indian not only is unable to comprehend certain aspects of his native tradition but also has lost respect for his grandfather as the representative of the ancient ways. Abel is "almost a grown man" when he has a riding accident: ". . . for days afterward there was a sharp, recurrent pain in the small of his back. Francisco chanted and prayed; the old man applied herbs and powders and potions and salves, and nothing worked" (p. 93). This incident may well have contributed to Abel's loss of faith in his grandfather and his native culture.

His inability to adhere to the rules of tradition brings about the final break between Francisco and Abel: "You ought to do this and that, his grandfather said. But the old man had not understood, would not understand, only wept, and Abel left him alone. It was time to go, and the old man was away in the fields" (p. 25). Abel's decision to leave is the final rejection of authority, grown out of the conviction that in the rigidness of his tribal environment he will be unable to find fulfillment and an identity. His leaving is a departure in dread, accompanied by fear of an unknown future in an unknown world.

Momaday stresses the young Indian's position between two cultures by means of Abel's shoes. The shoes are typical of the white man's fashion in the city and therefore conspicuous to traditional Indians. In some Pueblo communities tribal rules demand that shoes or boots can be worn only if the heel is cut off, to avoid injury to the sacred earth on which the community's existence depends.[52] Abel, however, does not share this orthodox view; to him the shoes are simply objects of good craftsmanship, admirable in their own right, like "the work of a good potter or painter or silversmith" (p. 98). As Abel steps out of his native community, he is wearing these shoes, having waited "a long time for the occasion to wear them" (p. 98). In this situation they signify the world he is about to enter, and as Abel realizes this he grows anxious and afraid:

But now and beyond his former frame of reference, the shoes called attention to Abel. They were brown and white; they were conspicuously new and too large; they shone; they clattered and creaked. And they were nailed to his feet. There were enemies all around, and he knew that he was ridiculous in their eyes. [P. 98]

Despite Abel's fears of what awaits him in the alien world of modern America, his departure is a necessary step toward his understanding of himself.

Abel's withdrawal from the tribe is the result of a disturbed communication between the old and the young generation. Anxious to preserve the ancient tribal ways, the old members of the pueblo have grown blind to the needs of the young. In the following section I examine Abel's struggle for an identity in the context of the tension between modern American and tribal cultures.

Between Two Worlds

When Abel returns to his grandfather after having served in the U.S. Army in World War II, he is drunk. His flight into alcohol indicates his inability to cope with the horror and turmoil of his recent past. Abel is confused. His drunken state reflects a lack of inner stability as a result of his bicultural situation. Alcoholism, in part a reaction to being cut adrift from native cultures and being unable to come to terms with the mainstream of American society, is a widespread problem among the American Indian population.[53]

During the two weeks Abel spends in his grandfather's house, he tries to halt his mental and physical disintegration and find his way back to the center of Indian life. He struggles to become attuned to the culture he left as an adolescent, and he tries to rid himself of the destructive influences of a war in an alien world.

On the morning after his return Abel climbs the hill outside the village. In the growing light of the new day, he looks out over the pueblo and the land. As he is standing there, a number of episodes from his boyhood and the war come to his mind. The series of flashbacks must be seen not merely as a technical device Momaday employs to make the reader familiar with the protagonist's past. In reliving central episodes of his childhood and adolescence, Abel tries to reintegrate himself into his environment, to imagine himself into an existence he can understand and with which he can identify. He re-creates previous experiences in his mind, trying to come to grips with his confused state. His recollections become a psychological process of searching for the roots of his confusion.

While Abel is very capable of comprehending the memories of his Indian boyhood, he is unable to come to terms with the months and years he spent away from the pueblo: "This— everything in advance of his going—he could remember whole and in detail. It was the recent past, the intervention of days and years without meaning, of awful calm and collision, time always immediate and confused, that he could not put together in his mind" (p. 25).

The shock of war is the determining factor in Abel's early manhood, as the vision of the eagles' flight was a central event in his adolescence. In the alien world he becomes subject to a dehumanizing military conflict. The dehumanization comes across forcefully in his recollection of his war experience through the recurrent reference to the tank as "the machine." The tank symbolizes the deadening force of an aggressive, technological society. The atmosphere of death and destruction is reinforced by another recurrent image pattern; damp, matted, wet, cold, and falling leaves intensify the scene's implications of decay and annihilation:

Then through the falling leaves, he saw the machine. It rose up behind the hill, black and massive, looming there in front of the sun. He saw it swell, deepen, and take shape on the skyline, as if it were some upheaval of the earth, the eruption of stone and eclipse, and all about it the glare, the cold perimeter of light, throbbing with leaves. For a moment it seemed apart from the land; its great iron hull lay out against the timber and the sky, and the center of its weight hung away from the ridge. Then it came crashing down to the grade, slow as a waterfall, thunderous, surpassing impact, *nestling* almost into the splash and boil of debris. He was shaking violently, and the machine bore down upon him, came close, and passed him by. A wind rose and ran along the slope, scattering the leaves. [P. 26]

The image of the machine as the embodiment of destruction and denial of life stands in sharp contrast to the crucial experience in Abel's youth when the eagles appeared to him as symbols of life and freedom.

It has already been pointed out that Abel had no stable identity when he left the pueblo; indeed, he entered the world of modern America because the restrictive environment of his home impeded his growth toward personal identity. During his absence from the Indian village his inner stability does not grow but is further disturbed by the traumatic events of the war. As an Indian among white soldiers he is denied a personal identity by his comrades. He is the "chief" who is "giving it to the tank in Sioux or Algonquin or something" (p. 100).

This statement by one of Abel's war companions shows why Abel is prevented from becoming assimilated. The dominant Anglocentric environment has stereotyped him as an Indian without regard for his individuality. In pressing him into this misconceived role, his peers not only shut him out from their culture but also deny his identity as a Jemez man.

Abel returns to the reservation in a state of identity confusion which is typical of adolescence. Even though Abel is approximately twenty-five years old, he is devoid of the sense of wholeness which is the basis for maturation into adulthood.[54] Erik Erikson wrote that "the young person, in order to experience wholeness, must feel a progressive continuity between that which he had come to be during the long years of childhood and that which he promises to become in the anticipated future: between that which he conceives himself to be and that which he perceives others to see in him and expect of him."[55]

For Abel progressive continuity is disrupted by his inability to accept tribal rules and by the damaging impact of his life outside the native community. The break from his culture and the effects of the war lead Abel into a state of confusion, isolation, and estrangement. With regard to such a crisis Erikson pointed out that "youth which is eager for, yet unable to find access to, the dominant techniques of society, will not only feel estranged from society, but also upset in sexuality, and most of all unable to apply aggression constructively."[56] Abel shows all these symptoms of identity confusion in his estrangement from the ritual and ceremonial practices of his tribe, in his relationship with Angela, and in his outburst of aggression which leads to the killing of the albino.

First Abel tries to reattune himself to the land and the culture of his tribe by searching for a sign in his environment: "He stood for a long time, the land yielding to the light. He stood without thinking, nor did he move; only his eyes roved after something" (p. 27). Abel is feeling his way back to a center which has been lost to him. Only by relating himself to this center can he reestablish order and overcome his inner chaos. His search is informed with religious meaning, as it aims at a communion with the land which is sacred to his people. This search for a sign, as Mircea Eliade pointed out, is a universal religious impulse in a state of disequilibrium: "A *sign* is asked, to put an end to the tension and anxiety caused by relativity and disorientation—in short, to reveal an absolute point of support."[57]

When a little later Abel sees his grandfather and some of the other Indians working in the fields, he acquires for a moment the old familiar sense of unity with his homeland: "The breeze was very faint, and it bore a scent of earth and grain; and for a moment everything was all right with him. He was at home" (pp. 31–32). But even as Abel recognizes that he has not entirely lost the ties to his native environment, he soon finds himself unable to enter the ceremonial life of his tribe.

Five days after Abel's return, the people of Jemez celebrate the game of the Chicken Pull. This activity was introduced by the Spaniards and adopted by many of the southwestern tribes. The Rio Grande Pueblos view the insertion of the rooster into the ground and its subsequent removal as a symbolic representation of planting and reaping. The scattering of the rooster's feathers and blood are representative of rain and are believed to increase the fertility of the land and the success of the harvest.[58]

Abel's participation in this ancient ceremony offers him an opportunity for reconciliation with his tribal culture: "For the first time since coming home he had done away with his uniform. He had put on his old clothes" (p. 42). His effort in the game, however, proves to be a failure: "When it came Abel's turn, he made a poor showing, full of caution and gesture" (p. 43). And when the albino as the victorious rider turns against Abel and starts beating him with the rooster in accordance with the rules of the game, he is unable to cope with the situation: "Abel was not used to the game, and the white man was too strong and quick for him" (p. 44). He is estranged from the old traditions and consequently fails to integrate himself into the cultural context of his community.

Another Pueblo ceremonial which could have been of help to Abel is the Pecos Bull Dance, which the Jemez people perform on August 1. Momaday witnessed the ceremony as a child.[59] He described it thus:

On the first of August, at dusk, the Pecos Bull ran through the streets of Jemez, taunted by the children, chased by young boys who were dressed in outlandish costumes, most in a manner which parodied the curious white Americans who came frequently to see the rich sights of Jemez on feast days. This "bull" was a man who wore a mask, a wooden framework on his back covered with black cloth and resembling roughly a bull, the head of which was a crude thing made of horns, a sheepskin, and a red cloth tongue which wagged about. It ran around madly, lunging at the children.[60]

Alfonso Ortiz noted that one purpose of burlesque and mock violence in Pueblo ritual drama is catharsis, the "purgation of individuals or community of rebellious tendencies so that they behave during the rest of the year."[61] The ceremony could have offered Abel a chance to vent his aggression against white Americans in a ritual way rather than in the hostile manner he later employs against the albino. This point was made by Lawrence J. Evers, who drew attention to Abel's isolation from the tribal community which once again becomes apparent on the occasion of the dance.[62]

Abel's reluctance to take part in the Bull Dance arises from his lack of identification with tribal rituals and perhaps also from his disbelief in their effectiveness. His loss of confidence after the Chicken Pull is a further obstacle to his participation in the event: "It was a hard thing to be the bull, for there was a primitive agony to it, and it was a kind of victim, an object of ridicule and hatred; and harder now that the men of the town had relaxed their hold upon the ancient ways, had grown soft and dubious. Or they had merely grown old" (p. 75). Momaday indicates in this context the increasing difficulty of adhering to the old traditions, which is a major problem, particularly for the young Indian generation represented by Abel. The ancient traditions tend to lose their meaning for young tribal members in their confrontation with mainstream America. This crisis in the Indian cultures adds to the identity problem exemplified in the figure of Abel.

A further indication of Abel's failure to reenter the Indian world of his childhood is his loss of articulation. His inability to find the proper words to acquire wholeness and communion with his culture and his homeland makes him aware that his return to the town has failed:

Abel walked into the canyon. His return to the town had been a failure, for all his looking forward. He had tried in the days that followed to speak to his grandfather, but he could not say the things he wanted; he had tried to pray, to sing, to enter into the old rhythm of the tongue, but he was no longer attuned to it. And yet it was there still, like memory, in the reach of his hearing, as if Francisco or his mother or Vidal had spoken out of the past and the words had taken hold of the moment and made it eternal. Had he been able to say it, anything in his own language—even the most commonplace formula of greeting "Where are you going"—which had no being beyond sound, no visible substance, would once again have shown him whole to himself; but he was dumb. Not dumb— silence was the older and better part of custom still—but *inarticulate*. [P. 57]

Some sense of the old harmony still remains, but Abel lacks the active power to reestablish harmony. This power is the power of the word.

As discussed in chapter 2, Momaday believes that the Indian relation to the world is based on the power of the word. The word links the Indian to his religious and mythological heritage. Indian culture is based on an oral tradition and maintained through the creative power of the word. If the word is lost, culture and identity are forfeited, as wholeness can only be established by the word. The following passage shows that Abel has indeed lost the power of words:

He began almost to be at peace, as if he had drunk a little of warm, sweet wine, for a time no longer centered upon himself. He was alone, and he wanted to make a song out of the colored canyon, the way the women of Torreón made songs upon their looms out of colored yarn, but he had not got the right words together. It would have been a creation song; he would have sung lowly of the first world, of fire and flood, and of the emergence of dawn from the hills. [P. 57]

As his imaginative re-creation of his childhood and adolescence was an attempt to understand his problematic situation, his effort to make a song is an endeavor to restore harmony between himself and the universe.[63] Abel's creation song would have been a bid for the creative power that heals, restores harmony, and provides wholeness. However, he "has not the right words" and thus remains isolated. It is not until his recital of the Night Chant at the end of the book that he regains his voice.

The second symptom of identity confusion, according to Erikson, the upset in sexuality, becomes apparent in the relationship between Abel and Angela St. John. After his failed attempts to find access to the tribal rituals and ceremonies, Abel tries to acquire some kind of stability in an intimate relationship with the white woman. This second endeavor proves to be as unsuccessful as the first. The insecurity Abel exposes in both his dealing with tribal roles and his relationship with Angela is a symptom of his confused identity. Erikson described the crisis of intimacy as the first postadolescent identity crisis. He pointed out that without a well-developed identity formation true intimacy cannot be achieved. "Where a youth," he continued, "does not accomplish such intimate relationships with others—and . . . with his own inner resources—in late adolescence or in early adulthood, he may settle for highly stereotyped interpersonal relations and come to retain a deep *sense of isolation*."[64]

Abel's inability to achieve true intimacy, then, can be seen as the result of the absence of meaningful relationships in his formative years. He grew up fatherless, lost his mother and brother in early boyhood, and never fully achieved an intimacy with the tribal community. There was also a possibly decisive, unsuccessful encounter with a young Indian girl during his adolescence (pp. 17–18). Abel's behavior toward Angela seems to indicate that this incident is still somewhere in the back of his mind. He tenaciously avoids exposing himself to humiliation and chooses to remain in the shell of his own self: "He would give her no clear way to be contemptuous of him" (p. 35).

Abel is portrayed as the stereotype of the mute Indian.[65] He avoids talking at any length and frequently does not react at all to Angela's questions. His fear of getting hurt and his inability to communicate his feelings are typical of his behavior: "His face darkened, but he hung on, dumb and immutable. He would not allow himself to be provoked. It was easy, natural for him to stand aside, hang on" (p. 35). His lack of articulation, which earlier in the novel prevented him from bringing forth a creation song, is now the main obstacle to an intimate relationship with Angela. She grows aware of a kind of powerlessness in Abel: "There he stood, dumb and docile at her pleasure, not knowing, she supposed, how even to take his leave" (p. 36).

Abel's failure to establish a relationship with Angela seems to be the result of his incomplete identity formation.[66] Throughout the novel he appears as a loner on a quest for a secure place, for a stability which he cannot find in an intimate relationship because he has not found himself. This dilemma accompanies Abel on his odyssey between Indian and modern American culture.

The third characteristic of identity confusion, the inability to vent aggression appropriately, leads to the climax of the first chapter, Abel's killing of the albino. This act of violence reflects Abel's inability to cope with the confusion he is subject to in his personal and cultural isolation. American culture has estranged him from his home: his endeavor to enter into the ceremonial life of his tribe has been unsuccessful; his attempt to establish an identity in an intimate relationship with Angela has failed. The resulting frustration is one source of the aggression Abel directs against the albino. Another is the deeply rooted fear which has dwelt in him since his early childhood— the fear that evil forces in the universe may exert their influence in him. This anxiety is common among Indian tribes. Abel's inability to comprehend the intricate nature of witchcraft leads to his individual and violent reaction against the albino, which could have been avoided through ritual.

The figure of the albino is a complex image of Abel's schizoid state of mind: his outburst of violence is an act of revenge against the "white man's world" and is at the same time the execution of an evil spirit. Frederick Hodge defined witchcraft as "the art of controlling the will and well-being of another person by supernatural or occult means, usually to his detriment."[67] The anthropologist Clyde Kluckhohn studied the phenomenon of witchcraft among the Navajos and observed that they showed an intense anxiety of evil forces and supernatural powers. He came to the conclusion that this anxiety must be "displaced from other sources—from immediate social situation or from generalized tension produced by white pressure, environmental insecurity or frustrations incident to the socialization process and family living."[68]

This result also holds true for the Pueblo Indians, as there are obvious similarities in the attitude toward witchcraft of the Navajos and Pueblos. According to Kluckhohn,

. . . there is no doubt that in both cultures belief in the existence of witches is manifested in expressions of fear of individuals and of places and objects held to be associated with witchcraft. Distrust and suspicion of certain persons unquestionably influence various behaviors, and there are occasional acts of violence.[69]

Abel's first encounter with the albino takes place during the Chicken Pull: "The appearance of one of the men was striking. He was large, lithe, and white-skinned; he wore little round colored glasses and rode a fine black horse of good blood" (p. 42). The albino turns out to be the winner in the game, even though Angela observes that in his movements "there was something out of place, some flaw in proportion or design, some unnatural thing" (p. 43). This is the first indication, apart from the physical otherness of the white man, that there is something strange about him. In the course of the game Abel finds himself confronted with the albino and loses out because of his alienation from tribal customs.

Although the albino is an Indian, he carries the stigma of an outsider and, in Abel's mind, seems partly associated with the evils of the white world. In the community he is believed to be a witch. Old man Francisco has a vague notion of his presence when working in the fields: ". . . he was suddenly conscious of some alien presence close at hand. . . . He was too old to be afraid. His acknowledgment of the unknown was nothing more than a dull, intrinsic sadness, a vague desire to weep, for evil had long since found him out and knew who he was" (pp. 63–64). Francisco can accept the existence of evil embodied in the albino. He has an understanding of the presence of sinister forces in the universe. Abel, however, cannot rationalize the inevitability of evil at this stage. It is not until his vision of the runners after evil later in the novel that he comprehends this idea.

Abel's latent fear of witchcraft is awakened by his encounter with the albino. Perhaps he is reminded of his childhood experience with the ill-reputed old woman Nicolás teah-whau (p. 13).

The fear of witchcraft is Abel's conscious motive for killing the albino, which makes his action an act of self-defense.[70] The problem, however, is more complex, for Abel's action cannot be seen simply in terms of the tribal context which allows the execution of witches. Abel's act of violence grows out of his frustration about his cultural estrangement and his feeling of inadequacy. It is possible that Abel recognizes himself in the figure of the albino, a mixture of Indian and white. Viewed in this light, Abel's act of destruction is an attempt to annihilate his own confused self. In doing so by culturally sanctioned means he is trying to find his way back to his tribal background. The albino, then, serves as a scapegoat.[71] The cultural ambiguity of the albino figure is highlighted in this scene:

Then he [the white man] closed his hands upon Abel and drew him close. Abel heard the strange excitement of the white man's breath, and the quick, uneven blowing at his ear, and he felt the blue quivering lips upon him, felt even the scales of the lips and the hot, slippery point of the tongue, writhing. He was sick with terror and revulsion, and he tried to fling himself away, but the white man held him close. The white immensity of flesh lay over and smothered him. He withdrew the knife and thrust again, lower, deep into the groin. [Pp. 77–78]

Abel's destruction of the "white immensity" which threatens to crush him appears not only as an act of self-defense against an assault by a witch but also against the corrupting forces of Anglo-American culture. This latter interpretation is reinforced by the scene's sexual implications—"the white man raised his arms as if to embrace him . . . , the blue, quivering lips . . . the hot, slippery point of the tongue, writhing" (pp. 77–78)—all of which suggest a homosexual assault.

Questioned on the ambiguity of this scene, Momaday accepted an interviewer's suggestion that Abel's motif for stabbing the albino is left "entirely open to interpretation." He explained his deliberately ambiguous presentation of the incident by saying that there is "an ineffable aspect to the killing so you simply point to it."[72] One critic pointed to the snake symbolism—"the scales of the lips" (p. 78)—and concluded that it is indicative of Abel's conception of the albino in traditional Christian terms of evil. He judged the killing as "more in accordance with Anglo tradition than Indian tradition."[73] There is, however, strong evidence to suggest that Abel is involved in the ritualistic killing of an incarnation of evil which is consistent with the laws of his tribal culture. Abel's statements at the trial that the killing was "the most natural thing in the world" and that "a man kills such an enemy if he can" (p. 95) give credence to such a reading. Moreover, the cruelty and messiness of the slaying are typical of witch executions. Kluckhohn pointed out that anthropological studies uniformly describe the killing of witches as acts of violent and gory sadism.[74]

The killing of the albino is a symbolic representation of the cultural conflict which Abel is trying to resolve. In the context of his native culture his act is justified and necessary. Momaday himself said that "not a person at Jemez would have held Abel liable."[75] Nevertheless, Abel's subsequent recognition of the ritual defenses against evil forces and his realization that evil can only be contained, but not eradicated, are fundamental steps to the resolution of his dilemma and his eventual understanding of his tribal tradition.

Many critics of *House Made of Dawn* have dealt with the

albino figure from an anthropological point of view. Only a few
have realized that the albino reflects not only Momaday's
knowledge of the Indian world of the American Southwest but
also his indebtedness to American literature. Charles Woodard
was the first critic to point out that the whiteness of the albino
owes something to the whiteness of the whale in Melville's
Moby-Dick.[76] A closer look at Melville's writings, however, reveals that *Moby-Dick* is only a minor influence on *House Made
of Dawn*. Momaday's novel shows a more obvious similarity to
Billy Budd, Sailor. This is by no means surprising—Billy
Budd was one of Momaday's great favorites as a graduate student.[77] Claggart, the albino's counterpart in Melville's story
has "an evil nature," is referred to as a "snake," and has a "pallid" complexion as the outer manifestation of his depraved
character.[78] Moreover, the story is permeated with homosexual
innuendo. Both Billy and Abel are inarticulate, both react violently in their respective crisis, and both are victimized.

The fascination of the albino figure in *House Made of Dawn*
lies as much in its connection with the Indian notion of witchcraft as in Momaday's adaptation of the great theme of evil in
American literature to the world of the Jemez Pueblo Indians.
The following section centers on the way in which Abel proceeds through various stages to his ultimate reconciliation with
his native culture.

Abel's Rite of Passage

The "Priest of the Sun" chapter is the most puzzling and haunting section of *House Made of Dawn*. The narrative voice is centered in Abel's consciousness as he is lying, delirious from alcohol and the brutal beating he received from Martinez, a
violent and corrupt police officer, on the beach outside Los
Angeles. Through multiple flashbacks Momaday reveals the
psychological situation of a man who is lost between two
worlds, torn apart culturally and spiritually, and drifting toward death. Abel is "reeling on the edge of the void" (p. 96),
but he does not fall. The very moment when Abel seems to

have exhausted all the possibilities of finding redemption holds the seed to his ultimate recovery. In the extremity of his situation Abel gains insights into the core of his native culture which lead him to a new understanding of his place in the scheme of things.

A gap of about six and a half years lies between the end of the opening chapter and the beginning of the next, "The Priest of the Sun." During this time Abel served his prison sentence for killing the albino and, after his release, settled in Los Angeles. However, the burden of the past proves too heavy and the pressure of life in the city too great to allow him integration into his new environment.

In this second chapter Momaday abandons a continuous plot line and operates instead with a device resembling the cutting technique employed in film. Whereas the series of flashbacks in the opening chapter showed a certain continuity by following Abel's growth, this characteristic is now absent. Without any apparent logical connections, fragmentary scenes from Abel's past alternate with blurred perceptions of his immediate environment. The flashbacks encompass scenes from Abel's childhood—Josie, Francisco, Vidal, and his departure from the village—from the trial and his stay in prison, and finally from his relationships with Milly and Angela.

The trial scene is of particular significance, for it is here that the issue of cultural relativism is addressed most explicitly. Abel registers the proceedings with detachment and a keen awareness that his case lies beyond his judges' frame of reference: "Word by word these men were disposing of him in language, *their* language, and they were making a bad job of it. They were strangely uneasy, full of hesitation, reluctance. He wanted to help them" (p. 95). Father Olguin, the Catholic priest in the pueblo, tries to explain Abel's perception of his victim as an evil spirit, admitting that the motivation behind and execution of the killing must ultimately resist comprehension by anyone outside the Jemez world. The nature of Abel's act is such that it cannot be assessed in terms of American law.

Abel states his own feelings on the issue with the conviction

of someone who believes himself to be in accordance with the
relevant law:

> He had killed a white man. It was not a complicated thing, after
> all; it was very simple. It was the most natural thing in the world.
> Surely they could see that, these men who meant to dispose of him
> in words. They must know that he would kill the white man again,
> if he had the chance, that there would be no hesitation whatsoever.
> For he would know what the white man was, and he would kill him
> if he could. A man kills such an enemy if he can. [P. 95]

The tragedy is that Abel's law and the law of his judges are
incompatible, resting on different cultural assumptions, and
that it is in accordance with his judges' law that he is sentenced
and sent to prison.

   This passage of *House Made of Dawn* is reminiscent of the
trial scene in Albert Camus's *The Outsider*. In fact, Momaday
declared that he had Camus in mind when he wrote about
Abel's trial.[79] Although for different reasons—philosophical
rather than cultural in nature—Meursault in *The Outsider* is
unrepentant of his killing. He too experiences his case with a
profound sense of detachment and isolation. Like Abel he
"wasn't to have any say," and "his fate was to be decided out of
hand."[80] Yet he too feels the need to help his judges: "Quite
often, interested as I was in what they had to say, I was tempted
to put in a word, myself."[81] In the end neither Abel nor Meursault can make himself understood.

   The sequence of sense perceptions and flashbacks in "The
Priest of the Sun" is connected by an underlying image pattern.
The intensity of these images, the apparent disjunction of time
elements, and the surface illogic—all typical of dreams and
hallucinations—account for the haunting, nightmarish effect
of this chapter. The reader gets only fragmentary impressions
of the conflicts which contributed to Abel's decline. Most of
the fragments remain obscure until Ben Benally's first-person
narrative in "The Night Chanter" chapter, which gives a coherent account of Abel's life in the city. But in allowing the
reader to enter Abel's consciousness in the final stage of his

decline Momaday conveys not only the protagonist's confusion but also the possibility that social and cultural barriers are the sources of Abel's disintegration. On the symbolic level Abel's isolation is evoked by the image of the fence: "There was a fence on the bank before him; at his back there was a broad rocky beach, tilting to the sea. The fence was made of heavy wire mesh. . . . There were cans and bits of paper and broken glass against the fence; . . . he could almost touch it. He raised himself to reach for the fence and the pain struck him again" (p. 92). Abel's inability to reach let alone overcome the fence is symbolic of his failure to break through the barriers between him and the mainstream of society. After realizing the source of his dilemma during his vision of the men running after evil, Abel finds the strength to reach the fence (p. 115). It is with its help that he manages to raise himself. Thus the fence symbolism stresses the theme of cultural segregation and at the same time emphasizes Abel's vision as the turning point of the novel.

It is not only the fragmentary structure which precludes any easy interpretation of this crucial chapter. Equally complex is Momaday's use of imagery; only when the seemingly unrelated symbols are combined in a coherent pattern does the full meaning of the beach scene surface. I have argued above that Abel has been suffering from the lack of stable identity, as evidenced by his position as an outsider in the community, his inability to identify with tribal rituals and ceremonies, and his failure to relate on a level of intimacy to his female partners. The process of degeneration resulting from this lack of stability reaches its climax in Abel's struggle with the murderous police officer and subsequently with death itself. The symbols which surround these events suggest that what is actually happening in this powerfully conceived scene is a rite of passage in which Abel progresses from lack of understanding to knowledge, from chaos through ritual death to rebirth.

The scene's setting is in itself suggestive. Abel is "lying in a shallow depression in which there were weeds and small white stones and tufts of long grey grass" (p. 92). It is a common feature of initiation ceremonies that the initiate is placed into a shallow grave from which he eventually rises as a new being.[82] Moreover, the scene happens at night. Darkness, according to Eliade, signifies in such rituals "the beyond, the 'infernal regions.'"[83] The beating Abel receives results from his attempt to get even with Martinez, who has tyrannized him. On the symbolic level this beating represents the initiatory mutilations which are frequent features of rites of passage. Abel's injuries are numerous: "His hands were broken, and he could not move them. Some of his fingers were stuck together with blood, and the blood was dry and black; . . . there was blood in his throat and mouth" (pp. 93, 95). These injuries point to his symbolic death, and it can hardly be a coincidence that amputations of fingers and the knocking out of teeth are common initiatory tortures.[84]

That Abel is lying on the beach, close to water, is of further importance in this context; although there is no suggestion that he actually comes into contact with the sea, he is closely associated with it and the small, silver-sided fish which dwell off the California coast. Water is traditionally a symbol of potential life, of creation and fertility, the element from which all cosmic manifestations emerge and to which they return.[85] Water creates and dissolves. According to Eliade:

Immersion in water symbolizes a return to the pre-formal, a total regeneration, a new birth, for immersion means a dissolution of forms, a reintegration into the formlessness of pre-existence; and emerging from the water is a repetition of the act of creation in which form was first expressed. Every contact with water implies regeneration: first, because dissolution is succeeded by a "new birth," and then because immersion fertilizes, increases the potential of life and of creation. In initiation rituals, water confers a "new birth."[86]

Abel's proximity to and association with water, then, suggest the dissolution of his state of estrangement and the potential for rebirth into his tribal culture.

Abel's connection with the fish reinforces the meaning of his transformation:

There is a small silversided fish that is found along the coast of southern California. In the spring and summer it spawns on the beach during the first three hours after each of the three high tides following the highest tide. These fish come by the hundreds from the sea. They hurl themselves upon the land and writhe in the light of the moon, the moon, the moon; they writhe in the light of the moon. They are among the most helpless creatures on the face of the earth. [P. 83]

The meaning of this seemingly unimportant descriptive passage becomes gradually apparent through the affiliation of Abel with the fish. Like them he is lying on the beach. He too is a helpless creature removed from the natural element of his native culture. In his delirious state Abel's thoughts constantly return to the fish, "His mind boggled and withdrew . . . and it came around again to the fishes" (p. 93). He feels a kind of sympathy for the "small silversided fishes spawned mindlessly in correlation to the phase of the moon and the rise and fall of the tides. The thought of it made him sad, filled him with sad, unnamable longing and wonder" (p. 91). Finally Abel is directly identified with the fish, "He had the sense that his whole body was shaking violently, tossing and whipping, flopping like a fish" (p. 106).

The fish imagery not only reflects Abel's suffering but also indicates the upward movement in his development after he has become aware of his situation. When Abel raises the energy to fight against and eventually escape the drift towards death, the fish too have found their way back to safety in the depth of the sea, as Abel will eventually return home to his tribal community: "And far out in the night where nothing else was, the fishes lay out on the black water, holding still against all the force and motion of the sea; or close to the surface, darting and rolling and spinning like lures, they played in the track of the moon" (p. 112).

The most complex symbol Momaday employs in this chapter is that of the moon. The common denominator in a number of scenes throughout the novel, it brings the various episodes together in Abel's and the reader's minds. The moon, of course, is also associated with the sea and the initiation ritual. Most important, however, it is Abel's realization of the cosmic significance of the moon which brings about his new understanding of a universal order. To appreciate the subtlety of this image pattern, we need to scrutinize in detail its various functions.

The connection of the moon with initiation rituals has already been mentioned. The moon's reappearance after her three-day "death" has traditionally been read as a symbol of rebirth. The Juan Capistrano Indians of California, according to James Frazer, declared, "As the moon dieth and cometh to life again, so we also, having to die, will again rise."[87] In a number of shamanistic initiation rites the novice is "broken in pieces" in analogy to the phases of the moon.[88] Among the Plains Indians it was customary to focus one's eyes on the moon in order to secure help in a moment of distress.[89] The Pueblo medicine-water chief implored the moon to give him power to see disease.[90] With this information the prominence of the moon image in Abel's consciousness becomes more readily intelligible.

However, it is not just the meanings of regeneration, spiritual assistance, and clearer vision which make the moon such a revealing image of Abel's struggle for recovery. His rise to a securer mode of being is effected above all by his growing awareness of the moon as a unifying and controlling force in the universe. Eliade pointed out that "the myths of 'quest' and of 'initiation trials' reveal, in artistic or dramatic form, the actual act by which the mind gets beyond a conditioned, piece-meal universe, swinging between opposites, to return to the fundamental oneness that existed before creation."[91] An important step towards Abel's understanding of cosmic unity lies in his realization that the moon controls the sea as well as the land: "Why should Abel think of the fishes? He could not understand the sea; it was not of his world. It was an enchanted thing, *too*, for it lay under the spell of the moon. It bent to the moon, and the moon made a bright, shimmering course upon it" (p. 91; italics added). This recognition of the moon's universal power to order and control the universe reflects Abel's growing reattunement to American Indian thought.

In the Southwest, as elsewhere among tribal peoples, the moon functions together with the sun as the measure of the yearly cycle in the life of the community.[92] The Santa Clara Pueblos believe that "the function of the sun, the moon, stars, the Milky Way, and other such features, is to make the earth inhabitable for human beings."[93] This idea has practical consequences for everyday Indian life. The belief, for instance, that the moon exerts a strong influence on the growth of plants has immediate impact on the process of sowing and reaping. At the beginning of *House Made of Dawn*, Momaday refers to the moon's influence on the communal work in the fields: "The townsmen work all summer in the fields. When the moon is full, they work at night with ancient, handmade plows and hoes" (p. 10). The holiness attributed to the moon by American Indians is alluded to in the "red and yellow symbols of the sun and the moon" (p. 84) which decorate the lectern in the Indian church in Los Angeles. Eliade noted that "the moon shows man his true human condition; that in a sense man looks at himself, and finds himself anew in the life of the moon."[94] If one subscribes to this idea, then Abel's rediscovery of his native heritage appears to be a result of his reattunement to a lunar rhythm.

Abel's understanding of the secrets of lunar control of the universe also arises from recollections and reinterpretations of some of his earlier hunting experiences. The image of the moon functions as an associative link to other scenes where animal imagery mirrors Abel's distress. One of these instances, the parallel between him and the fish, has already been discussed. The eagle hunt is another example: "Bound and helpless, his eagle seemed drab and shapeless in the moonlight, too large and ungainly for flight" (pp. 24–25). A third event of this kind occurs in one of Abel's recollections of his childhood. It is the hunting scene in which he recovers a shot water bird:

He took it up in his hands and it was heavy and warm and the feathers about its keel were hot and sticky with blood. He carried it out into the moonlight, and its bright black eyes, in which no terror was, were wide of him, wide of the river and the land, level and hard upon the ring of the moon in the southern sky. [P. 110]

The depiction of the dying bird strikingly resembles the description of Abel's own suffering in the face of death: "He awoke coughing; there was blood in his throat and mouth. He was shuddering with cold and pain. . . . He peered into the night: all around the black land against the star-bright, moon-bright sky" (p. 95).

In these instances the moon imagery connects Abel's present and past experiences. In recollecting the dying water bird, with its fearless black eyes, Abel can establish a link between his own desperate state and the reaction of the animal. The bird is part of the complexity of nature and is by nature without the fear of death. Abel too had a natural attitude towards death when, as a boy, he was still close to the Indian understanding of the universe (p. 15). His loss of identification with his heritage has led him away from this natural view of death and contributed to the intense fears which are haunting him now.

The moon, then, is strongly suggestive of a hope for rebirth. This is an entirely new perspective for Abel. If one recalls the scene in which he destroys the eagle because he felt pity and shame, it is obvious that Abel did not share in the traditional belief of many hunting communities that the spirit of the animal survives and returns in a new physical manifestation. If he had been attuned to the rituals of the hunters, as old man Francisco was on his bear hunt, he could have killed the eagle in the appropriate ritual way, with a sense of gratitude and appreciation rather than remorse.

Momaday uses a number of devices to reinforce further the connection between Abel and the moon. In two instances the course of the moonlight on the water functions as a bridge (pp. 91 and 109), and in the following passage a flock of birds serves as a link: "Then they [the birds] were away, and he had seen how they craned their long slender necks to the moon, ascending slowly into the far reaches of the winter night. They made a dark angle on the sky, acute, perfect; and for one moment they lay out like an omen on the bright fringe of a cloud" (p. 110).

Abel's recognition of the moon as a vital influence shows that he is beginning to return to the traditional Indian concept of the universe. The following passage, which comprises the three images of sea, moon, and fish, unites bird and fish imagery and thus widens the scope of Abel's vision to a universal dimension:

And somewhere beyond the cold and the fog and the pain there was the black and infinite sea, bending to the moon, and there was the cold white track of the moon on the water. And far out in the night where nothing else was, the fishes lay out in the black waters, holding still against all the force and motion of the sea; . . . And far away inland there were great gray geese riding under the moon. [P. 112]

Land and sea, man and animal are related in their connection with the moon. This notion coincides with the general idea of the interrelatedness of all elements in the Indian universe. By growing aware of this idea Abel discovers that he too is tied up in the totality of creation and has a legitimate place in it.

Another major step towards restoration and initiation into his tribal culture is Abel's vision of the runners after evil. Dreams and visions have always been of utmost significance in the lives of American Indian peoples. John Skinner commented on the religious nature of dreams in the Indian world: "Man succeeds first in his dreams. . . . man becomes in dreams and words before he becomes in deeds. A man becomes his successful dream, not his successful deed."[95] Abel's experience must be seen in the light of this statement. In his vision he catches, for the first time, a glimpse of the meaning of tribal ritual as he becomes aware of its importance for the relationship between the individual and the universe:

The runners after evil ran as water runs, deep in the channel, in the way of least resistance, no resistance. His skin crawled with excitement; he was overcome with longing and loneliness, for suddenly he saw the crucial sense in their going, of old men in white leggings running after evil in the night. They were whole and indispensable in what they did; everything in creation referred to them. Because of them, perspective, proportion, design in the universe. Meaning because of them. They ran with great dignity and calm, not in the hope of anything, but hopelessly; neither in fear nor hatred nor despair of evil, but simply in recognition and with respect. Evil was. Evil was abroad in the night; they must venture out to the confrontation; they must reckon dues and divide the world. [P. 96]

The vision confronts Abel with the ritualistic practices the elders of the tribe employ to maintain control over the supernatural. The race is connected with the ceremony of clearing the irrigation ditches in the spring. It is an imitation of water running through the channels, a magic bid for the vital supply of rain, and a ritual act to prevent the harvest from being influenced by evil powers.[96] This vision modifies Abel's view of his own actions in the past; he realizes that, although his destruction of the albino as a source of evil was in accordance with tribally sanctioned practices, Pueblo religion offers nonviolent ways of controlling supernatural powers. The ritualistic expression of human creativity through words in songs and prayers and through motion in dance and ceremonial races is the central instrument by which the Indian maintains a balance between himself and the universe.[97]

Abel's growing understanding of the cosmic order in terms of his tribal heritage leads him to the recognition that his estrangement from the center of Indian life has been the cause of his dilemma. This diagnosis of the source of his "disease" puts him on the road to recovery. Abel's previous inability to make sense of his situation is indicated in a flashback to his departure from the village, which is the continuation of the corresponding passage in the opening chapter (p. 25): "He tried to think where the trouble had begun, what the trouble was. There was trouble; he could admit that to himself, but he had no real insight into his own situation. Maybe, certainly, *that* was the trouble; but he had no way of knowing" (p. 97).

Now in his hallucinatory state the insight for which he had searched so long suddenly comes to him: "He had lost his place. He had been long ago at the center, had known where he was, had lost his way, had wandered to the end of the earth, was even now reeling on the edge of the void" (p. 96). This recognition epitomizes the entire development of the novel up to this point. Abel realizes that the Indian world of his boyhood is the only place where he can find a meaningful existence and an identity. As in a vision quest Abel receives a sign which shows him the way to personal wholeness.

Once Abel has by means of his subconscious gained insight into the meaning of ritual and the controlling forces in the universe, he is ready to establish a formal union with his tribal heritage through the ceremony of the Night Chant which Ben Benally conducts for him. The changes he undergoes as a result of his vision enable him to make the "spiritual commitment" of submitting himself to the healing powers of the Night Chant.[98] In doing so, he shows his newfound trust in the effectiveness of Indian ceremonials. In the Night Chant ceremony Abel, as the "patient," remains passive yet, but it is the first step toward his own conduction of a ceremony—the funeral rite after the death of his grandfather (p. 189)—and toward his participation in the ceremonial race that ends the novel.

The result of the Night Chant is the restoration of the wholeness Abel had lost in his crisis of identity and through his exposure to the disruptive forces of incompatible cultural patterns. American Indian ritual and song aim at the preservation of order and at the integration of the individual into the larger context of his environment.[99] Paula Allan remarked that through ceremonial practices "the isolated individualistic personality is shed and the person is restored to conscious harmony with the universe."[100] The Night Chant, then, reestablishes

Abel's inner balance and equilibrium with the world around him. In order to achieve this harmony Abel must regain his physical and mental wholeness and his power of the word.

Physical disintegration is the outward sign of Abel's inner conflict: "He had loved his body. It had been hard and quick and beautiful; it had been useful, quickly and surely responsive to his mind and will; . . .[now] his body was mangled and racked with pain. His body, like his mind, had turned on him; it was his enemy" (p. 93). The line "restore my body for me" (p. 134) in the chant is directed at the return of Abel's physical strength and his control over his body.[101] The line "restore my mind for me" (p. 134) aims at the restitution of Abel's mental wholeness and the coordination between his body and spirit.

Abel's lack of articulation stood at the center of his personal and cultural isolation. It was a syndrome of his estrangement from the oral tradition without which he remained cut off from his tribal heritage. Gladys A. Reichard stressed the fact that "the 'word' . . . is of great ritualistic value, and in order to be complete, man must control language. The better his control and the more extensive his knowledge, the greater his well-being."[102] The desire to regain power over the word finds expression in the request "restore my voice for me" (p. 134).

Finally, it is necessary to bring back the power of motion Abel lost in the course of his decline. Reichard pointed out the importance of the power of motion for the Navajos: "Man may breathe and speak, his organs may function well, but without the power of motion he is incomplete, useless."[103] The lines "Restore my feet for me, / Restore my legs for me, / Restore my body for me, / . . . Happily I recover. / . . . Happily I go forth. / . . . Being as it used to be long ago, may I walk" (p. 134) call for the return of Abel's power of motion. The race at the end of the novel shows that the request has been granted.

Abel's return to the Jemez world proceeds from a visionary, subconscious level through a ritualistic to a rational level. His recovery, which originates in his hallucinatory visions and is furthered through Ben's performance of the Night Chant, continues after his return to the pueblo. There he finds Francisco dying. For six days the old medicine man struggles against death, uttering memories of his life during the hours of dawn. Abel listens to his voice but initially fails to understand the meaning of his words. And yet the "voice of his memory was whole and clear and growing like the dawn" (p. 177). It reminds Abel of the secrets of the solar calendar which his grandfather had taught him many years ago, of the ceremonial races and festivities of Jemez, and, in the story of Francisco's bear hunt, of the traditional hunting ways and rituals. Francisco's final recollections seem to refresh Abel's knowledge of the ancient ways of his people; in the end they begin to make sense and carry meaning, for on the morning of the seventh day Abel for the first time conducts a ceremony: ". . . he knew what had to be done" (p. 189). Strictly adhering to the timeless practices of his tribe, he prepares Francisco for the funeral. In doing so he takes over the role of the dead medicine man.

Significantly, Abel's return to his tribal tradition takes place only a short time before dawn. This event is part of a coherent pattern of dawn images which permeate the novel. The book opens and closes with Abel running across the land at dawn. When Abel is lying on the beach after his fight with Martinez, struggling against death, he can hear the "sound of the city at night, ticking like a clock toward the dawn" (p. 92). If one takes the symbol of dawn to stand for rebirth, a new beginning, and creation, the reference to dawn at this point anticipates Abel's resurrection.

The connection between the symbol of dawn and the idea of creation is suggested in the following passage about Abel's attempt to bring forth a creation song: "He would have sung lowly of the first world, of fire and flood, and of the emergence of dawn from the hills" (p. 57). The first world, fire, and flood are references to the creation myths of many southwestern Indian tribes, such as the Hopi, Zuni, and Navajos. They hold in common the belief that they emerged to their present land after a migration through several underground worlds, in which they encountered floods or fire.[104] Dawn marks the moment of emergence from the underworld, the beginning of

tribal life, and the creation of tribal culture. Every new morning "is the moment of invigoration, when new life awakens
and all creation is astir—it is creation itself, an 'in the beginning.' . . . From the dawn comes generation and birth." [105]

At the center of the dawn image pattern stands the following
passage, which encompasses the historical migration of a tribe,
its cultural crisis, and its potential regeneration:

Man came down the ladder to the plain a long time ago. It was a
slow migration, though he came only from the caves in the canyons
and the tops of the mesas nearby. There are low, broken walls on the
tabletops and smoke-blackened caves in the cliffs, where still there
are metates and broken bowls and ancient ears of corn, as if the
prehistoric civilization had gone out among the hills for a little
while and would return; and then everything would be restored to
an older age, and time would have returned upon itself and a bad
dream of invasion and change would have been dissolved in an hour
before the dawn. [P. 56][106]

This short passage encapsulates the essence of *House Made of
Dawn*: the novel shows how a traditional Indian community
which is threatened in its cultural survival by an encroaching
alien world is struggling to defend itself against this influence.
The demand for strict adherence to traditional practices leads
to pressure within the tribe and thus aggravates the crisis. This
pressure may result, as in Abel's case, in identity conflicts
among young Indians, who, though rooted in their cultural
background, cannot ignore the reality of a modern age brought
about by an alien culture. Their need to develop their individuality within the tribal community must find the support of
their elders.

In the passage quoted above Momaday puts a cultural crisis
in its wider historical and mythological context. He points out
that the archaeological remnants of previous Indian generations
only seem to indicate the extinction of an ancient civilization,
because Pueblo culture has survived to the present. In referring
to the cyclical concept of time Momaday demonstrates his belief in the inherent potential of American Indian cultures to
survive historical crises. That the new rise of the old culture

should take place an hour before the dawn seems unimportant in the narrow context of this passage. In the larger context of the novel, however, it becomes most significant: Abel's celebration of the funeral rites for his grandfather "a while . . . before the dawn" (p. 189) is not only the moment when he finds his way back to his tribe but also, from a historical perspective, the point where Jemez culture gains new impetus in its struggle to survive a period of cultural encroachment and oppression. Like the Bahkyush people who had once journeyed along the edge of oblivion and recovered to become eagle hunters and rainmakers (p. 19), Abel, who is associated with this group as an eagle hunter, also returned from the edge of the void to become a dawn runner. As the Kiowas' migration from the north of the American continent to the south and east was "a journey toward the dawn" which "led to a golden age" (p. 118), the positive outcome of Abel's migration between two worlds can be seen as a hopeful beginning of a new period of Pueblo culture.

In much the same way as the reference to the cyclical concept of time indicates the potentially positive resolution of the historical crisis in Indian culture, the cyclical structure of the novel justifies a hopeful reading of Abel's future. At the close of the book Abel returns to the personal wholeness and harmony with the universe which were his main strengths at its beginning. Indeed the cyclical concept of tribal history and the cyclical movement of Abel's personal history interconnect at the end. Abel, whose dilemma is the product of historical crisis in Indian culture, overcomes his identity conflict and symbolically resolves the communal crisis of his tribe. Momaday's own comment on *House Made of Dawn* points in this direction: "I see the novel as a circle. It ends where it begins and it's informed with a kind of thread that runs through it and holds everything together." [107] This race, then, is a race for identity, both personal and communal. It finds its final resolution in the ceremonial race which shows Abel reconciled with his native culture and the Indian universe.

Many alienated characters in recent American fiction—

Ralph Ellison's *Invisible Man*, Faulkner's Joe Christmas in *Light in August*, and John Updike's Rabbit Angstrom in *Rabbit Run*—are running away from something and have no viable alternative to which they can turn. Abel is unique in that his running manifests an act of integration, not a symbol of estrangement. Momaday himself suggested this reading of the symbol by referring to its cultural context: "The man running is fitting himself into the basic motion of the universe. . . . That is simply a symbolism which prevails in the southwestern Indian world." [108] In one of his essays Momaday explained this ceremonial race which is "run at dawn before the spring cleaning of the Jemez irrigation ditches":

It is a stick race: the runners imitate the Cloud People who fill the arroyos with life-giving rain, and keep in motion, with only their feet, a "stick-ball" which represents the moving drift of the water's edge. The first race each year comes in February, and then the dawn is clear and cold, and the runners breathe steam. It is a long race, and it is neither won nor lost. It is an expression of the soul in the ancient terms of sheer physical exertion. To watch those runners is to know that they draw with every step some elemental power which resides at the core of the earth and which, for all our civilized ways, is lost upon us who have lost the art of going in the flow of things. [109]

Abel's running at dawn, singing the words of the Night Chant, marks the end of his struggle for identity. He has finally returned to his place in the house made of dawn. He has found the right words to articulate himself and he has a vision of the appropriate path to wholeness. The novel's final scene is charged with mythological overtones: according to a Pueblo emergence myth, Iatik, the corn mother, after creating the present world, called on the people to emerge from the previous world underground. As they entered their new environment they were blind. Then, the story goes on to explain, "Iatik lined them up in a row facing east and made the sun come up for the first time in this new world to shine upon them. And when its rays shone upon the eyes of the people, they were opened and they could see." [110]

In the primordial setting of dawn over the Jemez Valley,

Abel too "could see at last without having to think. He could see the canyons and the mountains and the sky. He could see the rain and the river and the fields beyond. He could see the dark hills at dawn" (p. 191). His new vision and voice are expressions of his communion with his native tradition and raise the hope that he may become the living link between the ancient past and a promising future for his tribal culture.

CHAPTER 5

The Indian Heritage:
The Way to Rainy Mountain

Two statements by Yvor Winters are particularly pertinent to an understanding of *The Way to Rainy Mountain*. Winters suggested that "unless we understand the history which produced us, we are determined by that history; we may be determined in any event, but the understanding gives us a chance."[1] Elsewhere he elaborated on this point: ". . . man lives and changes; but man has a memory, personal, historical, and racial, so that his changing is not absolute and should not be irresponsible. His changing may be growth, diminution, or disintegration, and the choice among these possibilities is his own."[2]

The Way to Rainy Mountain is Momaday's inquiry into his Indian past in an attempt to determine the extent to which it has shaped him and the degree to which he has become detached from the mythical worldview of his ancestors. It is a deeply personal journey. Momaday described its purpose thus: "In *The Way to Rainy Mountain* I was more concerned to reveal something to myself than to anyone else."[3] And in a different context he wrote: "If I don't understand my Kiowa background, I forsake a lot of my human potential. By understanding it as far as I can I fulfill my capacity for being alive as a human being."[4]

Momaday belongs to a large group of American Indians who, in the course of their successful integration into American society, realized that the link to their indigenous background had worn thin and that the knowledge of their racial past was about to be irretrievably lost. As Momaday realized, this recognition was crucial to the direction of his artistic work:

At a certain point in my life, and it was rather late, when I was in my early thirties, I began to wonder about my heritage which I had always taken for granted. I got fascinated in that business and made a point of looking at it and finding out as much as I could about it, which turned out to be a great intellectual exercise for me and a very fascinating thing.[5]

In another context he elaborated on the significance of this event:

I think of myself as an Indian because at one time in my life I suddenly realized that my father had grown up speaking a language that I didn't grow up speaking, that my forebears on his side had made a migration from Canada along with . . . Athapaskan peoples that I knew nothing about, and so I determined to find out something about these things and in the process I acquired an identity; it is an Indian identity, as far as I am concerned.[6]

While Winters's pronouncements may have sharpened Momaday's attention to the importance of his tribal heritage, there were at least two crucial experiences which initiated his conscious exploration of Kiowa tradition in the writing of *The Journey of Tai-me* and *The Way to Rainy Mountain*.

Momaday's encounter with the Tai-me bundle, the sacred Sun Dance fetish of the Kiowa tribe, was one of these events. Tai-me was the most powerful medicine the Kiowas possessed; it was worshiped as the bringer of good luck and exhibited for viewing only during the Sun Dance. After the last performance of this ceremony by the Kiowas in 1887, the Sun Dance doll remained in the possession of the Tai-me keeper, a Kiowa man responsible for the storing and opening of the medicine bundle. With the demise of the Sun Dance the bundle remained closed, and after the death of the keeper it was passed on to his daughter.

In 1963, Momaday's grandmother Aho told him that the Tai-me bundle was extant and could be seen on request. He traveled to Oklahoma with her and his father, Al, and visited this Kiowa woman, who, in a storytelling session, made him familiar with the nature of Tai-me and instructed him in the formalities of viewing the medicine bundle. Momaday, in keeping with tradition, had to make an offering of cloth and was then allowed into the presence of Tai-me. It was hanging from a small forked tree in a closetlike recess of a room. Momaday experienced "one of the most intensely religious feelings" he had ever known, the certainty of being in the presence of a sacred object.[7] In a manuscript fragment written some years after the journey, Momaday described the lasting effect of this experience:

From the time I stood before the Tai-me issikia I knew a certain restlessness. I felt that I had come to know something about myself I had never known before. I became more keenly aware of myself as someone who had walked through time and in whose blood there is something inestimably old and undying. It was as if I had remembered something that happened two hundred years ago. I meant then to seek after the source of my memory and myself. But there where not many who could help me. Aho was dead, Mammedaty had died before I was born. Theirs was the last generation, I believe, that could claim to be of the living culture of [the Kiowas].[8]

The second significant event followed naturally from the first. Momaday went to Rainy Mountain cemetery to mourn Aho, who had died shortly after their visit to the Tai-me bundle. His grandfather Mammedaty, his great-grandmother Kau-au-ointy, his aunt, and many great Kiowa warriors and chiefs are also buried there.[9] It appears that his physical presence in the realm of his dead ancestors reinforced Momaday's urgency to understand the connection between him and them:

When I go and walk among the stones of Rainy Mountain cemetery where my grandmother, in an unmarked grave, and my aunt, dead in infancy, are buried, I am conscious of something terribly important to my being. I could sense in that situation the vitality in myself, I could sense it but could not take possession of it until I had translated it into language. But that is only half the truth, I think. Language is not an aid at all, but an essence. My poem,

"Rainy Mountain Cemetery," is an act of understanding. Beyond that there is no other way. . . . It was important that I stood before my grandfather's grave at Rainy Mountain cemetery, and I had to put it into words.[10]

The immediate impact of confronting his ancestors' graves resulted in a sense of separation; the past seemed to be obliterated.[11] Yet at the same time it created in Momaday a determination to establish a bond with Mammedaty, Aho, and their common Kiowa culture. The obvious vehicle was the Kiowas' extant oral tradition, which became for Momaday a personal and academic preoccupation.

In much the same way as *House Made of Dawn*, *The Way to Rainy Mountain* gradually took shape over a period of six years following Momaday's revelatory encounter with the Tai-me bundle and his experience at Rainy Mountain cemetery. And, as in the case of the novel, Yvor Winters took a close interest in its development and contributed to it in several ways from its conception to the final publication.

The earliest published evidence of Momaday's research into the Kiowa oral tradition is his essay "The Morality of Indian Hating," in which he relates and interprets two Kiowa stories.[12] Within the framework of the essay, which consists of an expository presentation of the development of Indian-white relations combined with narrative passages, these tales serve as illustrations of the tribe's evolution. Winters's critical remarks on this essay in two letters to Momaday suggest not only his extraordinary sense of his student's literary talent but also his anticipation of the final structure of *The Way to Rainy Mountain*. Although Winters saw Momaday primarily as a poet, his first letter acknowledged the high quality of his prose:

The essay is very impressive. Your structure is that of controlled association. . . . You can write fine prose. The general exposition is excellent; some of the more personal details are superb: the Kiowa on horseback, Old Man Cheney and his Oklahoma sunrise. The diction here is plain but accurate: thus the united perception of physical detail and of the concept are there with real grandeur.[13]

Winters urged Momaday to continue to write poetry, but on the basis of the essay he encouraged him to develop his prose. In his second letter Winters returned to the article's structure and its potential for future projects:

> The form is flexible. It could be applied to primarily expository matter, to matter calling for exposition plus a narrative (fiction, historical, or conceivably legendary, although the task of giving adequate body to the legendary might be difficult and call for a good deal of research or imagination). But I think that you ought to pursue the possibilities for a time at least. I might result in a great book: a collection of such pieces, perhaps. [14]

Momaday's personal need to probe into his tribal heritage and his aspiration as a writer combined neatly in this new venture. While preparing for publication his edition of Frederick Goddard Tuckerman's poetry, he also focused his attention on retrieving the remnants of Kiowa oral tradition. He soon realized the extent of the deterioration in the tradition of American Indian oral poetry and mythology and the imperative for speedy research to salvage what was still within reach. [15]

Deprived of his grandparents as living sources of Kiowa tradition, Momaday collected stories from Kiowa elders. This fieldwork was greatly hampered by his lack of competence in the Kiowa language. The crucial role of interviewing informers and translating the recorded material fell to Momaday's father, Al, who passed on to his son his own recollections of traditional Kiowa life and the stories he used to hear as a boy. [16] However, the correspondence between him and Momaday shows that many details had been lost to his memory, a telling reminder of the fragility of an oral tradition. [17]

Like many contemporary American Indians, Momaday had to take recourse in written materials compiled by anthropologists, folklorists, and translators of Kiowa oral tradition. Some may object that Momaday's inability to speak Kiowa and his dependence on translations of Kiowa stories prevented him from capturing the true spirit of his oral heritage. Momaday himself, however, believes that his writing preserves the spirit of Kiowa language, if not the language itself. He contends that "there is no danger of the spirit of the language being lost . . . because the spirit proceeds out of the people themselves."[18] The works of James Mooney, Mildred Mayhall, Alice Marriott, and Wilbur S. Nye are a significant part of the raw material from which Momaday wrought *The Way to Rainy Mountain*.[19]

In the early stages of the project Momaday was interested only in a collection of stories. In a letter to the editor of his Tuckerman edition, Whitney Blake, he mentioned as a tentative title "The Tai-me Keepers: A Migration Literature of the Kiowas."[20] The first, privately published version appeared in 1967, entitled *The Journey of Tai-me*.[21] It contained all the traditional material subsequently published in *The Way to Rainy Mountain* and an additional six stories which were later collected separately.[22] The introduction, prologue, and epilogue, as well as the two poems which frame the final edition of *The Way to Rainy Mountain* are later additions.

The casting of the traditional material and the historical and personal commentaries in three distinct but complementary voices followed Winters's initial proposal to apply the structure of "The Morality of Indian Hating" to a more complex body of material. In a letter to Momaday he reiterated this suggestion and his conviction that the combination of personal comment and historical material would be very moving:

I wonder what would happen if you set yourself an exercise on a philosophical subject or a historical subject, to be done in a stanza somewhat like the crucifixion piece. Fort Sill, for example: not the historical, per se, but its various aspects as you look back. You are a long way from there, and yet you must be very close. Your father must have had eyewitness stories from his grandparents. That sort of thing as seen personally and in the long view of history might be very moving.[23]

Although Winters was thinking in terms of a poetic cycle, his ideas anticipated the changes Momaday made in transforming *The Journey of Tai-me* into *The Way to Rainy Mountain*.

In January 1967, before the completion of *The Journey of Tai-*

me, Momaday's "The Way to Rainy Mountain" essay was published.[24] Winters, who had been invited by the editors of the *Reporter* to write an appreciation of the piece, commented on its emerging structure, which would find its fullest manifestation in the final, book-length version:

> I think [Momaday's essay] one of the greatest pieces of short prose I have ever read. I should have trouble naming another; it is very short, yet it contains: the history of a people (the Kiowas) and the pathos of their combined grandeur and triviality; the biography of a Kiowa (Aho), in which the history is summed up; a commentary on both by the grandson and author. N. Scott Momaday can hardly drop a short phrase which does not haunt one. Nothing is wasted in this essay. Few poems stay in my mind as this prose stays.[25]

The overall structure of *The Way to Rainy Mountain* rests on the interplay among its numerous parts, which are interconnected by a multitude of cross references and associations. Behind its seemingly fragmentary construction lies a unified whole. The introductory essay and the twenty-four triads of mythical, historical, and personal narratives, which are subdivided into three chapters following the emergence, evolution to maturity, and decline of a Plains culture, are framed by two poems, and a prologue and an epilogue. The poems stand for, respectively, the mythical origin and historical end point of living Kiowa culture.

The first poem, "Headwaters," is a fine example of Momaday's skillful combination of syllabic and traditional meter.[26] Although the poem consists of a single stanza of eight lines, it separates metrically into two quatrains, the first in syllabic verse of eight syllables to the line, the second in iambic tetrameter. The rhythmic effect achieved in the second quatrain shapes and reinforces its content by imitating the rising movement of "this archaic force." Momaday attempts here to approximate the myriad forces he senses in nature, forces which are just beyond the reach of the poet's language.

"Headwaters" depicts the setting of the golden age of the Kiowas on the Great Plains. The hollow log in the intermountain plain refers to the emergence of the tribe from the underworld in the mountains of what is now Montana. The "archaic force" below the marsh and at the beginning of Kiowa existence is also the driving power along the way to Rainy Mountain, carrying the spirit of the people through the stages of their evolution. Momaday reinforces this point in the prologue by referring to the Kiowa migration as "an expression of the human spirit" and to his book as the vehicle through which this spirit prevails (p. 4).

The concluding poem, "Rainy Mountain Cemetery," not only suggests the end of Kiowa culture as a living entity but also reflects Momaday's reaction to his ancestors' graves, which motivated him to set out on his spiritual and physical journey along the Kiowa migration route. In the cemetery Momaday comes closest to his ancestors in spirit, but at the same time he becomes most acutely aware of his separation from them. The listener who yearns to hear the names of the dead remains enclosed by a wall of silence. The images of shadow, defined by the ancestral names, and of "the cold, black density of stone" impress upon the mourner the inexorable cleavage between the living and the dead. Momaday's only way of bridging this gap lies in an act of the imagination which is nourished by a quasi-religious penetration of the ancestral land and an immersion into the ancient stories of the Kiowas in which the spirit of the tribe has been crystallized.

The prologue is not only an unemotional, matter-of-fact stock-taking of the rise and fall of the Kiowas and the deterioration of the oral tradition which records tribal evolution but also a summary of the process and material through which Momaday's imagination takes hold of the racial spirit which binds him to his Kiowa heritage. The opening paragraph anticipates the three chapters of the main body of the book, "The Setting Out," "The Going On," and "The Closing In": "The journey began one day on the edge of the northern Plains. It was carried on over the course of many generations and many hundreds of miles. In the end there were many things to remember, to dwell upon and talk about" (p. 3). This opening points also to the central elements which constitute *The Way to Rainy Mountain*: "a landscape that is incomparable, a time that is gone forever, and the human spirit which endures." The work is "preeminently the history of an idea, man's idea of himself, and it has old and essential being in language" (p. 4).

The quotation applies to the evolution of a tribal consciousness in the course of the Kiowa migration as well as to Momaday's formation of a racial identity as a contemporary Kiowa. He noted that the "imaginative experience and the historical express equally the traditions of man's reality" (p. 4). Despite the collapse of Kiowa culture as a living organism, its modern heirs "remember their native culture and are able to live in relation to it."[27] Momaday suggests that "the Kiowa carries in his blood the meaning and full development of the plains culture."[28] By an individual and imaginative act he has raised the latent "blood memory" to a conscious level in *The Way to Rainy Mountain*.

Momaday's journey across the Great Plains was a journey into the tribal mind which evolved under the influence of this landscape. Momaday noted that "in the course of that long migration [the Kiowas] had become of age as a people. They had conceived a good idea of themselves; they had dared to imagine and determine who they were" (p. 4). In writing *The Way to Rainy Mountain*, Momaday responded to the responsibility of each successive generation to reaffirm this idea and sustain the tribal spirit. It is, as he stressed in the prologue, a deeply personal venture, "*one way* in which these traditions [mythical and historical] are conceived, developed, and interfused in the human mind" (p. 4; italics added).

The Way to Rainy Mountain should not be read as a historical document of Kiowa life, as the label "non-fiction" on a paperback reprint suggests.[29] It is rather a product of Momaday's imagination, as the following disclaimer shows:

. . . I'm not concerned to write the history of a people except as that history bears upon me directly. When I was writing *The Way to Rainy Mountain*, . . . I was dealing with something that belongs to the Indian world, and the Kiowa people as a whole, but I wasn't

concerned with that so much as I was concerned with the fact that
it meant this to me—this is how I as a person felt about it. And I
want my writing to reflect myself in certain ways—that is my first
concern.[30]

The prologue serves, within the overall concept of the book,
as an orientation for the reader. It tells how to order and con-
nect the stories and the historical/biographical accounts of the
three main chapters. The introduction extends the background—geographical, historical, and personal—against
which the subsequent triads become meaningful.

The opening paragraph of the introduction is a lyrical depiction of Momaday's ancestral land which plays a key role in his
exploration of Kiowa identity. The sense of isolation which the
vast landscape generates sets in motion Momaday's imagination and centers it on the land and his forebears. *The Way to
Rainy Mountain*, then, manifests ancestral piety and what has
been called "geopiety."[31]

The role of the imagination in the appropriation of man to
his environment has, in part, been discussed in chapter 2.
Momaday has repeatedly pointed out that "one's idea of the self
involves the environment. You don't really know who you are
until you know where you are in a physical sense."[32] The process of self-definition in terms of place involves sense perception and the formulation of an idea based on this perception.
In the end, landscape has existence in the mind of the perceiver
as a construct of the "physical eye" and the "eye of the mind."[33]
The final idea depends on individual memory, namely the remembered process of discovery of a certain place over many
years, and on a historical awareness of previous generations
whose lives unfolded in a given landscape.

"Geopiety" and ancestral piety are inseparable for Momaday
because they both pertain to the landscape of the Great Plains
in which the physical and spiritual migration of the Kiowas
took place. This landscape is the common denominator of
myths, legends, history, and biography, the focal point of racial
and individual memory. From the old woman Ko-sahn, Momaday received a sense of what the land means for the individual

who is its product. He wrote of Ko-sahn that "her roots ran deep into the earth, and from those depths she drew strength enough to hold still against all the forces of change and disorder. . . . And she drew therefrom the sustenance of meaning and of mystery as well."[34] Momaday relies on the land for the same reasons, and he stressed his conviction that this sense of the earth is beneficial to all persons. He made this point in what amounts to an urgent plea for a new awareness of man's rootedness in the land in this much-quoted passage from the final section of *The Way to Rainy Mountain*:

Once in his life man ought to concentrate his mind upon the remembered earth, I believe. He ought to give himself up to a particular landscape in his experience, to look at it from as many angles as he can, to wonder about it, to dwell upon it. He ought to imagine that he touches it with his hands at every season and listens to the sounds that are made upon it. He ought to imagine the creatures there and all the faintest motions of the wind. He ought to recollect the glare of noon and all the colors of the dawn and dusk. [P. 83]

"The remembered earth" is not only an individual but also a collective perception of the land, for it includes the way Momaday's ancestors viewed it generations ago. His view of the landscape is qualified by Kiowa oral tradition, in which the perceptions of his forebears prevail. When Wallace Stevens wrote that "sight / Is a museum of things seen," he meant that man's perception of his world is colored by concepts and interpretations he has assimilated from language, art, and memory.[35] How close Stevens and Momaday are on this point becomes still more apparent in the following quotation. For Stevens physical geography is really mental geography, a fiction created out of sense perceptions and the imaginative power of the mind. In "The Figure of the Youth as a Virile Poet" he wrote:

It is easy to suppose that few people realize on that occasion, which comes to all of us, when we look at the blue sky for the first time, that is to say, not merely see it, but look at it and experience it and for the first time have a sense that we live in the center of a physical poetry, a geography that would be intolerable except for the non-geography that exists there—few people realize that they are looking at the world of their own thoughts and the world of their own feelings.[36]

The same process of taking possession of a place in the mind, which Momaday has described as an elaboration of a "physical" by an "imaginative vision," finds expression in these lines from Stevens's "Notes toward a Supreme Fiction": "We reason of these things with later reason / And we make of what we see, what we see clearly / And have seen, a place dependent on ourselves."[37] For Momaday geography is not only "a physical poetry" but physical myth, legend, and history as well. This cultural significance is paramount in *The Way to Rainy Mountain*.

Jan Vansina, a scholar of oral traditions, pointed out that "the landscape, with its individual features, whether natural or man-made, can be used as a mnemonic device. It can give rise to well-known legends."[38] Yi-Fu Tuan, a student of psychological and philosophical aspects of geography, wrote on the same issue: "Landscape is personal and tribal history made visible; the native's identity—his place in the total scheme of things— is not in doubt, because the myths that support it are as real as the rocks, the waterholes, and the hills he can see and touch."[39]

The landscape and the oral tradition are particularly crucial for Momaday because the material culture of the Kiowas was relatively scarce owing to their nomadic life, and little of it is extant. But by involving himself in the landscape of his ancestors, he can verify the traditional stories and restore a sense of the way in which they grew out of the physical environment and his ancestors' daily experience.

A major function of the introduction is to depict how Momaday's personal attachment to Kiowa history depends on the living memories of Aho, his grandmother. If the landscape of Rainy Mountain is one door to Momaday's tribal past, Aho's recollections are another. Yi-Fu Tuan suggested that "to know a place is also to know the past. . . . But the communal past is not truly one's own past unless history extends without break into personal memories; and neither is vividly present unless objectified in things that can be seen and touched, that is, directly experienced."[40] Through Aho's personal memory Momaday gained access to the recent history of the Kiowas; through her racial memory, her knowledge of legends and myths, he learned about the tribe's migration and spiritual evolution. Using Aho's life as a focal point, Momaday moves from the final years of Kiowa culture back to the mythical emergence and subsequent migration of the tribe across the continent. He elaborates on the prologue's brief sketch of Kiowa evolution by summing up the crucial milestones of his ancestors' journey and by describing the transformation they underwent. This summary provides an overall framework into which fit the individual stories and documentary pieces of the three main chapters.

Aho was born around 1880, "when the Kiowas were living the last great moments of their history" (p. 6). She was "spared the humiliation of those high gray walls of Fort Sill [where the Kiowas finally surrendered to the U.S. Army] by eight, or ten years, but she must have known from birth the affliction of defeat, the dark brooding in old warriors" (p. 8). While she was very close to the horrors of cultural disintegration, she had also a clear notion of the earlier, glorious stage of her tribal history. Momaday contends that although she "lived out her long life in the shadow of Rainy Mountain, the immense landscape of the continental interior lay like a memory in her blood. She could tell of the Crows, whom she had never seen, and of the Black Hills, where she had never been" (p. 7).

The Kiowas encountered the Crows on the edge of the plains on their way east and south from the Yellowstone region, from where they set off in the late seventeenth century. They adopted the Plains culture and religion from this tribe. Two other factors changed the character of the Kiowas profoundly. The landscape they had entered allowed them a new vision into unknown distances. The sense of confinement and limitation in the northern mountains gave way to a sense of freedom in the plains. This experience was amplified by the acquisition of the horse, which revolutionized their way of life and created a new spirit of power and pride: the pedestrian mountain people of the north, whose existence had been fragile and cumbersome, emerged as highly mobile hunters and warriors.

With the acquisition of Tai-me, the sacred Sun Dance fetish, the Kiowas entered into an alliance with the sun, their highest deity. With the creation of the story of Tsoai in response to their awesome encounter with the rock formation of Devil's Tower, in Wyoming, the Kiowas established a kinship with the stars. Allied with the sun through Tai-me and related to the Big Dipper through the myth of Tsoai, they stood in good relation to the universe. Everything was prepared for the coming of their golden age.

It lasted roughly a century, from about 1775, and its decline was foreshadowed by the reversal of those signs which had heralded its arrival. In the early hours of 13 November 1833, just before dawn, a meteoric explosion occurred in the sky over North America. To the Kiowas the "Night the Stars Fell" signaled the loss of their kinsmen in the sky, a frightful omen for the destiny of the tribe. The disintegration of their world was close at hand. In the spring of the same year a large number of the tribe had been massacred in a clash with the Osages, and Tai-me had been lost. Four years later the Kiowas made their first treaty with the United States government. In the twenty years between 1833 and 1853 the tribe was reduced to half its number by several epidemics of smallpox and Asiatic cholera. In 1854 the Kiowas suffered a heavy defeat at the hands of the Sauk and Foxes. The loss of their horses and the butchering of the buffalo followed within a generation after the falling of the stars. And in 1887, little more than half a century later, the Kiowas held their last Sun Dance.

The killing of the buffalo destroyed the Kiowas' subsistence; the forced abolition of the Sun Dance, which the United States government perceived as idolatry, broke their spirit. With the loss of the buffalo, the animal representation of the sun, and their holiest religious ceremony, they were cut off from the life-sustaining power of the sun. Aho, who witnessed these times of turmoil, passed on her vision of deicide to her grandson. Her memories became his. Momaday ends his introduction by relating his sense of separation from Aho and by re-creating the life he used to know in his grandmother's house at Rainy Mountain.

It is against the "black and opaque" windowpanes of Aho's house that Momaday exerts the power of his imagination. The image of the empty house and the poet's urgency to repopulate it with its deceased inhabitants is reminiscent of part three of Wallace Stevens's "The Auroras of Autumn." Here Stevens re-creates in his imagination a mother and a family who have long since left a house: "Farewell to an idea . . . The mother's face, / The purpose of the poem, fills the room. / They are together, here, and it is warm, / . . . The house will crumble and the book will burn. / They are at ease in the shelter of the mind / And the house is of the mind and they and time, / Together, all together. . . ."[41] In the same way Aho, Mammedaty, and the other Kiowas who made their way to Rainy Mountain are at ease in the shelter of Momaday's mind.

Also significant in this context is Sonnet XVI of Frederick Goddard Tuckerman's "Second Series," which describes the deserted and decaying house of two sisters. Reminiscing about the life which once filled the home, the poetic persona confronts this scene of decline and loss:

> The house stands vacant in its green recess,
> Absent of beauty as a broken heart.
> The wild rain enters, and the sunset wind
> Sighs in the chambers of their loveliness
> Or shakes the pane—and in the silent noons
> The glass falls from the window, part by part,
> And ringeth faintly in the grassy stones.[42]

Past times and people live on in the poet's mind, and there only.

In another poem, Sonnet XVIII, Tuckerman focuses on the changed environment, a product of civilization which has replaced the wilderness. Momaday referred to this poem as "the very sensitive statement of a man who holds in his mind for a moment the inevitable fact of change."[43] Like Momaday in his confrontation with Aho's weather-stained house at Rainy Mountain, Tuckerman's persona attempts to reconcile recollections with present vision. The poetic voice concedes that "change with hurried hand has swept these scenes."[44] This fact can be softened only by the imaginative re-creation in the mind of a time that has gone forever:

> Yet for a moment let my fancy plant
> These autumn hills again: the wild dove's haunt,
> The wild deer's walk. In golden umbrage shut,
> The Indian river runs, Quonecktacut!
> Here, but a lifetime back, where falls tonight
> Behind the curtained pane a sheltered light
> On buds of rose or vase of violet
> Aloft upon the marble mantle set,
> Here in the forest-heart, hung blackening
> The wolfbait on the bush beside the spring.[45]

The conclusion of Momaday's introduction to *The Way to Rainy Mountain* touches upon the same themes: change and loss are a matter of course, facts of life which can be neither denied nor defied. Release from such inevitability can be derived only from the imagination. So Momaday, after depicting his dead grandmother's empty house, brings to life once more the joy which used to fill it. It is an intimation of the excitement of the Kiowas' summer reunions at Rainy Mountain in which Momaday took part as a child. He recalls the prayer meetings, feasts, and storytelling sessions to which the Kiowas came "to remind and be reminded of who they were" (p. 11), just as Momaday, in re-creating these times and events, reminds himself of who he is. The vitality of his imaginative life rises against a scene of stark finality: "Now there is a funeral silence in the rooms, the endless wake of some final word" (p. 12). This line anticipates the conclusion of the first stanza of "Rainy Mountain Cemetery," which evokes the same sense of resigned mourning in the presence of the dead: "The wake of nothing audible he hears / Who listens here and now to hear your name" (p. 89).

With the final image of the cricket against the full moon Momaday brings the introductory essay to its climax: "A cricket had perched upon the handrail, only a few inches away from me. My line of vision was such that the creature filled the moon like a fossil. It had gone there, I thought, to live and die, for there, of all places, was its small definition made whole and eternal" (p. 12). One critic has seen the cricket as symbolic of the Kiowa culture Momaday celebrates.[46] The cricket is more than an aboriginal icon, however. Momaday hinted at a deeper significance of the symbol in a letter to Gus Blaisdell, the editor of *The Way to Rainy Mountain*, in which he described the cricket as "one of the great images in our literature."[47] This remark, of course, refers to Tuckerman's poem "The Cricket," in which the insect stands as a symbol of death. Momaday described its function thus:

The ubiquity of Tuckerman's cricket is the ubiquity of death. Unlike man, who has severed his existence from primitive nature, the cricket is an integral part of nature. And, like death, it has absolute existence in a dimension incomprehensible to man. Therein lies the validity of the cricket as a symbol of death and of the inevitable frustration of man's quest to know the meaning of death.[48]

Momaday's cricket, too, is related to death. This connection becomes significant in Momaday's emotional response to his vision of the cricket: "A warm wind rose up and purled *like the longing within me*" (p. 12; italics added). This statement is deliberately ambiguous; it may be an expression of longing for the return of Aho and the time of Momaday's childhood or indeed a suggestion of his desire to join the dead. But, as in Tuckerman's sonnet, the poet does not yield to his emotions. Momaday wrote that "in *The Cricket* the death-wish is relinquished by an act both conscious and deliberate. What remains for the poet and his reader is not a reprieve, but the certain necessity of moral and intellectual responsibility."[49] The same is true of Momaday's response to the end of Kiowa culture. Out of his mourning for Aho grows an attitude of acceptance, a desire to hold on to cherished memories, and a determination to start afresh from Rainy Mountain: "Looking back once, I saw the mountain and came away" (p. 12). This "Coming Away," then, is the fourth stage of Kiowa evolution, a coming away from a glorious past the spirit of which continues to have a powerful presence in the life of modern Kiowa people. *The Way to Rainy Mountain* is the assertion of this spirit.

The three voices in each of the twenty-four triads which make up the main body of the book reflect three distinct perceptions of reality: the mythical-legendary, the historical-anthropological, and the personal. They are interrelated by a method of controlled association which results in a blending of these three dimensions of experience into a unique, personal view of the Kiowa world. While the associative links create a sense of unity, the separation of each individual voice—set off by differing type faces—suggests Momaday's distance from the mythical and historical experience of his ancestors. Only in his creative imagination, and through an associative process, can this distance be overcome.

It is clear that there is no attempt by Momaday to revive a primitive mentality, which for him, as a contemporary, intellectual Kiowa, is beyond reach. Neither are Momaday's intentions nostalgic. When he ends his unemotional sketch of the Kiowas' cultural collapse by referring to his thoughts as "idle recollections, the mean and ordinary agonies of human history" (p. 3), he admits his intellectual and emotional distance. It would be wrong to take Momaday's celebration of the Kiowas' heydays, their "time of great adventure and nobility and fulfilment" (p. 3), as a sign of nostalgic yearning for a return to this period. Separation and loss are inexorable parts of the human condition. Having accepted that, Momaday deals poetically with what is extant and representative of a heritage from which he can draw a sense of belonging and pride.

"The Setting Out," the first of the three chapters in *The Way to Rainy Mountain*, deals with the earliest stage in the development of Kiowa consciousness. The myths in this chapter refer to the Kiowas' emergence, their appropriation to the world surrounding them, and the satisfaction of their religious and emotional needs. According to H. A. Frankfort, myths are the product of prescientific man's speculative thought in his attempt to "underpin the chaos of experience so that it may reveal the features of structure—order, coherence, and meaning."[50] They reflect a world view dealing with the phenomenal world as a "Thou," which, according to Frankfort, has "the unprecedented, unparalleled, and unpredictable character of an individual, a presence known only in so far as it reveals itself. "Thou," moreover, is not merely contemplated or understood but is experienced emotionally in a dynamic reciprocal relationship."[51] Prescientific man experiences the world as animate, as a living presence to which he stands in a close personal relationship. Three characteristics of this particular attitude are useful for an understanding of the myths and legends in *The Way to Rainy Mountain*. According to Robert Redfield, precivilized man experiences a "primary indistinction of personal, natural, and sacred qualities" in the world he looks upon.[52] Second, his attitude to what surrounds him is "one of placation or appeal or coercion" in an attempt to maintain himself and the environment through responsible, reciprocal relations.[53] Finally, Redfield noted that "in the primary world view Man and Not-Man are bound together in one moral order. The universe is morally significant. It cares."[54]

The first story in "The Setting Out" is the Kiowa emergence myth. It introduces two themes which play a significant role in subsequent passages: separation and the creative power of language. Momaday, in a holographic addition to the original typescript, remarked that, first, the story "could be given the usual (and obvious) *psycho-biological overtones*: 'the hollow log' representing primordial vagina—primordial mother." Second, it is an etiologic myth, "giving the actual *reason* for the smallness of their tribe. The 'chosen people' feeling—small, but necessarily so." The story of the pregnant woman blocking the hollow log and preventing the remaining people from emerging suggests that separation was inherent in the creative act. And third, Momaday draws attention to the "unconceptualized I-Thou" relation: "'It made them glad to see so many things.' . . . Here one notices that there was no awe—no hint of the *numinous* (mysterium-tremendum etc.), the fascinans element enters in."[55] The subsequent act of calling themselves Kwuda, however, creates not only social unity but also a distinction between the group and the world around it.

The second, documentary passage of this opening triad provides additional information on the variants of the Kiowa tribal name. Momaday draws here, as in most of these passages, on James Mooney's *Calendar History of the Kiowa Indians.*[56] In the third section Momaday emulates his ancestors' "Coming Out" experience when he catches the first glimpse of the plains on his journey along the Kiowa migration route. Like the Kwuda he gradually becomes aware and takes stock of the world around him. He captures the moment of a newly awakening consciousness of the earth.

The opening story of the second triad relates another incident of separation and act of naming: the quarrel over an antelope udder leads to the splitting up of the Kiowas. The new group was called "the udder-angry travellers off."[57] Anthropological material from Mooney furnishes evidence as to the authenticity of the account. Historical records of an antelope drive during the horse era suggest that under extreme conditions the Kiowas reverted to their ancient hunting practices.[58] Momaday's description of a sighting of antelopes on his journey through Wyoming brings myth and documentation into a personal focus.

Section III opens with a story relating the coming of the dog to the Kiowas. Before the advent of the horse dogs were the only means of transportation. A dog appears to a man who is ostracized from the tribe and without food or weapons and offers him help against the daunting threat of enemies on the condition that the Kiowa take care of the dog's starving puppies. The parallel here is obvious: man and animal share an exposed, fragile existence, they understand each other (and each other's language), and by acting morally, reciprocally, and appropriately, they overcome their distress.

Sections IV to IX deal with the myth of how talyi-da-i, "boy medicine," came into the possession of the tribe. It established a form of sun worship which preceded that of Tai-me. Section IV begins by telling of the unification of man and deity. A Kiowa girl, lying in her cradle, is placed in a tree. A redbird attracts the child's attention and entices her to climb after it. The tree meanwhile begins to grow and carries the child into the sky. The girl changes into a woman and the redbird is transformed into a young man. He tells her that he has taken her away to be his wife. It is only then that the woman recognizes him as the sun.

The two passages which complete this triad are among the best examples of how effectively Momaday relates myth to his personal experience. The opening sentence of the second passage relates the landscape to the upward movement of the myth: "There the land itself ascends into the sky" (p. 23). In the third passage Momaday emulates the myth's reality in a poetic depiction of nature:

I have walked in a mountain meadow bright with Indian paintbrush, lupine, and wild buckwheat, and I have seen high in the branches of a lodgepole pine the male pine grosbeak, round and rose-colored, its dark, striped wings nearly invisible in the soft, mottled light. And the uppermost branches of the tree seemed very slowly to ride across the blue sky. [P. 23]

Section V has curious overtones of the biblical story of man's fall. The wife of the sun, who has given birth to a son, ignores her husband's prohibition to go near a certain bush and dig up its roots—pomme blanche, as the second passage explains. In doing so, she creates an opening through which she attempts to reach the earth by climbing down a rope. When the sun discovers her and his son's disappearance, he hurries to the forbidden bush and sees her dangling at the end of the rope halfway between sky and earth. He furiously kills the woman with a magic ring, leaving the child all alone. It is an ironic touch of this story that the woman's sin is the first step toward the arrival of the hero twins among the Kiowas.

Section VI relates how Sun Boy is captured by Spider Woman, who becomes his foster mother. Section VII tells of the separation of the boy into twins through the forbidden use of a magic ring. The next triad (section VIII) deals with an adventure typical of culture heroes in Indian oral traditions. More important, it illustrates through its three voices the creative and magical power of language, a theme which recurs in the Tai-me story (X), the stories of the arrowmaker (XIII) and the storm spirit (XIV), and the story of the buffalo with horns of steel (XVI).

The hero twins' defiance of their grandmother spider's warning not to throw the magic ring into the air leads to their capture by two malicious giants. They attempt to suffocate the boys by filling their cave with smoke, and it is only by uttering the word "thain-mom, above my eyes," a formula they learned from Spider Woman, that they escape death and return home. In the second passage of section VIII Momaday explains the attitude of preliterate man to language: "A word has power in and of itself. It comes from nothing into sound and meaning; it gives origin to all things. By means of words can a man deal with the world on equal terms. And the word is sacred" (p. 33). He also recalls his own experience of word magic: "When Aho saw or heard or thought something bad, she said the word zei-dl-bei, 'frightful.' It was the one word with which she confronted evil and the incomprehensible. . . . It was not an exclamation so much, I think, as it was a warding off, an exertion of language upon ignorance and disorder" (p. 33).

Section IX, in which the twins unwittingly kill their grandfather and precipitate the death of Spider Woman, brings the story cycle to a close. However, the account by Mooney in the second passage, explaining the religious significance of the hero twins for the Kiowas, anticipates the story of the two brothers in section XI and identifies it as a version of the talyi-da-i myth: ". . . one of the twins is said to have walked into the waters of a lake and disappeared forever, while the other at last transformed himself into ten portions of 'medicine,' thereby giving of his own body in eucharist form to the Kiowas. The ten bundles of talyi-da-i, 'boy medicine' are, like the Tai-me, chief objects of religious veneration" (p. 35).[59] Momaday believes that the tales of the twins once constituted an epic cycle which deteriorated and became fragmented. He noted that "there are several stories [in *The Way to Rainy Mountain*] about brothers, and I have an idea that they are the twins, though the connections got lost."[60]

Section X treats the most crucial event in the Kiowas "Setting Out" period, the coming of Tai-me. The Tai-me myth, as Momaday pointed out, "is not an entertainment nor even the journal of an old salvation; it is infinitely more. It is an emotional reaction to the elemental experience of being, the affirmation of an eternal reality behind all appearances; it is sacred."[61] Tai-me is a vision born out of hunger and despair and a reflection of the bond between man and not-man in a morally significant, caring universe. Momaday noted that the Kiowa's mind in his moment of extremity "is compelled to look beyond itself for meaning and for ease. It recoils from the present world and fastens upon another, a world of the imagination."[62] With Tai-me, the Sun Dance religion was added to the much older veneration of the sun based on the myth and medicine bundle of the talyi-da-i.

The second passage of section X describes the Tai-me fetish, as Mooney saw it at the end of the nineteenth century.[63] In the final passage of this triad Momaday relates his own encounter with the sacred bundle, the circumstances and impact of which were discussed at the beginning of this chapter.

The final triad (section XI) of the "Setting Out" chapter brings together three central elements of Kiowa religion: the hero twins, Tai-me (implicitly), and peyote. In the opening story of this triad, two brothers find a quantity of meat outside their tipi at a time of hunger and scarcity. While one of them refuses to touch the strange find, the other eats from it without fear. As a result he turns into a water beast and has to live in a lake where his brother visits him and tells him about the ways of the Kiowas.

This is another story of separation, and, as with the separation from their tribe of the seven sisters in the myth of Tsoai who united the Kiowas with the sky and the separation from her parents of the child who united the tribe with the sun, so the separation of the brothers results in the Kiowas' kinship to the water spirits. The reason for the brother's metamorphosis is somewhat obscure, and Momaday himself admitted that he had no explanation for it.[64] One possible interpretation is that the meat, presumably that of a buffalo, the animal representation of the sun, had not been sanctified by Tai-me and was therefore taboo.[65]

The second passage of section XI describes the sacrament of peyote, which the Kiowas see as the vegetable representation of the sun. They adopted the drug and the system of rituals and myths connected with it from the southern tribes along the Mexican border.[66] The third passage unites the various religious elements of this ritual in the figure of Mammedaty, Momaday's grandfather, who was a peyote man and a priest of the sun. His involvement in the Kiowas' most holy affairs represents a familial link to his grandson.

While the "Setting Out" chapter dealt with the evolving relations of the tribe with the supernaturals and with the external world in a movement from frailty to firm integration in the universe, the "Going On" chapter shows the Kiowas in control of their destiny and at the height of their freedom and power. Section XII illustrates their control over supernatural enemies; the story of the arrowmaker, which has been discussed in detail in Chapter 2 exemplifies their power to ward off evil through their belief in the efficacy of language. The magical properties of language are also at the heart of section XIV, in which words mediate between the Kiowas and the storm spirit, and section XVI, in which a buffalo hunter escapes a mythical beast through the aid of a magic voice.[67]

Two other stories, in sections XV and XVII, relate instances of the reconciliation of social discord and the sanctions against antisocial behavior. The final story of this chapter (in section XVIII) is an illustration of the freedom afforded the Kiowas by the acquisition of the horse. It shows their transformation from "half-starved skulkers in the timber," as Mooney put it, to daring buffalo hunters, raiders, and explorers. In their search for the home of the summer, they follow a southward course which takes them all the way to the jungles of northeastern Mexico. In his version of this story Wilbur S. Nye identified the place as "the jungles of Tamaulipas, where the Indians saw monkeys in the trees."[68]

The documentary and biographical passages in this chapter reinforce the grandeur of Kiowa culture through references to George Catlin's favorable accounts and paintings of the tribe and through the depiction of their majestic homeland in Momaday's poetic sketches of a sunset at Rainy Mountain cemetery (section XII, passage 3), of the figure of Old Man Cheney praying to the sun as dawn illuminates a soundless landscape (XIII, 3), of the calm and violent weather in the plains, and of seeking protection from tempestuous winds in the storm shelter of his grandmother's house (XIV, 2 and 3).[69]

Besides its celebratory accounts of Kiowa life at the height of its glory this chapter contains more inauspicious passages. The destruction of a heraldic tipi by fire in the winter of 1872–73 figures as an ominous sign of worse things to come (XII, 2). The moving passage of two old Kiowas reenacting a buffalo hunt captures the impending end of their culture. Their pathetic pursuit of the old animal, purchased for the occasion, nonetheless reflects a strength of spirit and an air of nobility at a moment when all the odds are against cultural survival (XVI, 2).[70]

Section XIX, the opening of the "Closing In" chapter, harks back to the previous stories of glory, while the remaining sections of this chapter record the steady decline of the Kiowas. The first story in this triad, a secularized version of the hero twin myth, reflects the courage, nobility, and mutual respect among Plains tribes. The third passage reinforces the glory of the Kiowa horse culture through Momaday's own familiarity with it. Framed by those two passages are two accounts of the grim end of the Kiowa horse culture: the destruction or confiscation of ponies after the surrender of the Kiowas at Fort Sill; and Mooney's account of the "horse-eating sun dance" which followed a winter of starvation. The Kiowas were in such a desperate situation that they killed most of their animals in order to survive. Mildred Mayhall concluded her study of the Kiowas by noting that "the culture ended as it had begun— with the dependence on the horse. Their horses were taken away from the Plains Indians . . . and their spirit was stifled. On foot, the 'centaur personality' was gone."[71]

The story of the horse which died of shame in section XX suggests the fading courage of the Kiowa warrior, whose moral deterioration stands in contrast to the nobility of the animal. The second passage in this triad records two sacrifices of horses, the different results of which indicate the precarious balance of Kiowa culture shortly before its collapse. The first sacrificial offering fails to prevent the arrival of "the white man's disease," smallpox. Gaapiatan's sacrifice, on the other hand, is received favorably: he and his family, according to Mooney, survived the epidemic.[72] Momaday's comment on the old man's action in the third passage of this triad stresses again the Kiowas' moral principle of reciprocity.

Most of the remaining episodes are drawn from Momaday's family history: the vignettes of Mammedaty in section XXI show him as in tune with natural and supernatural phenomena and in possession of powerful medicine. But even he yields to the pressures of cultural decline, as his act of violence against a horse indicates (XXII, 1). The theft of a valuable horse by a Pawnee and the disappearance of the bones of a horse which Mammedaty had preserved are two more incidents which reflect a gradual loss of power. The inexplicable and ominous event of the Tai-me bundle falling to the ground signals the tribe's impending spiritual breakdown.

The first story of the book's final triad points to the land as the place from which man emerges and to which he returns at the end of his life's journey. Momaday refers to it as "a declaration of love for the land, in which the several elements—the woman, the dress, and this plain—are at last become one reality, one expression of the beautiful in nature."[73] The stress is on the landscape and the beautiful dress, not on the name of the woman or the precise location of her grave. For Momaday this emphasis is peculiarly native, "a translation of the woman into the landscape, a translation particularly signified by means of the beautiful and distinctive dress, an *Indian* dress."[74] The third passage of the final triad, quoted earlier in this chapter, reiterates the sacredness of the land as the visible embodiment of a people's past.

The epilogue consists of another sketch of the incidents which brought the Kiowa culture to an end. Momaday connects them with the ominous meteoric display in 1833 which indicated to his ancestors "the sudden and violent disintegration of an older order" (p. 85). He concludes with a final example illustrating the significance of the oral tradition for the preservation of his heritage. The old woman Ko-sahn, whose story of the beginning of the Sun Dance Momaday recounts, has been important for his belief in the reality of a verbal dimension of existence.[75] In the story she entrusts to Momaday the verbal tradition is preserved in living memory. In the prologue Momaday wrote: "There are on the way to Rainy Mountain . . . many journeys in the one" (p. 4). Some of them are physical, some spiritual, others mythical. This final story draws attention to the most important journey of them all: the journey of words from one generation to the next which preserves all other journeys in the safety of language. In Momaday's writings the journeys and his heritage continue.

CHAPTER 6

Myths to Live By:
The Names: A Memoir

The Names: A Memoir records Momaday's experience of growing up as an Indian in modern America. It reveals the process of his symbolic and imaginative identification with his racial heritage. His recollections of his childhood and youth and the appropriation of ancient myths and ancestral stories to his life come together in the creation of a personal myth. In one of his earlier works Momaday described the deep impression which an old woman's composure and sense of place had made upon him: "It was as if she had said to me, 'Oh, I can tell you a story, and you can live well with it.'"[1] This statement is particularly appropriate in the context of *The Names*, for it is here that Momaday relates those stories in which his own life is concentrated. The myths and stories he lives by root him in the tradition of his ancestors, to which he adds what he finds valuable in other cultures. This chapter looks first at the literary background of the work and then examines Momaday's creation of his world of stories.

In 1968, only a few weeks before Yvor Winters's death, Momaday wrote to his friend: "Lately I have been thinking of a non-fiction book, an evocation of the American landscape, informed by autobiographical elements and the history of the Kiowas. I don't know, it's just a thought at this point. But I want to write an indigenous book."[2] The idea for this project emerged during his work on *House Made of Dawn*, when Frances McCullough, his editor, wrote to him expressing her astonishment at his unusual background:

Your remarks about your family and your childhood in the last letter are fascinating, and certainly you have a great story to tell. I have a suspicion (just by comparing the letter, the Rainy Mountain piece, and the novel) that perhaps the best way for you to deal with the material is to write a sort of autobiography about growing up Indian.[3]

At this point Momaday was already deeply involved in the exploration of his Kiowa heritage and had projected much of his boyhood into the world of *House Made of Dawn*. He was also familiar with and greatly impressed by Isak Dinesen's *Out of Africa*, which Winters had urged him to read.[4] Written after her return from Kenya to her native Denmark, it is a loving portrayal of the African landscape and its people. Perhaps the most striking features of her memoir are Dinesen's success in capturing the spirit of place and her sensitivity to the complex relations of the native people and their traditions to the physical environment. In *House Made of Dawn*, Momaday achieved a similar success in depicting the land as a physical and spiritual presence.[5] There is no conclusive evidence that Dinesen's work had a direct influence on Momaday at that point, although it is likely. However, when Momaday began to contemplate an autobiographical work, he consciously drew on *Out of Africa* as a model for *The Names*.[6]

With the exception of his early childhood among the Kiowas in Oklahoma, Momaday was as much an outsider to the cultures he describes as Dinesen was to the aboriginal people of Kenya. This status, however, did not prevent either of them from creating spiritual homes through their personal involvement in their respective landscapes. Momaday wrote: "If you have been to the hogans in Canyon de Chelly, or to the squaw dance near Lukachukai . . . you will never come away entirely, but a part of you will remain there always; you will have found an old home of the spirit."[7] And remembering his first morning in the Jemez Valley, he described his feelings by quoting from Dinesen: "In the highlands you woke up in the morning and thought: Here I am, where I ought to be" (p. 121).[8]

Both writers believe that individuals are molded by the particular location they inhabit. Momaday put it thus:

There was at Jemez a climate of the mind in which we, my parents and I, realized ourselves, understood who we were, not perfectly, it may be, but well enough. It was not our native world, but we appropriated it, as it were, to ourselves; we invested much of our lives in it, and in it was the remembered place of our hopes, our dreams, and our deep love. [P. 152]

In a sequel to *Out of Africa*, *Shadows on the Grass*, Dinesen wrote about the influence Kenya had on her: "Only during one time in my life, and only in connection with one kind of place and people, have phenomena of an outer world found their way into my dreams. It was in itself a strange and stirring experience."[9] Momaday has expressed his admiration of Dinesen's style, her descriptive power, and her skill as a storyteller on many occasions.[10] In *The Names* there are some striking instances which reveal not only a shared interest in subject matter but an apparent influence on Momaday by Dinesen's imagery.

The two writers are akin in the way they impose their imagination on the landscape. They are both aware that the landscape is, for the native people, above all mythical. Behind the physical properties linger the stories of creation, gods, and culture heroes, which endow geography with religious significance. Both writers have assimilated the oral tradition into their perception of the land. And they take their imaginative interaction with their environment one step further by populating it with figures from their literary backgrounds. Momaday wrote, "I saw Grendel's shadow on the wall of Canyon de Chelly, and once, having led the sun around Hokinini Mesa, I saw Copperfield at Oljeto Trading post" (p. 60). Dinesen describes a similar play of the imagination:

The fictitious characters in the books run beside your horse on the farm, and walk about the maize-fields. . . . All Walter Scott's characters were at home in the country and might be met anywhere; so were Odysseus and his men, and strangely enough many figures from Racine. Peter Schlemihl had walked over the hills in seven-league boots, Clown Agheb the honeybee lived in my garden by the river. [Pp. 363–64]

Dinesen's kind of imagery appears in numerous places in *The Names*. Momaday wrote, for instance, "Look, look, . . . how God has drawn the sky with light" (p. 80). Momaday echoes Dinesen not only in the notion of sublimity but in the image of a divine drawing, an example of which appears in her *Shadows on the Grass*: "We turned our eyes to . . . the wild geese and duck, in their purposeful line of flight across the sky, and we felt their course to have been drawn up by the finger of God."[11]

The title *Shadows on the Grass*, which refers to the spirits of the people Dinesen knew in Africa and who continued to populate the world of her imagination, echoes throughout *The Names*. One of the fundamental beliefs Momaday expressed in his memoir is that the spirits of his ancestors surround him, indeed that they are part of his being. He wrote about his grandfather Mammedaty: ". . . he came to be imagined posthumously in the going on of the blood, having invested the shadow of his presence in an object or a word, in his name above all" (p. 26). A drawing of Mammedaty which Momaday created as a boy is described as "so simply crude the likeness to some pallid shadow on my blood" (p. 93). The shadows of ancestral spirits, reflections of past existences, are ubiquitous influences in Momaday's life, as they were in the life of Pohd-lohk, the man who gave Momaday his Indian name. The thoughts of the dead happened upon Pohd-lohk like "shadows in his dreaming, and he imagined who they were and what happened to them" (p. 46). This shadow imagery serves as a reminder of the presence of the past in the here and now.

The beginning of the landscape description in the opening chapter of *The Names* is one example of shadow imagery: "The land settles into the end of summer. In the white light a whirlwind moves far out in the plain, and afterwards there is something like a shadow on the grass, a tremor, nothing" (pp. 3–4).[12] Momaday's comment after relating a tragic episode in the decline of the Kiowa horse culture is another case in point: "It was a simple story in the telling, but there were many implications, many shadows on the grass" (p. 50). There are a host of other examples with less overt echoes of Dinesen's title. When Momaday writes, "the shadows closed upon me" (p. 115), "shadows danced about" (p. 139), and "if in the sunrise I should see the long shadows running to the west (p. 147), the realistic description is loaded with a symbolic representation of the past. These shadows emerge from what Momaday calls his racial or blood memory, which nourishes his imagination. Toward the end of his memoir he writes, "My mind soared; time and again I saw the fleeting shadow of my mind moving about me as it went winding upon the sun" (p. 156). In this brilliant image Momaday captures the idea that he places his spirit in the physical world, a spirit real and accessible to posterity as the spirits of his forebears are real and accessible to him.[13]

Perhaps Isak Dinesen's eloquent statement best characterizes the kinship between her *Out of Africa* and *Shadows on the Grass* and Momaday's *The Way to Rainy Mountain* and *The Names*: "People work much in order to secure the future; I gave my mind much work and trouble trying to secure the past."[14] The subsistence of the past in the present is one of the main features of Momaday's and Dinesen's storytelling, dreaming, imagining; their concern is not a nostalgia for the past but the past as a vital dimension of their present being. Dinesen ends *Shadows on the Grass* with this comment on her relationship with her friends of the past: "You have kept me company through many years; I shall not again frivolously doubt your actuality, I shall, from now, leave to you the rich world of reality. And you may hand me over to those dreams of mine which will take charge of me."[15]

Through language and the artistic imagination both Dinesen and Momaday achieve their fullest humanity, of which the past is a determining part. It is a process which Momaday sees as central to the oral tradition of his ancestors and which Dinesen recognized in the customs of her African neighbors. In

Out of Africa she wrote: "The Masai when they were moved from their old country . . . took with them *the names* of their hills, plains and rivers; and gave them to hills, plains and rivers in the new country. . . . The Masai were carrying their cut roots with them as a medicine, and were trying, in exile, to keep their past by a formula" (p. 375; italics added). Dinesen, writing in her native Denmark about her spiritual home in Kenya, and Momaday, projecting himself from a distant residence in California into the worlds of his early life in Oklahoma and New Mexico, rely on the same strategy "to keep their past by a formula": the use of language as medicine in the hands of the storyteller and the treatment of names as magical carriers of the past. The title of Momaday's memoir points to this fundamental belief in a palpable reality of language.

While Dinesen's influence is perhaps most noticeable, other literary echoes abound in *The Names*. Camus's famous phrase "the benign indifference of the universe" resounds in Momaday's reference to "the vast, clear indifference of the night," which concludes his realization that the sky holds nothing "to be acknowledged beyond the occasional flicker of a star" (p. 22).[16]

Momaday's plea for an awakening to the wonder and fullness of human existence has the ring and vitality of Whitman:

Oh, it is summer in New Mexico, in the bright legend of my youth. I want you to see the very many deep colors of the distance. I want you to live, to be for an hour or a day more completely alive in me than you have ever been. There are moments in that time when I live so intensely in myself that I wonder how it is possible to keep from flying apart. I want you to feel that, too, the vibrant ecstasy of so much being—to know beyond any doubt that it is only the merest happy accident that you can hold together at all in the exhilaration of such wonder. The wonder: I want to tell you of it; I want to speak and to write it all out for you. [Pp. 154–55]

In a reference to his Kentucky ancestors' awareness that their tobacco's value consisted "not only in the cash for which it is given in trade, but also in the remembered wilderness that was

given up for it" (p. 19), Momaday is reminiscent of William
Faulkner. Faulkner attributed this kind of mindfulness of the
lost wilderness to characters such as Sam Fathers, who is of
Indian descent, and Ike McCaslin, in *Go Down, Moses*.[17]
Momaday and Faulkner share the belief that the past has a
fateful bearing on the present. The following passage from
"The Old People" reveals a concept of time similar to that
which is at the heart of *The Names*:

And as Sam Fathers talked about those old times and those dead and
vanished men of another race from either that the boy knew, gradually to the boy those old times would cease to be old times and
would become a part of the boy's present, not only as if they had
happened yesterday, but as if they were still happening, the men
who walked through them actually walking in breath and air and
casting an actual shadow on the earth they had not quitted.[18]

The magic of storytelling and the reality of ancestral shadows
are two themes which are also characteristic of Momaday's
memoir.

Momaday's reexperience of fearful hours as a child in a storm
shelter in Oklahoma resembles Proust's "involuntary memory,"
the sudden springing up of a past moment triggered by a
sound, motion, or scent. Momaday's memory of the dank room
arises spontaneously from the smell of moist earth, and, like
Proust's "resurrections," creates an experience of the past as
present: ". . . now and then," Momaday wrote, "I have been
reminded of it suddenly when I have gone into a cave, or when
I have just caught the scent of fresh, open earth steaming in
the rain, and I have been for a moment startled and strangely
glad in the presence of the past" (p. 6).

One reviewer aptly referred to *The Names* as "a portrait of the
artist as a young Indian."[19] The influence of Joyce on Momaday's memoir has already been mentioned briefly in chapter 2.
Both writers depict the development of their personae as growing up to an awareness of language. Words, and names in
particular, are crucial elements in the process of acquiring an

idea of the self. Moreover, language appears no longer as a mirror of reality but as reality itself. The myths Joyce and Momaday create represent uniquely personal worlds.

The creation of an inner world of language can be seen as a response to an outside world in which traditional values are losing their authority or have disappeared entirely, leaving the individual without reference points and a sense of stability. Since an ordered and unified reality is essential for a balanced human existence, the mind turns inward and builds its own world of images and words.[20] Momaday's identification with a racial tradition which has all but vanished from the modern world he lives in requires introspection and an imaginative re-creation of this tribal past. In this process Momaday resembles the old man at Jemez of whom he wrote, "I believe he looked . . . inward upon his mind and saw there, and there only, such things as were real to him" (p. 149). Language becomes more important as a reflection of the inner world of the imagination than of the outer world. This position is central to Joyce's *A Portrait of the Artist as a Young Man*, in which Stephen Dedalus ends a meditation on the nature of words by posing this question: ". . . was it that . . . he drew less pleasure from the reflection of the glowing sensible world through the prism of a language many-coloured and richly storied than from the contemplation of an inner world of individual emotions mirrored perfectly in a lucid supple periodic prose?"[21] The work makes it clear that the answer must be positive, the inner world being Stephen's "treasure" from which he draws sustenance.

The resemblance between *The Names* and *A Portrait* is perhaps most pronounced in the way language and myth are shown to create consciousness. This is how Joyce describes Stephen's appropriation of the world through language: Words which he did not understand he said over and over to himself till he had learnt them by heart: and through them he had glimpses of the real world about them."[22] Momaday communicates the awakening to his environment in similar terms: "And I know the voices of my parents, of my grandmother, of others. Their voices, their words, English and Kiowa—and the silences that lie about them—are already the elements of my mind's life. . . . Had I known it, even then language bore all the names of my being" (p. 8). The central personae in both works are introduced as parts of fictions. Stephen is created by his father as "baby tuckoo" inside a story, while Momaday's existence proceeds from the myth of Tsoai.

The mythical implications of the protagonists' names play a significant role in the shaping of their lives. Stephen's growing awareness of his name culminates in his realization that it is both mythical and prophetic. He makes it part of his life and strives to live up to it: "Yes! Yes! Yes! He would create proudly out of the freedom and power of his soul, as the great artificer whose name he bore, a living thing, new and soaring and beautiful, impalpable, imperishable."[23] In the end Stephen becomes the myth: like Daedalus, who forged the wings for his flight, Stephen sets out "to forge in the smithy of [his] soul the uncreated conscience of [his] race." And, as the last entry in his diary, "Trieste 1914," suggests, Stephen has "flown away" from Ireland in pursuit of his destiny.[24]

The Names, too, deals with the unity between myth and an individual's life. Momaday's Kiowa name, Tsoai-talee, is the symbolic tie to the mythical world of his ancestors. When Momaday was six months old, his parents took him to Devil's Tower, in Wyoming—Tsoai—a milestone on the Kiowa migration to the south. The Kiowas had made a story to account for the monolith. It tells of seven sisters and a brother; while they were playing, the boy suddenly changed into a bear and chased after his frightened sisters who, with the help of a talking tree, escaped into the sky where they became the stars of the Big Dipper. The bear, in his futile pursuit, left his claw marks on the bark of the tree which turned into Tsoai, "rock tree."

The purpose of this pilgrimage to Devil's Tower was to place Momaday in Tsoai's presence, "so that by means of the child the memory of the myth should be renewed in the blood of the coming-out-people" (p. 55). This ritual identification between Momaday and the mythical Kiowa landmark was formally completed by the old man Pohd-lohk:

Pohd-lohk spoke, as if telling a story, of the coming-out people, of their long journey. He spoke of how it was that everything began, of Tsoai, and of the stars falling or holding fast in strange patterns on the sky. And in this, at last, Pohd-lohk affirmed the whole life of the child in a name, saying: Now you are, Tsoai-talee. [P. 57]

In giving Momaday his Indian name, Pohd-lohk formally rooted him in the Kiowa oral tradition and created him in a verbal dimension of reality. The importance of this event can be assessed from Momaday's contention that "when a man is given a name, existence is given to him, too."[25] This statement also explains the opening words of the memoir as an assertion of existence through language: "My name is Tsoai-talee. I am, therefore, Tsoai-talee; therefore I am" (n.p.).

Pohd-lohk not only initiated Momaday into Kiowa culture but gave direction to his life. This is implicit in Momaday's observation that "Pohd-lohk believed that a man's life proceeds from his name, in the way that a river proceeds from its source" (n.p.). The myth of Tsoai is indeed a powerful presence in Momaday's life. It looms large in his imagination. For his ancestors the myth affirmed their kinship to the stars, for him his place in Kiowa tradition.

In a collection of stories entitled "Tsoai and the Shield Maker," Momaday elaborated and fleshed out the details of the miraculous transformation of the children in the Devil's Tower story.[26] Perhaps the best example of how important a place Tsoai occupies in Momaday's mind is this excerpt from a letter which illustrates how his view of the world is colored by his mythical past:

This past weekend I went into the Black Hills, to Devil's Tower (what a sad, inappropriate name for that unique, holy—but older than Christianity holy—place.) I discovered, I think, where the children were playing, where the girls were running, and the bear after them.. . . . There are no bears at the monument now, I am told. But, you know, . . . I am quite sure that a grizzly, an old thick animal, resides there somewhere in the Bear Lodge Mountains. He keeps an eye on Tsoai, surely. That is his trust. There is no Tsoai without the bear.[27]

The bear of the Tsoai myth also functions as Momaday's guardian spirit, as this confession suggests:

When I think back on my early education—those schools on the Reservation where I was sometimes the only kid who could speak English—I shudder; and I ask myself: How did I survive that? How did I come through that experience with my tongue in one piece? It was of course medicine. The bear was watching close by. The bear is always there.[28]

These and other examples which will be examined below are parts of Momaday's mythical world. Given his historical circumstances, Momaday's Kiowa identity can be established only through a retreat into the creative mind where he can commune with a world he could not experience in reality. Joseph Campbell suggested that ". . . just as in the past each civilization was the vehicle of its own mythology, developing in character as its myth became progressively interpreted, analyzed, and elucidated by its leading minds, so in this modern world . . . each individual is the center of a mythology of his own."[29] *The Names* is an imaginative reconstruction of childhood and youth, an account of a search for identity, and a portrayal of how past and present, myth and reality, dreams and visions come together in the mind of a contemporary American Indian.

In taking stock of his emotional, intellectual, and imaginative responses to the people, cultures, and landscapes of his own and his ancestors' past, Momaday comes to an understanding of himself as the unique individual he is. He seeks to account for his identity not merely by referring to the formative influences of various cultural environments—Kiowa, Jemez, Navajo, and Anglo-American—but by tracing a less tangible, racial component which he believes to be a determining force in his life. His projection into Kiowa antecedents constitutes for him "a way of learning" about his place in an ancient and ongoing tradition.[30] Like *The Way to Rainy Mountain*, Momaday's memoir is based on the premise that "the imaginative experience and the historical equally express the traditions of man's reality."[31]

While in *The Way to Rainy Mountain* mythical, historical, and personal experiences were only loosely connected by an associative structure, they now appear as virtually inseparable, interlocking images in the fabric of Momaday's consciousness. Past and present, reality and dream, the physical world and the imaginative world coalesce in his vision of existence. It is, to use the title of one of Momaday's essays, "a vision beyond time and place."[32] Chronological time dissolves as Momaday's memories move back and forth across the plane of his experience. In the web of his imagination life appears as an atemporal dimension in which tribal myths, ancestral stories, and personal recollections blend into a unified whole.

The notion of existence as a vertical rather than a horizontal configuration, as an upward surge from the roots of the individual to consciousness rather than a movement from past to present, finds expression in this central passage of Momaday's memoir:[33]

The past and future were simply the larger contingencies of a given moment; they bore upon the present and gave it shape. One does not pass through time, but time enters upon him, in his place. As a child, I knew this surely, as a matter of fact; I am not wise to doubt it now. Notions of the past and future are essentially notions of the present. In the same way an idea of one's ancestry and posterity is really an idea of the self. [P. 97]

The Names rests on the tenets regarding language and the imagination which have been examined in chapter 2. It is the clearest illustration of Momaday's belief that existence is a function of the imagination, that life is illusory, and that human existence finds its fullest realization in the medium of language. "Life," Momaday wrote, "is simply an idea, an idea of having existence in the scheme of things" (p. 128). He is not concerned with factual truth. He explores people and environments not to arrive at some objective veracity but to come to a subjective understanding, to assess their meanings as they affect him personally. In this process of appropriating self, environment, and history Momaday invents and distorts characters and incidents to create a larger, imaginative truth. In creating his own personal myth—"the bright legend of my youth" (p. 154), as he calls it—Momaday follows the same impulse which moved his storytelling ancestors to create the myths he inherited.

He illustrated the implications of the relationship between cultural background and individual expression when he described the meaning of prayer in Indian life, choosing the Navajo Night Chant as his example:

> The verbal formula is itself a religious context; that is to say, it is carefully prescribed and traditional. It is not the singer's own device but a current into which he enters and is sustained in his spirit. He believes that language is intrinsically powerful, that it is yet another and indeed indispensable dimension of the house in which he dwells. It is, moreover, the dimension in which his existence is most fully accomplished. He does not create language but is himself created within it. In a real sense his language is both the object and the instrument of his religious and artistic experience.[34]

From the outset Momaday stresses his awareness of participating in an evolving tradition, of writing in the spirit of his people:

> In general my narrative is an autobiographical account. Specifically it is an act of the imagination. When I turn my mind to my early life, it is the imaginative part of it that comes first and irresistible into reach, and of that part I take hold. This is one way to tell a story. In this instance it is my way, and it is the way of my people. [N.p.]

According to Momaday storytelling has always been "the life's blood" of a society.[35] "We invest ourselves and all our experience in stories"[36] because "the possibilities of storytelling are precisely those of understanding the human experience."[37]

Momaday portrays himself as growing up in a world of stories, the stories of his ancestors and his race. About his mother's experience with the Kiowas, for instance, he says that "it is a whole story, hers to tell; yet some part of it is mine as well. And there is a larger story. I think of where I am in it" (p. 8). As the stories of his personal and racial past gradually unfold, a unified impression of Momaday's self-image emerges.

In two passages Momaday depicts his discovery of language as a means of creation and control. The first of these episodes deals with man's dependence on language to create order out of the continuous flux of sense impressions. While this process is normally not experienced consciously, its absence results in the loss of control and stability which Momaday dramatizes in his description of a childhood nightmare.

He finds himself in a large, bare room without windows or doors. Gradually he grows aware of a presence in the room, an object that before long begins to move. The initial acknowledgment of the phenomenon causes surprise and a certain fascination rather than fear, but as the object grows and expands into a huge mass, reducing Momaday to insignificance and threatening to suffocate him, his terror has no end. He tries to cry out, but his voice fails him.

This symbolic event shows the helplessness of an individual deprived of the power of language and thus the essential means of control over his experience in the world around him. Momaday's reference to a phrase from the Navajo Night Chant, "Restore my voice for me," is appropriate in this context as part of a curing ceremony employed to restore the patient to wholeness and harmony. This traumatic experience seems to have had a lasting impression on Momaday by illustrating the precariousness of human existence outside the controlling influence of language:

How many times has this memory been nearly recovered, the definition almost realized! Again and again I have come to that awful edge, that one word, perhaps, that I cannot bring from my mouth. I sometimes think that it is surely a name, the name of someone or something, that if only I could utter it, the terrific mass would snap away into focus, and I should see and recognize what it is at once; I should have it then, once and for all, in my possession. [P. 63]

The crucial word may have been "zeidl-bei," with which, as Momaday learned in the course of his growing up, the old woman Ko-sahn "confronted evil and the incomprehensible."[38] The story of the arrowmaker, too, taught him the power of language to ward off danger.

The second crucial passage reveals the wonder Momaday experienced in his discovery of the creative power of language. He remembers a day in his childhood. In his grandmother's house he draws the head of a boy on a sheet of paper. The creative act arouses his interest; he tries to imagine the world surrounding his creation, to bring its character into sharper focus and make its existence accessible to himself. He achieves this by attaching a name to his drawing: "This is someone. Maybe this is Mammedaty. This is Mammedaty when he was a boy" (p. 93). He takes his step unconscious of its implications, but once the picture and the name have become an equation, he is overcome by a sense of wonder:

. . . I wonder at the words. *What are they?* They stand, they lean and run upon the page of a manuscript—I have made a manuscript, rude and illustrious. The page bears the likeness of a boy—so simply crude the likeness to some pallid shadow on my blood—and his name consists in the letters there, words, the other likeness, the little, jumbled drawings of a ritual, the nominal ceremony in which all homage is returned, the legend of the boy's having been, of his going on. I have said it; I have set it down. I trace the words; I touch myself to the words, and they stand for me. My mind lives among them, moving ever, ever going on. I lay the page aside, I imagine. [P. 93]

In this dual act of graphic and linguistic creation Mammedaty is resurrected in the likeness of a drawing and a name, and, equally important, the artist's relation to his personal and cultural ancestry is affirmed.

In *The Names*, Momaday continues his search for Kiowa precedents which he began in *The Way to Rainy Mountain*. But he

also takes into account his Anglo-American and French ancestors, tracing the maternal side of his family tree back four
generations to his forebears in Virginia, Kentucky, and Louisiana. Momaday combines the stories of the Galyens, Ellis's,
Scotts, and McMillans with imaginative evocations of the landscapes they inhabited. In part three the long stream-of-
consciousness narrative illustrates the impact of modern American civilization on Momaday and throws into stark relief his
growing up between two worlds.

This passage is based on his memories of living as an Indian
boy in a predominantly white community during World War
II. It reflects Momaday's awareness of being different from his
peers without being able to define this difference.[39] His con-
flicting loyalties to differing cultural models and his problems
in living up to his own image of what he thought an Indian
was supposed to be highlight the demands of his ambiguous
cultural situation. On the one hand he draws up lists of what
he considers to be Indian: Kiowa names, songs, and stories;
the Kiowa language he heard at Rainy Mountain; the ceremonies and dances he attended; the material culture he witnessed.
On the other hand television shows, motion pictures, and popular songs of the forties, American football, and the legend of
Billy the Kid feed his imagination and lead to confusion. His
remarks, "I don't know how to be a Kiowa" (p. 101) and "I *am*
proud to be so American" (p. 101), are only two hints of young
Momaday's difficulties in reconciling different cultural influences.

He imagines himself as an Indian-hater and as an avenger of
Billy the Kid's death, as a war hero and a football star. In the
latter role he adopts the image of a superhuman Indian: ". . .
we must stop Momaday he comes from nowhere from the sun
I tell you he's not human they say he's an Indian that he wears
an eagle feather has the eyes the heart of an eagle he must be
stopped the son of the rising sun" (p. 99). This is not the only
ironic use of the stereotyped Indian. Momaday remembers his
own frustration resulting from his inability to live up to the
image because of his nearsightedness: ". . . the Indians didn't

wear glasses not the Kiowas how can you hunt buffalo with glasses on I broke my glasses" (p. 108).

Momaday's adolescence among the Jemez and Navajo peoples of New Mexico added yet another cultural context to his Kiowa and Anglo-American experiences. Much of part four of *The Names* reveals the autobiographical elements which entered the world of *House Made of Dawn*.[40] While the Jemez, Navajo, and Anglo-American components are given great weight in *The Names*, the prevalent thrust is toward Momaday's Kiowa background. He complements his understanding of individuality as a result of one's immediate and singularly personal experience in the world with a belief in a racial determinant of identity. His search for a reconciliation of a modern, individualistic existence with a racial matrix is the pervasive undercurrent of his autobiographical work.

Momaday's conscious and symbolic act of immersing his modern individuality into Kiowa tradition signifies his particular place in history: he grew up without the support of the traditional, living Kiowa culture. In tribal societies the individual self is subordinated to a communal identity and to the natural and supernatural worlds. For Momaday as a self-conscious, modern individual, integration into a racial dimension is no longer a matter of course but the result of a conscious choice. This choice finds expression in a poetic fabrication stressing the importance of communal and familial allegiance. Momaday faces here a paradox: the autobiographical form he chooses is a product of modern consciousness, rooted in individualism and historicism, and based on writing. These three characteristics are, of course, alien to the tribal world Momaday is harking back to.[41] To accommodate this contradiction, Momaday emulates the tribal mentality by focusing on mythical and ancestral precedents before considering his individual existence.

The strategy Momaday chooses resembles that of two classic Indian life stories, those of Black Elk and Geronimo. Geronimo's story begins with an account of Apache emergence, the creation of their homeland, and the naming of the tribe.[42]

Only after the cosmic, geologic, tribal, and familial histories have been established does Geronimo consider his individual existence.[43]

Similarly, when Black Elk related the event of his life to John G. Neihardt, he stressed that the center of his account was not his individual existence but his vision and its implications for the Ogalala Sioux as a whole.[44] His tribal and familial descent are of primary importance: "I am a Lakota of the Ogalala band. My father's name was Black Elk, and his father before him bore the name, and the father of his father, so that I am the fourth to bear it."[45]

Momaday's dedication of *The Names* to "those whose name I bear and those who bear my names," his announcement that his story is told in the spirit of his people, his narrative of the Kiowa emergence myth, his careful reconstruction of his ancestry, and the great weight he places on the mythical implications of his Kiowa name are all designed to establish a communal and racial framework to which he can relate his individual existence. Unlike Momaday, Geronimo and Black Elk emerged from intact native communities, and their emphasis on racial and tribal existence in telling their life stories resulted from the absence of a concept of individuality. For Momaday this tribal mentality remains accessible only in his artistic imagination.

The structure of the work is another reflection of the link between Momaday's individual and racial existence. The prologue, relating the mythical emergence of the Kiowas, and the epilogue, which tells of Momaday's return to the place of origin, the hollow log, form an outer circle of racial precedent which surrounds Momaday's personal existence.

The four parts, too, are tied in a cyclical fashion. In the two opening paragraphs of the first part Momaday sets out to conjure up his ancestors and their worlds by pronouncing their names. At the end of part four he makes explicit the meaning of names as carriers of tribal precedent and personal memories. At this point the story comes full circle; the end refers back to the beginning. This inner circle demarcates a verbal dimension of reality in which a communal, tribal past has been merged with individual experience.

Many students of autobiography as a literary genre have made the point that it occupies the middle ground between history and fiction.[46] This is certainly true of *The Names*, in which Momaday takes great liberties with the autobiographical form. He employs novelistic techniques to create events and experiences to which he, as an autobiographer, cannot have had access. He freely enters other persons' consciousnesses, dramatizes encounters between his ancestors, or presents himself through the eyes of an omniscient narrator. Momaday explained this strategy by saying that "there is much room in autobiographical narrative . . . for speculation. It is speculation which is not fact in the ordinary sense, but neither is it fiction. I believe that this speculation, which is an act of the imagination, is indispensable to the writing of non-fiction prose."[47]

Perhaps the most revealing example of this speculative writing is Momaday's evocation of Pohd-lohk. His relation to the man who gave him his Indian name is central to an understanding of *The Names*, for Momaday creates himself in the image of Pohd-lohk and the myths with which the old man identified him. Their kinship is not a matter of inheritance but of a shared racial imagination. This is how Momaday explained his relation to and creation of Pohd-lohk:

[When Pohd-lohk was telling stories] he was drawing on the racial imagination, . . . on the memory of all his people. And I, when I wrote about him, and things that I imagined happened to him . . ., I too relied upon the imagination; I think of it as being not mine so much as the people's. It was his and all the Kiowas' imagination. That's what I was working with when I was writing about him. That part of the book is fiction in a way, because I imagined how he lived on a particular day in his life. He wasn't there for me to draw on any documents or histories, but I knew him well enough in my mind's eye, in my imagination, that I could write about him, and I think write about him truly. He did that in his stories, I do that in mine; it's been a long, growing tradition.[48]

The contribution of Pohd-lohk, Old Wolf, to Momaday's conception of self reveals a number of important premises concerning the determination of individual existence by a racial past. Old man Pohd-lohk is not only a prevalent figure because he established the link between Momaday and Tsoai. It is in the comparison of Pohd-lohk's experience to his own that Momaday makes the point of racial determination. That is to say that Momaday sees an important part of his existence following the same pattern which shaped Pohd-lohk's life.

Most notably, Momaday's journey of discovery into Kiowa history had a precedent in Pohd-lohk's calendar history, which consisted of records from an even older calendar painted on hide, the stories related to him by his elders, and finally the events he could recollect himself. Momaday described Pohd-lohk's chronicle as "an instrument with which he could reckon his place in the world" (p. 48); his own memoir served, of course, the same function. Moreover, both accounts appear as manifestations of an impersonal force which feeds the spirit of the Kiowa people. Momaday wrote about Pohd-lohk that "it was as if he could see in [the chronicle's] yellow, brittle leaves the long swath of his coming of age and sense in the very nature of it—the continuity of rude images in which the meaning of his racial life inhered—a force that had been set in motion at the Beginning" (p. 48). Momaday, too, is conscious that his life is directed by a power which connects him with the origin of his race: "I went on, farther and farther into the wide world. Many things happened. And in all this I knew one thing: I knew where the journey had begun, that it was itself a learning of the beginning, that the beginning was infinitely worth the learning" (p. 159). While Pohd-lohk searched in the "yellow, brittle leaves" of his ledger book for "the long swath of his coming of age"—the original meaning of swath is footstep, trace—Momaday wrote about his compulsion to place himself into the context of tribal tradition: "I invented history. In April's thin white light, in the white landscape of the Staked

Plains, I looked for *tracks* among the tufts of coarse, *brittle grass*" (p. 48; italics added).

Other parallels with Pohd-lohk are based on their share in what Momaday called the "scheme of remembered time" (p. 51), the stories preserved in the collective memory of the tribe. Despite the obvious differences in their individual circumstances, a part of their imaginative lives appears as virtually identical. It is this racial component which Momaday suggests to be constant in the flow of time. The stories of the falling stars and of Guadal-tseyn, the famous Kiowa horse, preoccupy their imaginations (pp. 50, 163, 48, and 166), and the ancestral names conjure up images of forebears in their minds (pp. 46 and 166). What seem at first only details of little significance suddenly suggest the repetition of experience when seen in the context of a generational sequence: "Through a window he [Pohd-lohk] saw a magpie drop down among the shadows, gleaming as it settled in the mottled light" (p. 47), and "I [Momaday] heard the wind running, and there were magpies huddled away in the shadows" (p. 166).

These parallels are, of course, symbolic and imaginative rather than factual. They are part of Momaday's myth-making effort to place himself in the racial matrix which produced Kiowa culture. The conscious integration of a tribal heritage into a modern self-concept is common among American Indians. The anthropologist John Bushnell, investigating the contemporary Hupa people of California, noted that they "have moved into the mainstream but continue to identify with a way of life that in reality is once removed in time or space and is largely ceremonial, symbolic, and emotional in its manifestation."[49]

Toward the end of *The Names* a symbolic scene captures all the ramifications of Momaday's relation to his past, both personal and racial. His fall from a rock near Jemez implies not only his loss of innocence but also the birth of his consciousness of his distance from and proximity to the world of his ancestors: "It was a strange thing in my life, and I think of it as the end of an age. I should never again see the world as I saw it on the other side of that moment, in the bright reflection of time lost. There are such reflections, and for some of them I have the names" (p. 161). In *The Names: A Memoir*, Momaday has collected these reflections—the names, stories, and myths he lives by.

CHAPTER 7

Momaday's Poetry

N. Scott Momaday described his poetic work as developing from a reflection of oral poetry to the strict formal tradition of English verse and then to syllabics and a kind of free verse. Yvor Winters's instruction in traditional English verse forms is clear in Momaday's early unpublished poems and also in some of the later works, particularly "Before an Old Painting of the Crucifixion" and "Plainview: 1."[1] Winters was also responsible for Momaday's experimentation with syllabics and postsymbolist imagery.

After his studies at Stanford, Momaday directed his attention to free verse and to what may best be described as prose poetry, while continuing to write syllabic verse. The stages by which Momaday described the evolution of his poetry are not strictly chronological or mutually exclusive. For example, of the published poems which antedate Momaday's studies at Stanford, one is in free verse, while another is an adaptation of Navajo verse patterns similar to the later syllabic poetry. These two poems will be examined in detail in the first section of this chapter.

Section two summarizes the poetic theory of Yvor Winters, which is essential to an understanding of Momaday's syllabic and postsymbolist poetry. The third section explores Momaday's place in the postsymbolist tradition by drawing connections among some of his poems and selected works of Paul Valéry, Wallace Stevens, Frederick Goddard Tuckerman, and

Yvor Winters. The influence of Emily Dickinson will also be considered in brief.

Sections four and five deal with two significant steps in Momaday's poetic development: his use of prose poetry for the treatment of his American Indian heritage, mainly in part two of *The Gourd Dancer*; and his return to a more formal technique in some of the poems he wrote in Russia, which are collected in "Anywhere Is a Street into the Night" along with a number of pieces in free verse. Finally, section six examines a little-known group of poems reflecting Momaday's preoccupation with the legend of Billy the Kid. Many of them have not appeared in print; others are hidden away in obscure publications.

The purpose of these six sections is to show the scope of Momaday's poetic work, both technical and thematic, and to examine the literary, cultural, and biographical aspects of his poetry through a close reading of selected poems.

Two Early Poems: "Los Alamos" and "Earth and I Gave You Turquoise"

"Los Alamos" is one of only a few extant early poems which show the influence of Momaday's reading of Hart Crane's poetry when he was an undergraduate at the University of New Mexico.[2] It stands in marked contrast to the poems of the Stanford period. "Los Alamos" was not collected in *Angle of Geese and Other Poems* and *The Gourd Dancer* because Momaday had "lost track of it" after its publication in the *New Mexico Quarterly*.[3] The poem is Momaday's first explicit statement about the clash between technology and nature, between a world of organic wholeness and the potential destructiveness of modern civilization. Crane's attempt to reconcile these oppositions in "The Bridge" made him "a very important figure" for Momaday the young poet.[4] The most striking similarity between Crane's poetry and "Los Alamos" is that poem's oblique imagery which often borders on the obscure. Some of its lines resist paraphrase and require lengthy glosses.

This style would almost certainly not have brought the approval of Yvor Winters, whose influence contributed to the great precision and clarity of Momaday's later poems. Winters corresponded with Crane and, despite considerable differences of opinion, had great regard for his work. Their disagreement was mainly on the issue of the romantic ideal of automatic writing and Crane's bias toward the connotative use of language. Winters could empathize with Crane, since in his own early poetic experiments he had followed a similar path. But his subsequent conversion to a more formal and rational poetry distanced him critically from Crane's work. Winters reflected on the issue:

[Crane] told me once that he often did not understand his poems till after they were written; and I am fairly confident that this kind of experimentation was common in Crane's generation and earlier, and in fact it is still common in certain quarters. I know that I myself engaged in it with great fascination when I was young, and I know that certain other persons did so. The result is likely to be a poetry which frequently and sometimes wholly eludes paraphrase by at least a margin, but which appears constantly to be suggesting a precise meaning.

. . . one may say that wherever the poet's sensibility to the connotation of language overbalances his awareness of the importance of denotation, something of the kind is beginning.[5]

The characteristics which Winters attributed to Crane's poetry can be found in Momaday's "Los Alamos." But while the similarities between Crane and Momaday in this poem's form and style cannot be overlooked, the contrast in the poets' moral judgments on the relation between nature and technology could not be more striking. Crane was preoccupied with a reconciliation of the two, whereas Momaday has stressed the threat science poses for the wilderness. Crane suggested the presence of the same organic wholeness in man-made constructions that he discovered in nature, a position Emerson had adopted before him in his "Art" essay. Momaday sees technology and nature as fundamentally at odds. He could not have chosen a better focus for making this point than Los Alamos.

Ironically, Momaday uses the bridge image to argue exactly the opposite of the case Crane put forward in celebrating the triumph of modern advance in "To Brooklyn Bridge."[6] This contrariness, however, is not immediately apparent because of the oblique nature of the opening lines. They demand careful scrutiny. Since "Los Alamos" is not readily available it is quoted here in full:

Steel spans and spurns our filtered vision
To the crossed hairs of promise, the magnified self-image.
In the near distance, audible in time,
Exiled voices hover and collide.
Beneath gray girders skaters groove the water
And crumble bread for snowbirds.

Children, though uprooted and wedged from the earth,
Humanize this statuary.

Machinery is scattered over the earth like hurled coins.
I have heard the angry monotone
Retching into troughs the pins of war
When I walked in the wood to hear rain.

The stark, impersonal lamps on the bridge
Destroy the symmetry of her straining shadows.
The desert smiles and waits
And there the night settles, transfixed by the moon.

Confidently,
Uniformed men pace the corridors of Purgatory
And every wrist and wall is shackled to a timepiece
That, through the disinfected chambers,
Rap against the unknown like a blind man's cane.

I have dreamed a city peopled
By one sufficient man
And faithful reproductions.[7]

"Steel spans" refers to the physical arch of the bridge across Los Alamos Canyon, connecting the atomic laboratories with the town. The bridge is portrayed as "the magnified self-image" of scientific man. This seemingly positive image of the bridge is further reinforced by the reference to "the crossed hairs of promise," the bridge's two carrying elements on which the whole construction rests. If this were the whole story, Momaday's depiction would be very much in the Cranean vein. However, this poem is not about technological triumph but the destructive potential of technology with which the Los Alamos name is inextricably connected.

It was here, in laboratories hidden away in a mountain landscape of majestic beauty, that the first nuclear weapons were developed and built which in 1945 brought death and destruction to Hiroshima and Nagasaki. Nowhere else could the contrast between natural beauty and the horror of unchecked scientific research be more evident than in this small town on the eastern slope of the Jemez Mountains, some thirty miles from Momaday's boyhood home.

His angry criticism of the destructive potential in the modern world sets the tone in this early poem. In a rather oblique way the first two lines undercut the image of the bridge as a statuary of promise. The "crossed hairs of promise" which seem to signify the triumph of the bridge's construction simultaneously bring to mind the hairline cross of an aiming telescope, a device to increase the deadly efficiency of modern weaponry. This connection is corroborated by Momaday's reference in the third stanza to a shooting site. One may even argue that, in line with Crane's liking for puns, Momaday has amplified his anti-image with a pun on "crossed," suggesting betrayal. In this light the meaning of the first line becomes more readily apparent: the adjective "filtered" signifies an incomplete vision, a vision which takes in only part of the whole truth. And this truth is the darker side of technology which, in Momaday's view, is obliterated by a naively optimistic belief in the benefits of science. The steel of the bridge, with its connotations of destruction, spurns, that is, rejects disdainfully, a distorted vision which perceives only the blessings of modern technological accomplishments, not their inherent dangers.

Against the stark outline of the bridge Momaday sets organic life: there are skaters on a nearby ice rink. These children, whose voices are exiled, are "uprooted and wedged from the earth," yet they give a human touch to the "statuary" through their play on the ice and enjoyment of the snowbirds they feed. The following two stanzas develop the theme of the encroachment of the technological on the natural world. Stanza three is an impressionistic sketch of a gun site where "machinery is scattered over the earth like hurled coins," the simile pointing to the rapacity and greed which underlie destruction. "The angry monotone retching into troughs the pins of war" are bombers dropping their loads on practice targets. It is their noise which the poem's persona hears when he comes to listen to the rain in the wood. In the context of Los Alamos, the central image of this line evokes the vision of the destruction of Hiroshima and Nagasaki.

If in the previous scene it was a mechanical sound which drowned the sound of nature, in the fourth stanza it is artificial light which interferes with the light of the moon: "The stark, impersonal lamps on the bridge / Destroy the symmetry of her straining shadows. / The desert smiles and waits / And there the night settles, transfixed by the moon." While these lines exemplify the kind of romanticism which is absent from Momaday's later poetry—the pathetic fallacy in the third line of this stanza is a particularly obvious example—the belief they express in nature's superior strength and ability to outwait the onslaught of a technological world remains one of Momaday's deep convictions.[8]

The fifth stanza leaves the world of nature behind and enters a breeding ground of human destruction: the nuclear research installations at Los Alamos. Momaday paints a disturbing portrayal of the presumptuousness of scientific man who, in his arrogance, fails to realize that he has become a prisoner of his own achievements. The uniformed men seem to be laboratory guards who are shackled to the clocks they have to check on their rounds. The final line of this stanza underscores the dangerous nature of man's desire to discover the secrets of ultimate destruction.

The poem reaches its climax in Momaday's nightmarish vision of a world to which activities like those at Los Alamos can lead. The suggestion of cloning in the final lines epitomizes the extremes of automation and totalitarianism. This is particularly ironic in connection with the two unmistakable resonances of the line "I have dreamed a city peopled," which echoes not only Martin Luther King's "I have a dream" but also the image of the Puritans' "City on the Hill" emblem of the ultimate fulfillment of the American destiny. Momaday deliberately touches upon these connotations to heighten the absurdity inherent in man's dream of mastery over the universe. Such a dream is, in Momaday's view, a nightmare.

"Earth and I Gave You Turquoise," another poem which predates Momaday's Stanford period, is quite different in form, tone, and content. It was written, according to Momaday, in 1958, "at one of the second grader's desks of the Jemez day school, one night when [he] had come home from college for a weekend."[9] It was the first poem to be published in Momaday's career and probably belonged to the pieces he submitted for the Wallace Stegner Creative Writing Fellowship which eventually caught Yvor Winters's attention at Stanford.[10]

Under Winters's instruction Momaday followed Charles Gullans and Thom Gunn in writing syllabic poetry, a method which, according to Momaday, originated at Stanford.[11] He described syllabics as "a departure from the traditional English meter, based upon the number of syllables to the line, no matter how they were going together accentually." This form allowed him "a much freer kind of expression than . . . iambic pentameter or tetrameter," which he had been mastering for years.[12] One of the interesting aspects of "Earth and I Gave You Turquoise" is that its metrical form—syllabic verse of seven and five syllables to the line—suggests that Momaday had experimented with this method before he came under the influence of the Winters circle. The poem's form, however, is also reminiscent of American Indian verse translations.

This technical similarity carries over into the poem's content. It is both an evocation of the oral tradition and a moving elegy on the death of a Navajo woman. Momaday remembered that the idea for the poem came to him at Jemez, "perhaps it was on or about one of the feast days when the Navajos came from Torreon in their covered wagons." The things he saw and heard on this occasion "put him in mind of the Navajo country, Dine bikeyah, in which there are wonderful memories." [13]

The opening stanza of "Earth and I Gave You Turquoise" sets up the tragic event around which the poem revolves. It expresses the happiness the poetic persona shared with the woman and the sudden turn of fortune which separated them: "Earth and I gave you turquoise / when you walked singing / We lived laughing in my house / and told old stories / You grew ill when the owl cried / We will meet on Black Mountain." Turquoise is cherished among the Navajos as a bringer of good fortune and well-being. [14] Momaday learned from them that "a turquoise stone will improve the vision of the eye." [15] The second line echoes a common formula of Navajo chants, in which walking is synonymous with living: "Happily may I walk, . . . happily in earthly beauty may I walk. . . . With it happy all around me may I walk." [16] The woman's singing is a ritual designed to maintain perpetual harmony with and well-being in the universe. The anthropologist Gladys A. Reichard made the point that "to the Navajo, song is a necessity; it is an inspiration, a hope, a protection and comfort, a guide to one in want of a procedure, a means of transforming frustration into power." [17]

The references to song and storytelling illustrate the couple's involvement in their culture and the happiness they derive from it. They are at peace with each other and the universe. However, this balance is fragile. The owl, a bird of ill omen, heralds the presence of evil, disease, and death. The Navajos believe that ghosts appear "just before the death of some family member, in human form or as coyotes, owls, mice." [18] The final line of the opening stanza expresses the hope for a reunion of the two lovers on Black Mountain, west of Chinle, New Mexico. Momaday referred to this place not because it has a particular ceremonial significance to the Navajos or any religious connection to their dead but because he was once told that

"there are still Navajos at Black Mountain who have never seen
a white man." Thus, the reference suggests primarily a "condition of isolation . . . rather than a geographical location."[19]

The second stanza develops the hope for reunion into an idea
of an afterlife which is individualistic in character and identical
with worldly existence. Momaday's depiction of the lovers'
meeting in death is a romantic projection which conflicts with
the Navajo notion of death. Reichard pointed out that, according to Navajo belief, death destroys not only man's body but
his individuality as well.[20] She stressed that all her informants
"repudiated the idea of a *personal* immortality."[21] Clyde Kluckhohn suggested that "the Navahos seem to have no belief in a
glorious immortality. Existence in the hereafter appears to be
only a shadowy and uninviting thing."[22] Another aspect of
Navajo attitudes toward death is relevant for an understanding
of line five of this stanza, "I speak your name many times."
This is at once an expression of the lover's grief and an evocation of the dead woman, whose essence rests in her name. This
concept of immortality in language is typical of an oral culture.
The memory of the dead in the tribal mind manifests one form
of existence beyond the confines of an individual's life.[23] It is
not insignificant that the persona utters the name only to himself and avoids it in the presence of other people, as lines three
and four of stanza three indicate. The Navajos' deeply rooted
fear of the dead prevents them from naming the deceased in
public.[24] The final line of stanza two, "The wild cane remembers you," suggests a lasting association between man and his
environment which extends beyond death.

Stanzas three and four describe the continuation of life under
the shadow of grief; social events are conveyed in terms of the
absence of the loved woman. Momaday's reference to Moon
Woman as a mediator between the living and the dead is somewhat obscure. Moon Woman may be related to or identical
with Spider Woman or White Shell Woman in Navajo mythology. Momaday often heard about Moon Woman while he
was growing up. Her significance in the poem seems to be
metaphorical rather than mythological; Momaday remembered

that he "was thinking of a path, especially, the trace of a comet, or the track of the moon on sand or water."[25] It is the first example of this image, which recurs frequently in Momaday's later prose and poems, such as "New World," "The Colors of Night," "The Delight Song of Tsoai-talee," and in several passages of *House Made of Dawn*.

The last stanza describes the continuing presence of the woman in the lover's mind. In his natural environment he experiences epiphanies which bring him close to his lost companion. The blackness of the crow may simply be a reminder of the woman's hair. If one accepts Adolph Bittany's claim that "many of the Navaho say that the after-death-spirit dwells here or there or is manifested in various animals," the bird may actually be a manifestation of the woman's spirit, not unlike Poe's raven.[26] The three final lines suggest that the passing of time has not eased the sense of loss, and that the longing for a speedy reunion remains unfulfilled.

"Los Alamos," "Earth and I Gave You Turquoise," and "Eve My Mother, No," which is discussed in chapter 3 of this book, are of interest for the examination of Momaday's poetic development because they exemplify the standard of his poetry before he received his formal training from Yvor Winters. The nature and consequences of this training are the subject of the following two sections.

The Influence of Yvor Winters

During Momaday's four years at Stanford, Yvor Winters was undoubtedly his most important artistic and scholarly influence. Winters's emphasis on morality and reason as the central pillars of literary expression and his insistence on form and control gave new impetus and direction to Momaday's poetic development. The full extent of his indebtedness to his tutor can be appreciated only if one recalls the basic tenets of Winters's poetic theory.

Winters was essentially concerned with a moral evaluation of literature and poetry, in his view, was the highest form of literary expression.[27] He perceived poetry as a "technique of contemplation, of comprehension."[28] It enabled man to come to a rational and emotional understanding of the human condition and allowed him to make moral judgments.[29] Winters contended that since the poet is dealing in language which is "essentially conceptual and denotative," he would inevitably create confusion and obscurity if he tried to shift his emphasis from the rational, conceptual level to the level of pure connotation.[30] It was from this critical position that Winters attacked what he considered the "general deterioration of the quality of poetry since the opening of the eighteenth century."[31] He was particularly resentful of the romantics' distrust of the rational faculty and the resulting "destruction . . . of conceptual understanding, in the effort to reach pure connotation" in their poetry.[32] Winters saw the associationist theories of the eighteenth century as one source of the "disastrous" influence of the romantic theory of literature.[33]

Theorists of poetry, drawing on Locke's and Hobbes's ideas of associationism, tried to develop a concept whereby ideas could be expressed purely in terms of sense perceptions. Winters rejected these experiments as foolish: "No matter how ideas may have arisen," he maintained, "they cannot at this late date be equated with the impressions of sense."[34] He saw such, in his view, flawed experiments at the center of most romantic theories in Europe and America. The result was, according to Winters, inevitable: "Since ideas cannot really be expressed purely in terms of sense-perceptions, we are merely given pure sense-perception."[35] Associationist experiments and the romantic preference for the connotative aspect of words over their conceptual content were the two basic factors which Winters blamed for what he perceived as widespread poetic obscurantism.

While Winters believed that any attempt to express ideas in terms of pure sense perception was doomed to failure, he discovered one useful application of the associationist theory: an associative structure could be employed in the organization of a poem, providing the vital link between its sensory details and the conceptual context, and thus preventing vagueness and obscurity.[36] Winters emphatically expressed the need for such a poetic technique by suggesting that men are not just rational but "also sensory animals, and we live in a physical universe, and if we are blind to the impressiveness and meanings of our physical surroundings, we are limited. It ought to be possible to employ our sensory experience in our poetry in an efficient way, not as ornament, and with no sacrifice of rational intelligence." He referred to this poetic technique as "controlled associationism."[37]

Central to this "post-Symbolist method," as Winters also called it, is the establishment of a theme or the introduction of an abstract idea in conceptual terms.[38] This rational framework is then entwined with sharp sensory details. The controlled association of abstract theme with imagery leads to a charging of images with meaning. Image and concept are fused and operate simultaneously. Winters found this principle successfully employed in the poetry of Paul Valéry. French poetry was one of Winters's keen interests. In the works of Stéphane Mallarmé, Arthur Rimbaud, and Paul Verlaine he found an intentional "dissociation of sense-perception and feeling on the one hand from conceptual understanding on the other." Winters did not advocate their poetic technique and described these three poets as "the most distinguished apologists for, and practitioners of, deliberate obscurity."[39]

Paul Valéry inherited their clarity of sensory perception, but he used it in the context of abstract statement. Winters wrote, ". . . in Valéry . . . we get the sharp sensory detail contained in a poem or passage of such a nature that the detail is charged with meaning without our being told of the meaning explicitly, or is described in language indicating such meaning indirectly but clearly."[40] Winters referred to Valéry's "Le Cimetière Marin" as one of the classic examples of the postsymbolist method. It will be discussed in detail below, with other representative poems such as Frederick Goddard Tuckerman's "The Cricket" and Wallace Stevens's "Sunday Morning."

While Winters insisted that good poetry depends on a careful combination of rational statement and sensory perception, he also demanded that it reflect an appropriate emotional response to the abstract theme and that this emotion must be justified by reason. The poet's moral attitude was to be defined not only by the logical, paraphrasable content of his work but also by his emotional reaction to its themes. This combination of reason and feeling had direct bearing on poetic form, which was one of Winters' chief preoccupations. In "The Morality of Poetry" he wrote, "This feeling is inseparable from what we call poetic form, or unity, for the creation of a form is nothing more nor less than the act of evaluating and shaping (that is, controlling) a given experience."[41]

According to Winters form reflects the poet's "refinement of contemplation" and "moral attitude toward that range of experience of which he is aware."[42] Form is not "something outside the poet, something 'aesthetic,' and superimposed upon his moral content; it is essentially a part, in fact it may be the decisive part, of the moral content."[43] Winters leveled many attacks on what he saw as a detrimental flaw in much of modern writing, namely "the fallacy of expressive, or imitative form."[44] Attempts to deal with the subjects of chaos or fragmentation in modern life by rendering them in chaotic or fragmentary form he considered to be self-defeating: "Form, in so far as it endeavors to imitate the formless, destroys itself."[45] It was the task of the writer to give form to his subject, not surrender to it. The following statement throws the issue into clearer relief:

. . . many writers have sought to seize the fluidity of experience by breaking down the limits of form, but . . . in doing so, they defeat their own ends. For . . . writing, as it approaches the looseness of prose and departs from the strictness of verse, tends to lose the capacity for fluid or highly complex relationships between words; language, in short, reapproaches its original stiffness and generality; and one is forced to recognize the truth of what appears a paradox, that the greatest fluidity of statement is possible where the greatest clarity of form prevails.[46]

Winters's early experimental poetry, written between 1920 and 1928, was in free verse. He changed to traditional meter early in 1928, when he realized that the other technique would prevent him from achieving the poetic mastery he admired in the works of Valéry, Stevens, and Charles-Pierre Baudelaire.[47] The theoretical reasons for this shift became apparent to him only in the course of the following years. He summarized the theoretical underpinnings of his strictly controlled poetic form:

. . . poetry is written in verse; verse is exceptionally rhythmical language and is usually metrical. Meter controls rhythm and renders rhythmical structure more precise, not merely in its general outlines but in its versifications. Rhythm is expressive of emotion, and the language of verse makes possible a more precise rendition of emotion, a more precise relationship of emotion to rational content, than would otherwise be possible. The use of versification introduces complexities into the management of grammar and syntax, and makes it possible to use them more emphatically or more subtly or both; and the new kinds of precision made possible (and therefore necessary) by versification enforce the need for greater precision of diction than one can hope to find in prose.[48]

This brief summary of Winters's basic principles regarding the function and character of poetry makes Momaday's artistic debt to his tutor more readily apparent. Momaday shares Winters's moral stance on literature.[49] Many of his poems exemplify the postsymbolist method which Winters taught out of his conviction that it was "potentially the richest method to appear," providing "a greater range of thinking and perceiving than we have had before."[50] Winters and Momaday agree on a number of philosophical positions which I will discuss below in the context of specific poems. Many of Momaday's literary preferences—his interest in antiromantic American literature, in Frederick Goddard Tuckerman, or his admiration for Emily Dickinson, Wallace Stevens, and Isak Dinesen—were induced by Winters. Despite their close relationship, however, Momaday's original talent was not stifled by his rigorous training at Stanford. When he felt the need to go beyond the formal demands of his mentor, he did not hesitate to alter his style. And he succeeded in holding on to his inheritance of tribal poetry.

Momaday and the Postsymbolist Tradition

Yvor Winters named a number of poems which he considered classic examples of the postsymbolist method in their clarity of sensory perception coupled with abstract statement. Among these are Valéry's "Le Cimetière Marin," Tuckerman's "The Cricket," and Stevens's "Sunday Morning." Looked at closely, they form a group to which Momaday's "Before an Old Painting of the Crucifixion" is an obvious complement. Since Winters used these poems as models for the poetic method he passed on to his students, this kinship is hardly surprising. The four poems are related not only in their technical execution but also in their theme. They are extended meditations which focus on the natural world and lead to a rational assessment of death.

The epigraph of "Le Cimetière Marin," taken from Pindar's Pythian Odes, could introduce all four poems: "My soul, do not seek immortal life, but exhaust the realm of the possible."[51] Valéry explained the validity of expressing abstract philosophical concepts through precise descriptions of the external world:

Do you not see that our mind experiences, discovers then, in this aspect and harmony of natural conditions, precisely all the qualities, all the attributes of knowledge: clarity, depth, vastness, measure. . . . It is, as it were, lured, initiated to universal thought. . . . I see the very simple origin . . . of those notions of infinity, depth, knowledge, universe, in the presence of a superabundant light, a stretch of water, mobility, in the constant impression of majesty and omnipotence.[52]

Valéry's meditation in "Le Cimetière Marin" develops in an oscillating movement between the sea and a symbol of death, the graveyard; in Momaday's poem the painting of the crucifixion and the recollection of the sea generate philosophical considerations. The silence which informs the sea, "the massively tranquil, visibly contained" sea, captures the imagination and suggests eternity in both poems.[53] The poets' meditations on death, triggered by the cemetery and the crucifixion scene, conclude with rejections of immortality. While Momaday's poem ends with a courageous acceptance of life in an indifferent universe, rendered in a tone of complete emotional control, Valéry, after exposing immortality as "a pretty fiction, and a pious ruse!" returns to the sea in the closing stanzas of the poem and rejoices in it as a symbol of new vitality which helps man to live in the face of ultimate annihilation.[54]

As to Tuckerman's "The Cricket" and Stevens's "Sunday Morning," a number of observations in Momaday's reading of Tuckerman's poem in the unrevised introduction to his Stanford dissertation are particularly useful for establishing the link between these poems and "Before an Old Painting of the Crucifixion." At the center of Tuckerman's scrupulous depiction of nature is the cricket, which has existence in its sound. If in Momaday's crucifixion poem it is the overbearing calm which "preoccupies" the poet's mind, here it is the "pipings" of "acres of crickets," "above, beneath," and all around, which cast a spell on the listener.[55] The entrancing drone is likened to the rising and falling of the sea, an association which is reinforced in the third stanza (lines 44–49). Then Tuckerman establishes the cricket as a symbol of death: "Thou bringest too, dim accents from the grave." The hearer hopes to find an answer to the ultimate mystery of death in the cricket's drone: "Might I but find thy knowledge in thy song" (line 89). Such knowledge, however, remains beyond human reach, and the poetic persona concedes this truth without resentment or despair. In his acceptance of an existence overshadowed by death yet sustained by the beauty and mystery of nature, the protagonist draws a conclusion based on reason and moral responsibility. This is how Momaday views the moral implications of Tuckerman's poem:

For Tuckerman the ultimate question is not how to die, but how to live in the face of death. "The water and the waste shall still be dear," he says, and in the next century Wallace Stevens is to make substantially the same affirmation in the last stanza of *Sunday Morning*. But each of these utterances is made without the sustenance of an unfaltering trust. And, like *Sunday Morning, The Cricket* is not a poem that consoles.[56]

"Sunday Morning" was, according to Momaday, "one of Winters' great glories."[57] Winters taught Momaday a great deal about the poem in the course of a seminar and through his explication in *In Defense of Reason*.[58] Stevens's influence on Momaday's poetry has been noted by a number of critics.[59] The parallels between "Sunday Morning" and "Before an Old Painting of the Crucifixion" illustrate this kinship particularly well.

Stevens's poem is a meditation on death which deals critically with the idea of Christ's immortality. Moreover, the philosophical inquiry is provoked by a calmness over the sea which impresses upon the female persona's mind the lingering presence of death: "She dreams a little, and she feels the dark / Encroachment of that old catastrophe, / As a calm darkens among waterlights."[60] The following lines of this first stanza deepen the silence which informs the sea, reinforce the notion of death, and establish the link to the crucifixion:

> The pungent oranges and bright, green wings
> Seem things in some procession of the dead,
> Winding across wide water, without sound.
> The day is like wide water, without sound,
> Stilled for the passing of her dreaming feet
> Over the seas, to silent Palestine,
> Dominion of the blood and sepulchre.[61]

The image of the "water without sound" is echoed in "Before an Old Painting of the Crucifixion" by "that calm which inhabits wilderness, the sea." In both cases it signifies a dimension which is real yet unintelligible, functioning as a powerful "memento mori."

In the final stanza of "Sunday Morning" this image of death is coupled with a denial of the possibilities of transcendence and resurrection: "She hears, upon the water without sound, / A voice that cries, 'The tomb in Palestine / Is not the porch of spirits lingering. / It is the grave of Jesus, where he lay.'"[62] In

Momaday's poem Jesus' cry is absorbed by a nonhuman universe which gives no response to his ultimate sacrifice; the poet is forced to conclude that death is final, immortality a fiction. I am not suggesting here that Momaday was conscious of these poems' influence and certainly not that he was borrowing. These three poems, however, have undoubtedly been important in shaping Momaday's poetic skills and perceptions, and this seminal impact is clear in such a poem as "Before an Old Painting of the Crucifixion."

Winters's poetry was, of course, available to Momaday, and he read it during his formative period as a poet at Stanford.[63] Winters's and Momaday's statements on the question of death demonstrate that they share a resentment of religious and romantic notions. According to one of his colleagues at Stanford, Winters believed death to be annihilation.[64] Momaday remembered that Winters "had very little patience with people who did subscribe to the Christian answer to death."[65] He voices this impatience poetically in "A Fragment."[66] In another poem, "A Song in Passing," he restates his belief in the finality of death and declares that the idea of paradise is only an illusion.[67]

Perhaps most similar in tone, imagery, and theme to Momaday's "Rainy Mountain Cemetery" and "Before an Old Painting of the Crucifixion" is Winters's meditation on the finality of death and the ineffectuality of Christ's sacrifice entitled "To the Holy Spirit—From a Deserted Graveyard in the Salinas Valley."[68] The desert landscape which Winters depicts in the opening stanza is informed with a sense not only of timelessness, evoking the cleavage between human and geological existence, but also of stubborn resistance to the presence of man. As in "Rainy Mountain Cemetery," the silence and heat of noon center the mind on the gravestones as markers of death. They signify nothingness, not the transcendence of spirit.

The third stanza of Winters's poem directly addresses the Holy Spirit, concluding with the recognition that the Holy Spirit is beyond the reach of rational investigation. In the final stanza Winters shifts his focus back to the forgotten dead in the cemetery. The argument now widens to include the question of Christ's resurrection and its impact on human history. It is in these considerations and in the final judgment that Winters's poem resembles most closely the argument and conclusion of Momaday's "Before an Old Painting of the Crucifixion": Winters refuses to enter into speculations which go beyond the stark finality of death suggested by the graves; instead, he doubts Christ's resurrection and denies the relevance of Christianity.[69]

This discussion of Momaday's metaphysical poems would be incomplete without a reference to the poetry of Emily Dickinson. Momaday gave tribute to her profound influence on his personal and artistic development: "She taught me a good deal about language—and in the process a good deal about the art of intellectual survival."[70] In her poems he found the "mystery and miracle of language" and a way to make the human condition endurable by dealing with it in words.[71]

Particularly significant in this context are those poems by Dickinson which Winters described as capturing "the tragic finality, the haunting sense of human isolation in a foreign universe." In these her greatest poems, according to Winters, "the explicit theme is a denial of [the] mystical stance, is a statement of the limits of judgment."[72] Unlike many of her contemporaries who adopted Emerson's transcendental philosophy, Dickinson perceived no correspondence between the natural world and a higher divine realm. To her nature represented the antagonist to human existence. Her position is best illustrated in two stanzas from "What mystery pervades a well!"

> But nature is a stranger yet;
> The ones that cite her most
> Have never passed her haunted house,
> Nor simplified her ghost,
>
> To pity those that know her not
> I helped by the regret
> That those who know her, know her less
> The nearer her they get.[73]

There is no mystical union here between man and nature, but
an immitigable antagonism. The indifference of nature of human presence is also one of the sustained themes in Momaday's
poetry. And there is agreement on another important position.
Momaday, like Dickinson, struggles in numerous poems with
what Winters called "the inexplicable fact of change, of the
absolute cleavage between successive states of being."[74] This
change is most dramatically concentrated in death. Poems
which exemplify this change include Dickinson's "A Light exists in Spring," "As imperceptible as Grief," and "There's a
certain Slant of light" and Momaday's "Comparatives," "Rainy
Mountain Cemetery," "Angles of Geese," and "Before an Old
Painting of the Crucifixion." Both poets perceive and acknowledge change without pretending that its underlying mystery
can be explained.

In a discussion of "There's a certain Slant of light," Momaday
draws attention to Dickinson's kinship with Frederick Goddard Tuckerman and to both poets' opposition to the transcendental movement. The attributes he isolates in their work significantly inform his own poetry:

The final stanza of Miss Dickinson's poem, "There's a certain Slant
of light," reads as follows:

> When it comes, the landscape listens—
> Shadows—hold their breath—
> When it goes, 'tis like the Distance
> On the look of Death—

"Distance" is but an appellation of the incomprehensible. To approach it, as Miss Dickinson does in this poem, is one thing; to
enter upon it another. The dividing line is always tenuous, but, in
Emersonian terms, it scarcely can be said to exist. Nor can it be said
to exist in terms of Christian mysticism. Neither Tuckerman nor
Emily Dickinson is a Christian mystic, and neither is a pantheist.
The assertion of both poets that nature is at last impenetrable is a
position consistently held. It is the essence of their departure from
the Emersonian tradition.[75]

In Momaday's own work we approach the incomprehensible in
the dark stone of the ancestral graves in "Rainy Mountain Cem-

etery," in the angle of geese in the poem of this title, in the calm over the sea in "Before an Old Painting of the Crucifixion," and in the "hazy southern distances" in "The Omen," the first section of "The Gourd Dancer."

The title of "Before an Old Painting of the Crucifixion" and the reference to its location, at the Mission Carmel on the coast of the Monterey Peninsula in California, are two crucial pieces of information which help to keep the poem free from obscurity. They establish from the outset the two central scenes, the mural and the sea, on which the poetic mind focuses. The meditation on death, time, nature, and eternity develops in a process of controlled association between these two scenes. Like Valéry's 'Le Cimetière Marin," the poem is written in iambic pentameter, with six lines to each stanza.

The first stanza opens with the poetic persona in the process of reviewing mentally the crucifixion scene. The "human act" of ultimate sacrifice is rendered in precise, unemotional language which heightens the sense of despair, the keynote of these first lines.[76] Christ's desperate cry on the cross has found no echo, but has subsided instead into an indifferent natural world, has waned "in vacant skies, in clearings where no other was." There it remains latent, implied in "desolate calm," forcing its presence on the human mind. Despair, Momaday suggests, does not transcend itself. It is simply an inherent part of nature. He concludes the first stanza by rejecting the romantic notion of nature's capacity for consolation: "There is no solace there." This statement anticipates the judgment of the futility of Christ's sacrifice with which the poem concludes.

The theme of human despair which has been associated with a silent universe is, in the second stanza, related more specifically to "wilderness, the sea," and places "where no peace inheres but solitude." Its inseparability from death is restated. In the following lines the calm is further scrutinized in its relation to the experience of Christ. As Winters has noted, Momaday does not attempt to speculate on the nature of Christ's experience, since its uniqueness precludes description.[77] The calm implies a realm beyond death and therefore inaccessible to the

human mind. Momaday's rational position precludes any notion of transcendence; the calm is nothing beyond the inscru-
table fact of calm; neither art nor pseudonym can give it meaning beyond itself. It is nothing so much as a mystery and a
"vague contagion."

The second half of the opening line in stanza three shifts
focus from the painting on the wall to the sea, which the protagonist had scanned before he entered the mission. The following remarks by Momaday explain this experience of transition and serve as an exegesis of the third stanza:

The painting is old; the colors have faded and the landscape in the
painting has become faint, the details more and more indistinct.
The quality suggests the sea, reminds me of the sea which I have
seen only a few minutes before, suggests the fainter appearance of
the innumerable waves, all running together, blending into a field
of constant motion, so constant in fact that motion appears to be
suspended—The sea, in spite of all its motion and sound, appears
to be as mute and still as the landscape of the mural. (But there is a
crucial difference, that expressed in the fourth and fifth stanzas). My
view of the sea becomes transfixed; the ocean, in the perfect balance
of motion and motion suspended, is a symbol (in a sense much more
than a symbol) of eternity, declares eternity. The mural but implies
eternity. Looking at the sea, I had the sense of perceiving what I
have elsewhere called "The pale angle of time and eternity." A line
of cormorants cut across the scene, drew my eyes back to the land,
imposed upon me the realization that I have existence in time.[78]

Unlike the sea, the mural "but implies eternity." Momaday
explores the reasons for this in the fourth and fifth stanzas. He
opens by interjecting a central claim which appropriately
marks the midpoint of the poem: "Not death, but silence after
death is change." This declaration undercuts the view of death
as a stage of transition from a worldly to a heavenly existence.
More specifically, in connection with Christ, it denies the possibility of resurrection and immortality. True change is only
the calm which follows death, and that, as it cannot be com-
prehended, causes despair and a sense of futility. One reason

the mural implies only eternity, then, is that the crucifixion does not mark the beginning of eternity, of immortal life, but is a cruel expression of the transitoriness of human existence. Another reason is the transience of the mural itself: it is fading to the point of becoming indiscernible.

What seems to suggest eternity in the mural is its timeless landscape: "Judean hills, the endless afternoon, / The farther groves of arbors seasonless." And yet, its effect is only a temporary fixation of "the mind within the moment's range." The last two lines of stanza four highlight the concreteness and finality of death: "Where evening would obscure our sorrow soon, / There shines too much a sterile loveliness." The sterile loveliness of sunshine which engulfs the crucifixion scene prevents any softening of the cruel facts. It is a stark antipode to the romantic notion expressed in Emerson's much-quoted sentence, "Nature always wears the colors of the spirit."[79]

Stanza five also associates the mural with the sea. In the painting "no semblances remark the cold / unhindered swell of time, for time is stayed." While the swell of the ocean symbolizes eternal change, time in the mural is frozen. But since the flow of time is suspended, the scene it portrays bears no relation to the present; Christ's Passion is isolated and fades into oblivion.

The final stanza is a rational evaluation of the poem's central issues of death and immortality. The two facts referred to in the opening line are "the actual crucifixion of Christ and the representation of the event by the artist, the creation of the painting itself."[80] Neither of them has stood the test of time; "the critical expanse" of centuries has yielded none of the changes which were promised. It was a period of geological, not human time. Christ's sacrifice turned out to be an act of no consequence. The hope of immortality is stifled by an indifferent, nonhuman universe. The final image of time advancing "like flecks of foam borne landward and destroyed" turns the eye back to the sea. The sea alone reflects eternity, an eternity in which man has no part.

In the context of this poem it is worth noting a related piece which Momaday wrote during his stay in Moscow. As it has not been published, it is quoted here in full:

> The Nickname of Nothing
> A flat and brittle wind has lain all night
> Against the fields. And it would wear away
> The summer from the seed and leave at last
> A carrion harvest. It saddens me
> Who knew the winter well and kept the count
> As each dusk darkens to oblivion.
> The sound insinuates a long silence,
> And once I thought it was the name of God,
> Old as the sun, as terribly lucent,
> And had only to learn it in my time
> That it should be familiar and found
> Upon the final turning of my tongue.
> I shall not find it there; it is no name,
> Or else it is the nickname of nothing.[81]

Again Momaday couches his philosophical thoughts in a depiction of nature. The universe appears destructive and hostile to the human condition. The suggestion that silence may be an expression of divine presence is rejected; "the name of God / Old as the sun" is an illusion. This image echoes Stevens's line from "Sunday Morning," "We live in an old chaos of the sun."[82] The final lines express the realization that a search for a transcendent reality in nature is illusory. Momaday takes up this and similar issues in a number of other poems, among them "Rainy Mountain Cemetery," which has been discussed in chapter 5.

"Angle of Geese" is another disturbing statement on the question of death.[83] The poem is difficult and its context not immediately obvious. Momaday himself realized this and considered adding the epigraph "For a friend on the death of his child" to the title.[84] This clue would have made the poem more easily accessible and could have avoided some misunderstanding.[85]

The poem deals with the incomprehensibility of death and the problem of communicating individual experience in the face of extinction. The first stanza states plainly that language has no power to embellish the crude fact of death. Death is too overbearing to be mediated by words. They cannot soften the existential experience of grief which the "recognition" of "the dead firstborn" has caused in the mourners.

The second stanza shows how man has learned to deal with such a crisis: "Custom intervenes: / We are civil, something more: / More than language means, / The mute presence mulls and marks." "Civil" suggests civility, but also sobriety, decency, and graveness. The act of human solidarity expressed in the silent convention of mourners goes beyond language. And yet even this ritualistic gesture cannot bring relief. "The mute presence" merely mulls, stupefies, and marks, separates.

The third stanza amplifies these ideas. "Almost of a mind, / We take measure of the loss; / I am slow to find / The mere margin of repose." "Almost" in the first line indicates that the sense of communion is incomplete, that the fact of death must be faced individually. And if it is difficult to advance to the margin of death, it is, by implication, quite impossible to penetrate to the core of the mystery.

The second half of "Angle of Geese" presents a different scene of death, this time from the realm of what Winters called "the essential wilderness."[86] The poem's two halves contrast death in the human context and in the context of wild nature. Stanzas four to six are a poetic version of a similar depiction of death in Momaday's *House Made of Dawn*, where Abel and his brother, Vidal, kill a goose. After Vidal shoots the bird, the rest of the flock are "ascending slowly into the far reaches of the winter night. They made a dark angle on the sky, acute, perfect; and for one moment they lay out like an omen on the bright fringe of a cloud." While "the dark shape [is] floating away in the blackness," Abel recovers the dying goose; "its bright black eyes, in which no terror was, were wide of him, wide of the river and the land, level and hard upon the ring of the moon in the southern sky."[87] In this scene the moon stands for a cosmic order to which the bird firmly belongs. In "Angle of Geese" the perfect symmetry of the flock, "the pale angle of time and eternity," suggests a dimension of reality that is incomprehensible to man. Man's existence has become detached from primitive nature, severed from the dimension of reality of which the goose, and death, are integral parts.

The pronoun "it" in the fourth stanza, "And one November, / It was longer in the watch, / As if forever, / Of the huge ancestral goose," refers back to "margin of repose" in the third stanza. The "huge, ancestral goose," progenitor of the flock which flies on and continues the chain of life, meets death "without hope and hurt." It is tied up in the web of nature in which death is a necessary matter of course, not a matter of emotion or meditation. The bird's gaze is "wide of time," seeing existence perpetuated eternally in the ongoing flight of "the dark distant flurry." The separation of the goose from the archetypal triangle powerfully depicts individual mortality against the background of immortal patterns.[88]

The second half of "Angle of Geese" portrays death as a universal force which is beyond concern for individual manifestations of life. This suggestion makes human reflection on death as described in the first three stanzas appear futile, and it deepens the sense of helplessness and destitution which is the inevitable outcome of any attempt to explain the mystery of death. Like "Before an Old Painting of the Crucifixion," "Angle of Geese" offers no solace, only a stark portrayal of the inscrutability of death which overshadows human and nonhuman existence.

"Comparatives" is closely related in theme and structure to "Angle of Geese." In syllabic verse of alternating lines of three and five syllables, it reflects on the inescapable fact of death in the juxtaposition of two scenes of extinction. The first stanza opens with a picture postcard view of an exotic coastline: a glistening sea, palm trees waving in the breeze, white sails on the water—"the seaside of any day."[89] The word "except," followed by a colon, marks the shift from pure description to philosophical considerations which undercut and qualify the superficial beauty of the initial scene. The ubiquity of death in a magnificent universe is thrown into sharp focus by the "cold, bright body, / of the fish / upon the planks, / the coil and crescent of flesh / extending / just into death."

If the dying fish in the first stanza illustrated the physical presence of death, the comparatives in the following lines add the dimension of time, specifically geological time. The fossil fish, caught forever in the rock of "the distant inland sea," bears witness to the uniformity of death over space and time. The single common denominator in the contrast of the dying fish on the beach and the petrified fish among the remnants of an ancient ocean is the agony of annihilation. The fossil fish symbolizes finality and timelessness. Momaday's description of it—"a shadow runs, / radiant, / rude in the rock"—gives it a degree of animation which connects this emblem of death millions of years ago with its contemporary manifestation.

The final judgment of "Comparatives" indicates that acknowledgment and acceptance of death as an integral part of the universe is man's only option. The imagery in which this conclusion is couched resembles that of "Before an Old Painting of the Crucifixion": "[Death] is most like / wind on waves—/ mere commotion, / mute and mean, / perceptible— / that is all." Although death is an inescapable fact of existence, it is neither comprehensible nor communicable.

Among the earliest examples of Momaday's postsymbolist, syllabic poems are "The Bear" and "Buteo Regalis," which were written during his first year at Stanford and are the first two in a sequence of animal poems. Both deal with the mystery of nature. Despite the precise rendition of the bear, the animal appears more as the ghost of a disappearing wilderness than a living creature. It displays an intended kinship with Faulkner's Old Ben.[90] "Buteo Regalis," like "The Bear" descriptive in character, captures the flight of a hawk ready for the kill. The elegance of its descent and the prey's instinctive knowledge of danger are combined in a sharp portrayal of nature's splendor and asperity.

"Pit Viper" is the third in this sequence of animal poems. One version of it, differing greatly from the published poem, appeared in Momaday's Stanford collection of 1960. Both versions of "Pit Viper" probe the question of nature's "archaic force," as Momaday called it in "Headwaters." Because of their equal merit and interest, both poems shall be considered here, the published version first.[91]

The opening lines of "Pit Viper" convey the mystery inherent in a snake's shedding of skin through a precise, close-up rendition of a moment of renewal and regeneration in nature. The snake appears as a symbol of perpetuity, a creature which seems to defy death. It is at home not only in the "evergreen shade" of the forest but in the life-forbidding desert—the image of "inland seas" also appears in the poem "Comparatives"—and in "catacombs" with their connotation of death.

The second half of the poem focuses more closely on the meaning of the snake's annual metamorphosis, moving from description to metaphysical inquiry. In a brilliant shift of perspective Momaday replaces the external view of the creature with the snake's perception of the process of renewal: "Blurred eyes that ever see have seen him waste, / Acquire, and undiminished: have seen death—/ or simile—come nigh and overcome." The "blurred eyes" of the snake register the process of rejuvenation with profound detachment, as if the mind behind the eyes were unconnected to the body. Momaday creates a center of changelessness within change, a symbol of antiquity and knowledge of nature's working. The snake is not merely an instinctual creature. It is mindful, "almost wise," and signifies the essence of the wilderness. This essence remains undiminished in the natural processes of growth and deterioration, birth and death.

This is the unpublished version of "Pit Viper":

> Free of nothing it knew, could know, his brain
> Is lodged in darkness. Only the new skin,
> Kindled to flares along his length, responds.
> By the evergreen mast where he has lain,
> What pain his pits have sung is seasonal.
> He will descend as vision through his scales
> Ever down inland seas of quarter-moons,
> Alone always, at dusk, when placid winds
> Arise, purl, effect a quiet tumult
> In salvo on the crests of gypsum dunes.[92]

Here, too, Momaday draws a distinction between the snake's mind and body. On the descriptive level only the reptile's body appears covered in light, while its head remains in shadow. On the metaphysical plane the creature possesses a knowledge of nature's mystery which defies illumination and can only be inferred from the snake's physical response to the impulses it receives from a natural rhythm. The sloughing of the skin results from one such impulse and is accompanied by the acute, even painful increase in sensitivity of the viper's pits, its most important sensory organs.

The image of the snake as a bearer of primordial knowledge of the earth is reinforced in this version of "Pit Viper" by an association with its habitat. The "evergreen mast," a metaphor for the tree where the snake is resting, is part of a portrayal of the landscape which focuses on its geological evolution from an ancient sea bed to desert. Momaday depicts the desert as a petrified ocean. The grayish white layer of gypsum and limestone, containing fossils and shells, marks the surface of the snake's domain from which it descends to "inland seas of quarter-moons." The lunar rhythm which once controlled the rise and fall of ancient tides now bears upon the snake. And the winds which used to whip up the crests of waves now "effect a quiet tumult / In salvo on the crests of gypsum dunes." The parallel between the metamorphoses of snake and landscape suggest a mysterious, unchanging force behind the changing surface of nature.

Syllabics and postsymbolist imagery are the hallmarks of the poems Momaday wrote under the supervision of Yvor Winters. But as a group these pieces represent only one aspect of Momaday's poetic work. Equally significant are the poems which emerged as a direct reaction against the rigidity of Winters's technical demands.

During the years immediately following Momaday's studies at Stanford he neglected poetry and concentrated on prose. It was a period in which he distanced himself from Winters's poetic principles, and, when he resumed writing poetry, he did so in a much looser style of prose poetry. Thematically, he focused on his American Indian background, and technically he emulated in some of his poems the typical verse pattern of Navajo songs. This change of direction, however, did not result in a permanent rejection of his earlier method. He returned to syllabics and combined this technique with traditional meter, as, for instance, in "Headwaters." The poems Momaday wrote in Moscow show that free verse and a more formal, controlled poetry continue to coexist in his poetic expression. The following two sections of this chapter focus on Momaday's poetic work as it developed after his training at Stanford.

Momaday's "Aboriginal" Poems

This section is devoted to Momaday's poetic statements on his American Indian heritage and his particular treatment of the American earth. Most of the poems I will discuss belong to part two of Momaday's *The Gourd Dancer* collection. While many of them are written in a loose style approaching prose, there are also examples of syllabic and free verse as well as one sonnet. This variety of styles suggests a greater ease of expression compared with the rigid and formalized work of Momaday's Stanford period.

In three short pieces of prose poetry, similar in style to those in *The Way to Rainy Mountain*, Momaday evokes different stages in the evolution of Kiowa life. "The Stalker" shows the fragility of Kiowa existence before the acquisition of the horse; "The Fear of Bo-talee" is a salute to the heroism and humanity of a Kiowa warrior at the height of the horse culture; "The Horse that Died of Shame" combines a story of an act of cowardice, signifying the decline of the Kiowa spirit, with a description of the way in which this traditional tale prevails in Momaday's imagination and dreams and affects his vision of the world around him. In a fourth poem of similar character, "The Story of a Well-Made Shield," Momaday tries to approximate the inexpressible potency he senses in nature.[93]

"The Delight Song of Tsoai-talee" reflects an aboriginal ethic which holds that man is an integral, but not dominant part of creation.[94] It is a prayer of thanks for having existence in a world of endless wonder and beauty. Momaday, one of whose Kiowa names is Tsoai-talee, introduced an early version of this poem with the following words: "It is a day to sing a song, or to run deep into a sunlit field, or to sit easily with someone who is old and alone. It is a day to rejoice. On such a day as this I would tell a story to a child, I would deal in delight. I would say, and the child would say after me: 'I am a feather in the bright sky.'"[95]

The lines which follow illuminate a particularly native attitude toward the natural world, and its form is a deliberate emulation of Navajo song patterns. Mary Austin, whose life and work in the Southwest and study of aboriginal American verse gave her a deep insight into the Indian's sense of the land, described the embeddedness of Indian life in the natural environment, which is at the heart of Momaday's poem, in these paragraphs:

> Man is not himself only, not solely a variation of his racial type in the pattern of his immediate experience. He is all that he sees; all that flows to him from a thousand sources, half noted, or noted not at all except by some sense that lies too deep for naming. He is the land, the lift of its mountain lines, the reach of its valleys; his is the rhythm of its seasonal processions, the involution and variation of its vegetable patterns. . . .
>
> . . . By land, I mean all those things common to a given re-

gion . . . : the flow of prevailing winds, the succession of vegetal cover, the legend of ancient life; and the scene, above everything the magnificently shaped and colored scene.[96]

The use of parallel structures, repetition, and accretion is a common feature in Navajo songs. The final six lines of the poem, which are separated from the main body, correspond to the traditional evocation of personal harmony which concludes many Navajo chants. Such evocations are designed to place the singer into the center of the universe, surrounded by the four cardinal directions, the spirit world above, and the underworld below. The following example is a case in point:

> May it be beautiful before me
> May it be beautiful behind me
> May it be beautiful below me
> May it be beautiful above me
> May it be beautiful all around me
> In beauty it is finished.[97]

"The Delight Song of Tsoai-talee" is a contemporary appropriation of the individual to the universe, based on native tradition and resulting in harmony and delight.

The four poems of the "Plainview" sequence are, as the title suggests, reflections on the world of the Kiowas in the southern plains.[98] "Plainview: 1" and "Plainview: 3" are evocations of the Oklahoma landscape at Rainy Mountain, near Mountain View, the home of Momaday's father. "Plainview: 2" and "Plainview: 4" deal with Kiowa history; the first poem delineates the glory and decline of a Plains culture, the second relates the extraordinary captivity story of Milly Durgan among the Kiowas. The widely differing forms of the four poems indicate Momaday's technical virtuosity and scope.

Momaday introduced the first publication of "Plainview: 1" by saying: "I remember having been at Rainy Mountain in a stormy season, and I write a commemorative poem, a sonnet."[99] The poem is one of the clearest examples of Momaday's kinship with Wallace Stevens. The landscape Momaday creates is more than the sum of carefully selected and precisely observed details. Momaday rendes the scene in terms of its impact not only on the senses but also on the imagination. It is this poetic strategy, the creation of a landscape of the mind, which is also the hallmark of Stevens's work. Stevens's poems fuse reality and imagination to create a fiction, a constructed world particular to the poet alone. One critic has summarized the relevance of this theory to geography: "The idea that place is made of an integration of human concept and external reality and that man's familiar scenes are dependent on his imagination—this idea is basic to an understanding of the supreme fiction." [100]

In "Plainview: 1" Momaday composes a fiction out of sense perceptions—light and shadow, sound and motion, shapes and color—combined with the result of his imaginative response to the ominous mood which informs a landscape under the threat of an approaching storm. The eleven magpies the persona sees are figments of the imagination, "illusions," as the last stanza makes clear. But at the same time they are an integral part of the poet's reality; the poem proceeds in relating the imaginative magpies to the physical world. The resulting reality is a synthesis of sense perceptions and imagination.

"Plainview: 2" is an emulation of indigenous poetic patterns: as with "The Delight Song of Tsoai-talee," its parallel structures, repetition, and accretion are characteristic of American Indian chants. The poem is an elegy on the decline of the Plains Indian world. The peoples of the plains—among them the Kiowas, Comanches, Cheyennes, Arapahos, and Dakotas—reached their golden age after acquiring horses from the Spaniards. Horses gave them mobility and power, both as buffalo hunters and warriors. It is therefore appropriate to render the disintegration of these cultures in terms of the demise of a horse. Deprived of the animal around which his culture flourished, the old Indian is left with memories and dreams of a better time. His flight into alcoholism is an expression of his inability to adapt to new circumstances as well as a way of easing the pain of his nostalgia.

"Plainview: 3" is a celebration of the sun, the central object of veneration among the Plains tribes. Momaday renders the spectacle of sunrise impressionistically, using concrete language and images. Three metaphors are compounded in this depiction of the rising sun: "a pendant / of clear cutbeads, flashing; / a drift of pollen and glitter / lapping, and overlapping night; / a prairie fire."

"Plainview: 4" deals with the extraordinary story of Milly Durgan, whose experience epitomizes the drama of frontier life in Texas and Oklahoma at a time when white settlers were still at the mercy of powerful Kiowa raiders. When she was eighteen months old, Milly Durgan was kidnapped in a raid led by the Kiowa warrior Little Buffalo at Elm Creek, Young County, Texas, on 13 October 1864. While the other captives were later ransomed, Milly was adopted by the famous Kiowa warrior, Au-soant-sai-mah, and given her Indian name, Sain-tohoodie. Most Kiowa captives were treated as slaves, but Milly was raised by kind foster parents and enjoyed the wealth, status, and protection of a respected family. She worshiped the Kiowa idols, Tai-me and the Ten Grandmother bundles, and when the first Baptist missionaries arrived at Rainy Mountain, she fiercely resisted their demand that she adopt the new religion. It was only in old age that she converted to Christianity. She married the Kiowa chief, Goombi, and never regretted her Indian existence when, late in life, she learned about her true origin.[101] After a brief visit to her relations in Texas she returned to the Kiowas in Oklahoma.[102]

In a manuscript version of "Plainview: 4," Momaday described this remarkable woman: "She was made much of in her time, for she had come over an unimaginable distance and crossed the native strain with a hard, exotic blood—a frontier intercession."[103] The two worlds of Milly Durgan are reflected in Momaday's use of excerpts from American folksongs and his emulation of Kiowa oral tradition. The introduction of the first prose section, "Once upon a time I saw the people there," indicates that Momaday is creating an oral tradition out of his direct knowledge of the Kiowa captive and his imaginative re-creation of her life.

The middle section takes the form of a folksong. In the manuscript version the two final lines of this passage read: 'Aye, Milly Durgan, you've gone from your home / Away to the prairie with red men to roam."[104] While this version refers to the kidnap only, the two lines in their published form are ambiguous: they suggest not only Milly's forceful removal from her home in Texas by the Kiowas but her departure in death from her house at Rainy Mountain. It is now her spirit which roams the prairie.

The excerpt from "Shoot the Buffalo" that concludes "Plain-view: 4" is a reminder of the tragic consequences for the Kio-was of the encroachment of the settlers and buffalo hunters. It must have been particularly traumatic for Milly Durgan to see her adopted culture destroyed by people of her own blood. The four poems of the "Plainview" cycle are celebrations of a place in which Momaday is rooted by birth and of a time which prevails in the poet's mind.

"The Gourd Dancer" is a tribute in four sections to Momaday's grandfather Mammedaty, whom he never knew in person but came to know in his racial memory and the verbal dimension of Kiowa lore.[105] Momaday is a successor to his grandfather in the Gourd Dance Society. Thus, the poem makes a statement about the relation between generations in the larger context of Kiowa history and, on a metaphysical level, about the notion of immortality and individual human life in an oral tradition.

In a number of prose works Momaday has directed his energy at salvaging the memory of his ancestor, most notably in *The Names* and in two of his *Viva* columns.[106] In "A Memory that Persists in the Blood" he deals with the giveaway in honor of Mammedaty which is the subject of the fourth section of "The Gourd Dancer." He points out that the event took place ". . . some years ago, before I was born. And yet it is an important event in my mind, important to me and to my understanding of an Indian heritage. I remember it, as it were, in the way that we human beings seem at times to remember Genesis—across evolutionary distances. It is a memory that persists in the blood, and there only." [107]

The first section of "The Gourd Dancer" is entitled "The Omen." Consisting of two quatrains in blank verse, it establishes in its opening line the centrality of the Kiowa homeland. "This place" is the repository of tribal myth and history, the focal point of Momaday's personal and racial heritage. Through the use of grammatical inversion in lines two and three, Momaday stresses the dependence of blood memory and the passage of time—the receding sun and the seasonal rhythm stand as images of change—on the changeless, everlasting land. Memory and time have existence only in relation to place.

Lines five and six describe the physical landscape, but they also suggest its effect on the human imagination. "A vagrant heat" intimates the flux and intensity of memories, while "shadows turning like smoke" evoke the elusive and indistinct imaginative responses to the physical environment. The omen refers to the owl, a bird which symbolizes transmigration in Kiowa thought. [108] The owl, a creature animated by the souls of the dead, functions as a catalyst for Momaday's epiphany of his grandfather. "Remote within its motion, intricate with age," the bird signifies the world of the past. In its distant and aloof nature, it is a challenge to the human imagination.

In this context the owl carries a second meaning. It refers to Mammedaty, who was an owl prophet. According to a newspaper description of the Gourd Dance, he "received the medicine of the owl when he was cooling off at a creek and a screech owl spoke to him. At a later time, he went into a cataleptic state, visiting the land of the dead. He became knowledgeable about the spirit world." [109] In the light of this biographical detail it becomes apparent that Momaday is presenting a landscape twice perceived: once by Mammedaty, whose encounter with the owl made him a medicine man, and then by the poet himself, who conceives of the bird as a carrier of an ancestral spirit. Momaday and Mammedaty are linked by memory and the imagination, which in turn are moored to the land. Change within constancy finds expression not only in the cycle of seasons but in the chain of generations passing through the Kiowa world.

The poem's second section, "The Dream," reinforces the notion of ancestral interrelatedness established in "The Omen." It consists of Momaday's dream of his grandfather's dreaming about dreaming, a deliberate construction of a chain of imaginative experiences, dreams, and recollections which constitute the oral tradition. Again, the opening line establishes the fixed point as "this house," to which everything else is related. This first sentence, "Mammedaty saw to the building of this house," suggests more than just a physical activity. The verb points beyond its primary meaning of "attending' to" the construction of the building; Mammedaty is involved in a spiritual activity, having envisioned the house and pursued this vision as a matter of course. Momaday establishes a link between the sound of the hammers, implied in the silence after the day of work, and the sounds of nature, which take over when human activity rests. The blows of hammers find an echo in the drumbeats of Mammedaty's imaginative dance. The magnificent image, "a low, hectic wind upon the pale, slanting plane of the moon's light," owes something perhaps to the opening line of Emily Dickinson's "There's a certain Slant of light."[110]

Mammedaty's dreaming of the imaginative in the last three lines of this second section is described in terms of the physical. The dream of "the summer breaking upon the spirit" is likened to the drumbeats and gleaming gourds of the Gourd Dance. Implicit in this poetic strategy is the notion that the worlds of dream and reality are the same, an idea corroborated by Momaday's beliefs in the illusory nature of existence and the reality of dreams.[111]

Section three, "The Dance," of "The Gourd Dancer" opens with an inversion: at the end of "The Dream" Mammedaty was dreaming of the Gourd Dance; now he is actually dancing, dreaming of the mythical past which gave rise to the Gourd Dance ceremony. This inversion is designed to dissolve even further the separation between the real and the ideal dominant in Anglocentric thought but alien to American Indian philosophy.

In the third line Momaday again takes up the images of wind and "the pale slanting plane of the moon's light." Momaday's use of the verb "glance" is an example of the richness and economy of his language. In its first meaning, "to strike a surface obliquely so as to go off at an angle," "glance" refers to the wind being deflected by the slanting plane of the moonlight.[112] In a second meaning, "to flash or gleam with quick intermittent rays of light," the image is linked to the flashing and gleaming of the gourd rattles. In its third meaning, "to make sudden quick movements," it is related to the "mincing steps" of the dancer. While the first meaning establishes a connection within the poem, the second and third meanings point beyond its immediate context to the story about the beginning of the Gourd Dance.

The three lines "The long wind glances, moves / Forever as a music to the mind; / The gourds are flashes of the sun," suggest that Mammedaty, in his dream, is drawn toward the mythical origin of his dance. The story of the origin of the Gourd Dance tells of a young man who, on a solitary quest, encounters an enemy in the shape of a wolf. He kills the wolf-like man. "Then," the story continues, "the young man took up the enemy's arrows in his right hand and held them high and shook them. They rattled loudly like dry leaves in a hard wind, and to the music the young man danced around the dead enemy."[113]

The sound and motion of the wind in Mammedaty's dream evoke the music to which the hero in the story is dancing. As the landscape in "The Omen" is a landscape twice perceived, so the wind is a music twice heard. It is "a music in the tribal mind," where it prevails. The motion of the wind relates to the movement of the dance, suggesting a kinship between ritual and nature. The same expression of ritual in terms of nature informs the line "The gourds are flashes of the sun." While the stress here is on the visual impression, the image also evokes the sound and motion of the rattling arrows, again a reminder of the Gourd Dance's origin. In taking the "inward, mincing steps," both in the dance and in the imagination, the past becomes alive for Mammedaty in "old processions and returns." The ritual creates a realm in which time is suspended and the accumulated experience of the race is accessible to the participant.

The second stanza of "The Dance" elaborates on Mammedaty's place within Kiowa tradition. His being is contained in his ritual garb as well as in his name and the story of the giveaway. His part in the Gourd Dance ensures cultural survival. By simulating an eagle's flight, the eagle-feather fan effects Mammedaty's extension not only into the natural world but, more important, into the tribal past and future. His hold upon "the deep ancestral air" constitutes a privilege as well as a responsibility. Momaday's careful use of the word "air," with its double meaning of song and life, implies that through a scrupulous adherence to ritual and song the Gourd Dance will keep Kiowa tradition alive and breathing. The adjective "concise" in the description of Mammedaty's handling of the fan suggests language in being "marked by brevity of expression or statement; free from elaboration and superfluous detail."[114] Momaday appears to draw a deliberate parallel between the motion of the fan and the style of his writing about it, indicating his personal investment in the perpetuation of Kiowa tradition both as a Gourd Dancer and as an artist.

The final section of "The Gourd Dancer," "The Giveaway," amplifies the significance of language in Kiowa culture. Momaday's imaginative reenactment of the ceremony in Mammedaty's honor is framed by two statements on the physical and verbal dimension of human existence. According to Kiowa thought a name is "as much part of the owner as his hand or his foot."[115] It is never dealt with lightly. A name contains the essence of its bearer, not only during his lifetime but beyond it. This attitude toward names is typical of oral cultures. Mammedaty, on hearing his name spoken in public, is aware of the seriousness of the impending event. He is "thoughtful, full of wonder, and aware of himself and of his name." Momaday draws attention to this dual existence in body and language which constitutes the central premise of the oral tradition. It is in the verbal dimension that life becomes timeless. Existence in place is temporary; in language it is eternal, as long as the old stories continue and the names prevail in the memory of the people.

Momaday conjures up the giveaway ceremony in all its dignity and excitement. The black horse, Mammedaty's gift of honor, is a symbol of the life force, of "the wild way." Its excitement is analogous to Mammedaty's in view of the seriousness of the occasion. For the ceremony is not only a matter of honor; it represents the making of a tradition. In that his name is attached to the ceremony, which is perpetuated as a story in Kiowa oral tradition, he is being immortalized. The giveaway is thus something of an initiation ceremony in which Mammedaty enters the verbal dimension of existence which goes on forever in the tribal mind.

In "New World" Momaday combines syllabic verse and imagistic expression with the ambiguity and creativity of sound typical of the oral tradition to generate a sense of the aboriginal perception of the universe. The poem was published simultaneously in *The Gourd Dancer* and as part of an essay entitled "A First American Views His Land," in which Momaday adumbrates the moral implications of the relationship between Indians and their land.[116] Some statements from this article are useful for putting the poem into perspective. Momaday noted that "Native American oral tradition is rich with songs and tales that celebrate natural beauty, the beauty of the natural world."[117] "New World" exemplifies the oral-aural quality of some of Momaday's poetry because of not only its subject matter but also its subtle use of imitative sound and phonic effects. These effects come alive when the poem is read aloud or, better still, when one listens to Momaday's own reading of it.[118]

"New World" is a hymn to the beauty of nature. If the language, at times, has a biblical ring to it, the implication is clearly that the scene generates a religious experience in the beholder, a sense of communion between man and earth. Momaday expressed this communion: "The first truth is that I *love* the land; I see that it is beautiful; I delight in it; I am alive in it."[119] It would be wrong to see the poem merely as an attempt to reconstruct the scene as it presented itself, in the beginning, to "First Man." As in "The Gourd Dancer," the landscape is mythical, but it is also contemporary. If the perceiving eye can take hold of the mystery of the natural world, its field of vision extends across time to the moment of creation. Momaday describes the experience: "It was simply exciting to be overtaken by the dawn, to see the world emerge from the darkness. There is something like Genesis, like Creation at that hour of the day; and outside, breathing deeply of it, you feel intensely alive."[120] "New World" is more than a poem; it is a prayer for communion with the universe and for the strength which emanates from the beginning of the world.

Momaday's poetic construction of the natural world rests on the use of juxtapositions and the careful selection of minute details. The main oppositions are earth and sky, sun and moon, light and shadow, heat and cold, motion and motion suspended. The poem's structure is cyclical: after setting the scene in the first stanza, Momaday follows the course of a day from dawn to noon in stanzas two and three to dusk and night in the last stanza.

The three opening words, "First Man / behold," are characteristic of American Indian creation myths, in which a creator lines up the people to view, for the first time, their new world.[121] The notions of creation and procreation are sustained by the images of rain and pollen, two fundamental elements in the chain of life. The sun, implicit in the glittering of leaves and the glistening of the sky, and the wind as carrier of pollen and seed are other life-giving agents. Momaday indicates that what he selects for description is beautiful not only in its appearance but in its interrelatedness and function within nature. Sky and wind attain a distinct concreteness: the sky is conceived of as a surface reflecting the sunlight; the "winds that low and lean upon the mountains" have almost a personal character. "Low" suggests not only sound, a voice, but also movement, as the winds lower themselves on the mountains for support. Apart from alliteration, which occurs frequently throughout the poem, the choice of words with phonic effects is the most striking device Momaday employs and the one most closely related to the oral tradition.

Another example of such ambiguity of sound is the word "borne" in "Pollen / is borne / on winds." In print the distinction of "borne" and "born" is obvious, but it is much less so in the poem's true medium of sound, where the verb's suggestiveness of birth connects with the explicit theme of creation in the first stanza. The unusual choice of the archaic word "hie" in the second stanza is justified by the homophonous character of the word, suggesting at the same time the rapid motion and height of the eagles at dawn. Similarly, "plain" in "eagles / hie and / hover / above / the plain" resonates with the additional meaning of "plane," evokes an image of light as in "The Dream" section of "The Gourd Dancer," and anticipates the "planes / of heat" in the third stanza. The verb "lie" in "shadows / withdraw / and lie / away / like smoke" is another case in point. Not only does it suggest the retreat and eventual disappearance of shadows, it simultaneously connotes the deceptiveness of the phenomenon.

In this second stanza Momaday also succeeds in creating a sense of the space and height of his world. He uses a double perspective, one angle of vision from below, focusing on the eagles in the sky, and one from the eagles' vantage point above, centering on the pools of light on the plain. Finally, the image of the moving shadows is a powerful evocation of the passage of time as the sun approaches its pivotal point at noon.

The opening of the third stanza suggests a slowing down of life in the heat of noon. Through the use of long vowels Momaday achieves an effect of phonic mimesis. The second sentence, "Bees hold / the swarm," is of twofold interest. On the level of sound "Bees hold" is a play on "behold" in the first stanza, a deliberate repetition with a variation, another call to be mindful of the natural world. On the conceptual level this sentence raises the question of the relation between the parts and the whole; inasmuch as the bees hold the swarm, the swarm unites the bees. It is a small example of the mystery of nature: the interrelatedness of individual parts which form an organic whole.

The final stanza opens with a stark silhouette. Momaday's images of animal life immobilized in the cold of the approaching night have the quality of abstract line drawings. In the atmospheric cold motion is suspended, "foxes / stiffen" and "blackbirds / are fixed / in the /branches." The latter image is reminiscent of Wallace Stevens's solitary blackbirds sitting "in the cedar-limbs" on a snowy and dark winter afternoon.[122]

The final image of moonlight over the river is rendered by one of Momaday's typical poetic devices, inversion: "Rivers / follow / the moon, / the long / white track / of the / full moon." It is, of course, the moonlight which follows the track of the river; but in ignoring logical order, Momaday creates a sense of wonder and mystery. He points to a dimension of reality which is closed to the analytical mind. The vision of the river following the moon is an imaginative transformation, a mode of reality based on belief rather than knowledge, and therefore mythical in character.

In "The Eagle-Feather Fan," Momaday turns his attention to ritual. The poem reflects his participation in the annual Kiowa Gourd Dance ceremonials at Carnegie, Oklahoma.[123] It captures some typically indigenous assumptions about human existence: the belief in magic, the belief in the value of tradition, the belief in the unity of creation, and the belief in the relationship of reality and the imagination.

Central to the magical world view is the idea of power, or medicine. It is conceived of as an intrinsic element of the natural order, a force which the individual can appropriate through ritual and utilize in his dealings with the world.[124] The opening lines, "The eagle is my power, / And my fan is an eagle," indicate the connection between the dancer and his power through the ritual implement of the eagle-feather fan. The fan "is real," not a symbol of power but power itself. No distinction is made between the physical and spiritual, the "real" and the imaginative; such a separation would be alien to the American Indian view of the universe. The equation of the fan's beaded handle with "the twist of bristlecone" suggests the ancient nature of the ritual and its potential for tapping the life force. Bristlecones are among the oldest known living trees, and Momaday has noted "the impulse of life" in these "thorns of the ancient earth." [125]

The next lines express man's ritual extension into and identification with the natural world: "The bones of my hand are fine / and hollow; the fan bears them. / My hand veers in the thin air / of the summit." The bones are fine and hollow like those of an eagle's wing; moreover, Momaday makes the point that the fan bears the hand rather than the other way around, as one might expect. This inversion implies first and foremost that ritual sustains human existence and, second, that man's ritual activity sustains the ceremony.

Through his adherence to tradition, his capacity for belief, and the power of his imagination, the Gourd Dancer can transcend the individual boundaries of human existence and unite himself with the cosmos. The association of power with the eagle, eagle with the fan, fan with the bristlecone, and the Gourd Dancer with all of them suggests the infinite chain of creation of which man is one small link.

If ritual is one form of human expression which ensures man's link to tradition and the web of life, the oral tradition is another. In "Carriers of the Dream Wheel," Momaday explores the verbal dimension of American Indian cultures. [126] An individual inherits his tribe's accumulated wealth of orally transmitted stories and songs, "the dream wheel," which shapes his existence and his perception of the world around him.

The first four lines of the poem establish the reciprocal relation between the dream wheel and its carriers. The imaginary realm of histories and myths, visions and songs, survives in their voices, and the keepers of the oral tradition have existence in and through it. It is a fundamental tenet of American Indian thought that the world came into existence through language, that nothing truly exists unless it has existence in language. This theory of creation is intimated in the lines "It [the Dream Wheel] encircles the First World, / This powerful wheel. / They shape their songs upon the wheel / And spin the names of the earth and sky, / The aboriginal names." The concluding six lines combine the ancient and contemporary aspects of the oral tradition: as long as this heritage is kept alive in the communal experience of American Indians, they will continue to know who they are and what their destiny is.

The sequence of eight prose poems which constitutes "The Colors of Night" is a product of Momaday's stay in Moscow in 1974.[127] He has described the poems as "quintessential novels, concentrated stories of time, place, and presence."[128] In attributing a color to each of the sections Momaday creates a spectrum, a dark prism which makes up night. He explained that he "was not thinking of traditional Indian colors," but "of times of day, and trying to associate all the colors of night into one thing."[129] Traditionally, of course, night is the time of Indian storytelling; the poetic sequence manifests a slice of the oral tradition, revealing a number of characteristic ethical and epistemological issues. The stories are imbued with a sense of wonder and mystery which accounts for their peculiar charm.

The first story, about a man who retrieves and cherishes the bones of his dead son, is a moving example of the respect for the deceased which is common among Indian peoples. Moreover, the old man's proclamation "that now his son consists in his bones" powerfully attests to his belief in the indestructibility of a man's essence or, to use the Christian term, his soul. The color white refers to the polished bones which "gleam like glass in the light of the sun and the moon." The story is a poetic treatment of a historical incident recorded by James Mooney:

In the spring of 1870, before the last sun dance, the son of the noted chief Set-ängya ("Sitting-bear"), . . . had made a raid with a few followers into Texas, where . . . he had been shot and killed. After the dance his father with some friends went to Texas, found his bones and wrapped them in several fine blankets, put the bundle upon the back of a led horse and brought them home. . . . While on the march the remains were always put upon the saddle of a led horse, as when first brought home, the [funeral] tipi and the horse thus burdened being a matter of personal knowledge to all middle-age people of the tribe now living. He continued to care for his son's bones in this manner until he himself was killed at Fort Sill about a year later, when the Kiowa buried them.[130]

The second section, "Yellow," is an etiologic myth about how it came about that dogs howl at the moon. Enchanted by the yellow brilliance of moonlight on a river, and inspired to sing what is to be his death song, a boy follows the mystery of sound and vision and drowns in the swirling waters. The story is, however, primarily concerned not with death but with meta-morphosis: the boy emerges from the river as a dog, howling at the moon, presumably reproaching the moon for its deceit. As in the first poem, death is presented as a matter of transfor-mation rather than annihilation.

In the third section, "Brown," Momaday makes a humorous claim against empiricism. The secret of how terrapins evade a flood by climbing to higher ground defies the most scrupulous observation. The implication here seems to be that although nature has been stripped of many of its wonders by analytical, scientific investigation, there still remain mysteries which frus-trate reason and feed the imagination.

Section four, "Red," deals with the moral implications of magic. A man has used his "powerful medicine" to create a woman out of sumac leaves, and he lives with her for a while. The title of the poem refers to the woman's skin color, which resembles that of pipestone. When the man mistreats her, he loses both his magic power and the woman, who disintegrates and becomes part of nature again, "leaves scattered in the plain." Once more, the story bears witness to the belief in the infinite possibilities of creation, transformation, and decon-struction.

The fifth section, "Green," is a puzzling statement on the nature of reality: "A young girl awoke one night and looked out into the moonlit meadow. There appeared to be a tree; but it was only an appearance; there was a shape made of smoke; but it was only an appearance; there was a tree." Momaday's oral reading of this passage shows a declining stress from the first "there," which carries great weight and functions as a demonstrative and prepositional referent, putting the existence of the tree beyond doubt, to the third "there," which is no more than an unstressed reference to an indefinite object.[131]

Despite this variance of stress and the repetition of "it was only an appearance," Momaday's intention is obvious: he is trying to eliminate the distinction between appearance and reality. Human reality goes beyond what is verifiable by reason; it is constituted as well by dreams, visions, and illusions. Momaday had noted that "there are modes and modes of existence."[132] The reality of a tree, he seems to say, is valid, whether it is a product of sense perception or of the imagination.[133]

In the following section, "Blue," Momaday qualifies the nature of reality in an important way: reality, he suggests, is ultimately a function of language; only what has existence in language can be said to be real. The parable of the child who appears in a camp and talks to the people in an unintelligible language is the account of a vision the reality of which is denied because it cannot be transformed into language: "After all . . . how can we believe in the child? It gave us not one word of sense to hold on to." Had the child given his name, he would have acquired an identity and a sense of reality.

Section seven, "Purple," relates the transgression of the sacred rules which regulate the relation between man and the animal world. A man has slaughtered a buffalo, the animal representation of the sun, for no reason other than sport. His fellow people witness the sacrilege with shame and grief. The moral implications of the story are amplified by its etiologic character. The buffalo's hump and spine are transformed into a mountain on the western horizon, and its blood, bright and purple, colors the setting sun, darkens, and creates the night sky. The results of these metamorphoses are permanent reminders of the sacrilegious act in the people's physical environment.

The final section, "Black," is another illustration of the existence of mysterious forces in the universe which cannot be accounted for but have to be believed. What the woman who "steals into the men's societies and fits her voice into their holiest songs" represents remains in doubt. However, what is important is not what she is but *that* she is, timeless, ever-present, inexplicable. At the end of a sequence of poems which centers on a world of magic and mystery, she stands as the embodiment of mystery itself.

"Colors of Night" is an attempt to give some clues to the way in which American Indians view the world. Theirs is a mythical world view, a fact which accounts for the difficulties a non-Indian reader may have with this poetic cycle. Momaday once quoted Isak Dinesen's remark that "it is not necessarily bad that a story should only be half understood." [134] If the eight poems generate a sense of wonder and delight, they have fulfilled their purpose. If they set in motion the reader's imagination and motivate him to expand and retell them, they indeed acquire the status of "quintessential novels" which Momaday intended for them.

The concluding five poems of part two of *The Ground Dancer* are evocations of different landscapes, delineating various human reactions to the natural world. [135] "The Monoliths" seems to refer to the three awesome stone columns which tower over Monument Valley. The four-line poem suggests that the poetic persona experiences simultaneously a communion with and separation from his environment. While the wind upon him makes him part of the scene, the monoliths are of an order which defies his approach. Defined by the contrast of stone against light, they appear as pillars of eternity, generating the sense of awe and wonder which enters the human mind when man is obliged to relate his existence to the grandeur of the world around him.[136]

"North Dakota, North Light" is a reflection on the terrible powers of winter. Man and animals seem frozen in a dazzling, brilliant winter landscape. After an opening statement on the encroaching presence of cold, Momaday frames the remainder of the poem by references to "the sheer, lucent plane," repeated with slight modification in the final line, ". . . the sheer, shining plane." The only motion in this scene of extraordinary beauty is the wind which is deflected from the hunter's weapon: "A glassy wind glances / from the ball of bone in my wrist."

Life has come to a total halt. The rabbits in the foreground rest under the force of the sky which is "clenched upon them" like the claws of a bird of prey. The hunter, too, seems motionless, arrested by the deadening cold. Significantly, its effect is both physical and mental: ". . . and I cannot conceive / of summer; / and another man in me / stands for it, / wills even to remain, / figurative, fixed, / among the hard, hunchbacked rabbits." The cold is so overwhelming that it halts even the imagination; the pronoun "it" in line eleven refers back to "summer," suggesting that there are two separate manifestations of the persona, one for winter, another for summer. This distinction may indicate man's spiritual and physical subordination to the cyclical, seasonal rhythms of nature. Since the summer manifestation is powerless in the face of wintry forces, it wills to remain "figurative, fixed," submitting itself to their reign as do the "hard, hunchbacked rabbits."

"Winter Holding off the Coast of North America" addresses itself to man's instinctual fear when he confronts irresistible natural forces. Momaday captures this abstract idea in the word "dread" in the opening line. The simile and images which follow evoke this notion through clear sensory details and communicate tightly controlled emotions in response to the facts of human vulnerability and insignificance.

The simile "like a calm" and the adjective "colorless" simultaneously describe and explain the sense of dread. The powerful forces at work are beyond visual and auditory perception, but they are nevertheless real and make themselves felt. They are defined in terms of cold and suspension of motion and represent a kind of anti-life. This theme is suggested by Momaday's use of the adjective "dead" to describe the approaching cold. The poem is related to "Before an Old Painting of the Crucifixion," in which the latent presence of death also informs the calm of the sea. The only reference to human presence in "Winter Holding off the Coast of North America" is "the stricken palm," an image of man's exposure and fragility which evokes the crucifixion.

The last stanza, in its depiction of the natural world charged with an irresistible and inexorable destiny, belongs to Momaday's most powerful poetic statements: "Out there, beyond the floes, / On the thin pewter plane, / The polar currents close, / And stiffen, and remain."

While the previous two poems dealt with hostile, life-denying winter landscapes, "To a Child Running with Outstretched Arms in Canyon de Chelly" communicates the exhilaration and joy derived from the spectacular scenery near Chinle, New Mexico, where Momaday spent a brief part of his childhood. The poem can therefore be seen as a projection of Momaday's own wonder and delight into the figure of the child. The idea of "spirit of place" is related to aesthetic and historical considerations in this poem. The play of light and shadow as well as the natural stone sculptures which abound in the canyon appeal to the aesthetic sense.

But it is not only in geographical terms that "the backdrop is immense." Rock paintings and ruins of cliff dwellings are silent witnesses to the culture of the Anazasi, the Ancient Ones, who lived in Canyon de Chelly centuries before the Navajos made it their home. Here also the Navajos made their brave if futile stand against Kit Carson's military expedition in 1864, which led to the enforced relocation of the tribe known as the Long Walk, perhaps the darkest chapter in Navajo history. But the Navajos returned, and their sense of belonging to a homeland of majestic beauty is ample reason for excitement and joy.

"Long Shadows at Dulce" is written in syllabic verse of six syllables to the line and consists of four individually numbered stanzas, each of which represents a miniature poem in its own right. These four stanzas capture in a highly personal, imagistic manner the mood and activities of autumn at Dulce, a small town on the Jicarilla Apache Reservation in northern New Mexico. [137] Although only two months are referred to by name, the four stanzas form a sequence from September to December. In its progression through the season, its compressed imagistic form, and perhaps even in the title the poem shows parallels to Yvor Winters's poetic cycle "The Magpie's Shadow." Winters's one-line poems are reflections on a year at Madrid, a coal-mining camp twenty miles south of Santa Fe where he taught grade school in 1922 after recovering from tuberculosis. Momaday's poem is a commemoration of impressions during a brief stay at Dulce where he worked as a schoolteacher in 1958.

In the first stanza Momaday addresses the ambiguous nature of September. His characterization of the month as "a long illusion of itself" presumably refers to the transition from summer to fall which lies in the air but is nothing more than a vague presence defying sensory perception. The third line, "the elders bide their time," is ambiguous: it may refer to old people who await the approach of winter, perhaps of death; simultaneously it alludes to the elderberry trees which seem to defer the change of color, the sign of the arrival of autumn.

Stanza two captures the joy and excitement among the children when, at the end of summer, the sheep are rounded up in the camps and the community gathers for social activities. Stanza three communicates the atmosphere of November by way of an extended metaphor. It is the time of the bear hunt: "November is the flesh / And blood of the black bear, / Dusk its bone and marrow." The sense of melancholy and the slowing down of life which announces the coming of winter are brilliantly reflected in the image of the final stanza: "In the hud-

dled horses / That know of perfect cold / There is a calm, like
sorrow."

These five poems which conclude part two of *The Gourd
Dancer* reflect not only a greater freedom and flexibility in po-
etic expression compared to the Stanford period but also a shift
from the largely abstract, philosophical themes explored under
Winters's supervision to more immediate, personal concerns.
The self-exploration in terms of his American Indian back-
ground, which Momaday pursued in prose in *The Way to Rainy
Mountain*, is the central theme in the second part of *The Gourd
Dancer*.

Poems from a Journey to Russia

Momaday's four-month stay in the Soviet Union was a period
of great creative productiveness. One reason for this surge may
have been his deep sense of isolation, which stirred his imagination and resulted in the poems collected in the third part of
The Gourd Dancer. [138] The experience of being detached from
his immediate environment found expression in "Krasnopresnenskaya Station," in which Momaday deals with his loneliness. [139] The concluding line of stanza two, "I have no prospect
here," suggests the deep rift between himself and the persons
surrounding him. This second stanza indicates that the poem
is closely related to "Anywhere Is a Street into the Night." [140]
Both poems reflect the same setting and experience: the poetic
personae sit by the window of a metro train; and the window
stands as an image of the imagination, which provides relief
from social isolation.

In "Krasnopresnenskaya Station" the protagonist wonders
why the people "keep so, to themselves, / in their trains, in
the deep streets." While in reality he has no access to them,
his imagination allows him to find "a street into the night"
which leads him out of his isolated condition. Stanzas three
and four spell out this imaginative process. First, the poetic
persona enters the mind of a girl on the train: "I suppose /
she does not remember herself; / she dreams of the lindens at Ar-

khangelskoe." [141] After establishing this contact with another stranger, the persona develops their imaginative relationship: "She would speak of ordinary things; / I would listen / for the hard resonances of the river, / the ice breaking apart in the afternoon." [142]

The imaginative process referred to in "Anywhere Is a Street into the Night" gave rise not only to Momaday's writing of poetry but also to his drawings and sketches. His exploration of this new artistic medium presumably led to his discovery of the Japanese painter Hokusai, to whom the poem "For the Old Man Mad for Drawing, Dead at Eighty-nine" is dedicated. [143] Hokusai, who lived from 1760 to 1849, has been described as "one of the greatest masters of the popular school" of Japanese painting, "a man of great vitality and a terrific worker with an insatiable curiosity, who allowed nothing to escape his searching eyes; no scene was too small or too sublime to escape his brush." [144]

The general theme of the poem is the infinite possibilities of the imagination. That Momaday poetically expresses the creative powers of the visual art of drawing indicates how the two forms of expression preoccupied him. The poem's epigraph, ". . . at ninety I shall have penetrated to the essence of all things," stems from Hokusai's epilogue to his collection of prints entitled *One Hundred Views of Fuji Mountain*. He wrote it when he was seventy-five years old and signed it "Gwakyo Rojin, the Old Man Mad About Drawing." [145] It represents a brief overview of his career and his aspirations:

I had a habit for drawing the forms of things from the age of six, and had published by the time I was fifty, quite a number of books of pictures; but all I had produced before the age of seventy is not worth taking into account. At seventy-three I have learned a little about the structure of birds, animals, insects and fishes, and also how plants and trees are brought forth. Therefore, I shall have made still more progress when I am eighty, and penetrate the mystery of things at ninety, and certainly have reached a divine state at a hundred. And when I am a hundred and ten, anything I do, whether it be a dot or a line, will be looking as if alive.[146]

There is a certain irony, or tragedy, in Hokusai's death a year before his aspired mastery over the mystery of all things. Momaday takes up this point to speculate about what might have happened: in setting up a contrast between appearance and reality he suggests that, had Hokusai reached the age of ninety, "there might have been here / not apparently / a corpulent merchant and his pillow / but really three long winds converging on the dawn." At this point of ultimate artistic mastery the supremacy of the imagination over reality would have been established.[147]

"Abstract: Old Woman in a Room" deals with the reflections on life by a woman waiting for death. It is dedicated to Olga Sergeevna Akhmanova, who was the head of the English Department at the University of Moscow. The poem's language is, as the title suggests, abstract. The inescapability of the room as the final scene of meditation, as a place in which a whole human life is concentrated, is suggested by the monotonous repetition of "here." Like the ticking of a clock, it recurs seven times in the poem. Each of the five stanzas opens with "here" or "and here"; in the central stanza both lines begin with "here"; and the final word is "here."[148]

The poem's somber mood is set in the opening stanza, which depicts the room as a place for stock-taking. The Day of Reckoning comes to mind on reading the second line, "But where you come to reckon recompence." In the second stanza the room is a void in which a vague sense of regret enters the mind. "The will's disease"—Momaday uses the word literally in the sense of "dis-ease"—suggests the rise of doubt over decisions and aspirations which have shaped a life. "And otherwise / Here is no reparation in surmise" extends the previous point in suggesting that speculation on what might have been yields no consolation. The white light on the woman's white hair only heightens the "darkness and despair" which engulf her. In the extremity of this situation "death is dear," not as a way of redemption but simply as a release from the burden of old age. Though death is impending, the woman remains captive in her state of reflection, struggling with doubts and regrets, held back by "essences of anguish" in a life which is no longer appreciated.

"Crows in a Winter Composition" is another of Momaday's meditations on the land which reveals his position on the value of the human imagination.[149] The first stanza presents a scene of emptiness and silence, a landscape devoid of definition, content, and depth. The observer's response is not explicit, but it appears to have been a sense of mystification, of dissolution of the self in a realm outside of space and time. In much the same way as the line of cormorants in "Before an Old Painting of the Crucifixion" reminds the poetic persona of his existence in time, the abrupt intrusion of the crows into the winter composition interferes with and brings to an end the protagonist's absorption in an indefinite and unintelligible scene. This reminder of the observer's existence in a world of well-defined, concrete reality results first in a feeling of being "ill at ease" and then in hostility: "The crows . . . stood in a mindless manner, / on the gray, luminous crust, / altogether definite, composed, / in the bright enmity of my regard, / in the hard nature of crows."

Inasmuch as the landscape is a void, it is threatening to man as a rational creature because it deprives him of any frame of reference. Conversely, the "mindless" crows are firmly integrated and at home in this dimension. However, by its very lack of definition the scene is charged with infinite possibility and potential, posing, as the clearly defined crows cannot, a challenge to the human imagination.

Momaday seems to be playing here with the tension between the real and the ideal, between a well-defined, ordered, and concrete reality which is intelligible but ultimately dull and an abstract, vague dimension which is incomprehensible yet appealing to the observer's imagination. In suggesting a bias toward the supremacy of the imagination over reality, Moma-

day strikes a Stevensian note. The poem's setting resembles
that of "Thirteen Ways of Looking at a Blackbird."[150] And his
lines "The several silences, / Imposed one upon another" are
reminiscent of Stevens's reference to the earth as "the mute, the
final sculpture / around which silence lies on silence."[151]

The protagonist's temptation to indulge in a realm of pure
imagination is tempered only by his admission that this dimension is ultimately beyond reason. It is possible that, on one
level of this poem, Momaday has dramatized one of Winters's
central concerns, the relation between poetic imagination and
reason. If Momaday is the poem's persona, then he is drawn
strongly toward the ideal, reality having only limited appeal
to him.

The last two poems to be considered in this section deal with
two of Momaday's friends whom he remembered in his Russian
domicile. "The Gift" is one of four poems in the original typescript written in commemoration of his friendship with Bobby
Jack Nelson.[152] They met as undergraduates at the University
of New Mexico. The four poems reflect the fellowship and the
competition between two young aspiring writers. Nelson left
the United States for Australia to write the book he published
under the title *The Last Station*.[153] While Momaday knew that
he could draw on his imagination for his writing, Nelson
needed to be in the physical locale he wanted to deal with in
his fiction.[154] The first two pieces of the original sequence refer
to the effect the separation from his friend had on Momaday:

1. On Standing in Good Relation to Each Other

I knew that neither you nor I
Could look the other in the eye.

2. Envy

You fled to distant continents to live;
(I stayed at home and struggled to forgive).
You ventured here and there and everywhere;
(I kept indoors and envied you the air).

"The Gift" is the third poem of the original sequence.[155] It portrays a matured friendship between the two men:

> Older, more generous,
> We give each other hope.
> The gift is ominous:
> Enough praise, enough rope.

Competition has given way to mutual support; the gifts of hope and encouragement they exchange hold the promise of greater artistic freedom and success. The realization of this promise is acknowledged in the final piece:

> 4. On Limits that We Knew and Exceeded
>
> Bobby Jack, we rode the range together;
> We rode beyond the end of our tether.

This poetic sequence is a tribute to a relationship which has been significant in more ways than one: Nelson and Momaday supported each other at a crucial point in their careers; Momaday read his manuscripts to Nelson;[156] and they shared flights into "mad, mad poetry."[157] Finally, and perhaps most important, it was Bobby Jack Nelson who drew his friend's attention to the Wallace Stegner Creative Writing Fellowship which was to affect Momaday's artistic development so profoundly.[158]

"Forms of the Earth at Abiquiu" was written to commemorate Momaday's friendship with the painter Georgia O'Keeffe.[159] In 1972, Momaday visited her at her home in Abiquiu, a small town forty miles north of Jemez Springs. It was the first of several visits during which Momaday expressed his admiration for her work. The objects he describes in the poem—skulls, bones, stones—are significant not only because they figure prominently in O'Keeffe's paintings but because they revealed to him an understanding and admiration of the natural world with which he could immediately identify. He learned about her love of wine and goat cheese, and on subsequent visits he never failed to bring along a small supply for their "late luncheons."[160]

Their common interest in painting and in the New Mexico landscape dominated their conversations. O'Keeffe's fascination with stones and rocks found expression in a series of paintings on which she was working at the time of Momaday's visit.[161] These paintings may have inspired Momaday to make her "the gift of a small, brown stone" which she greatly admired.

The mutual understanding between the two artists grew out of their deep involvement in the landscape they shared. Momaday sensed that O'Keeffe had been molded, physically and artistically, by the environment of the Southwest. He was intrigued by her hands, which he had expected to be elegant and feminine from the photographs of Alfred Stieglitz, taken in 1919.[162] But, Momaday noted: "When I first saw her I marvelled because her hands were huge and very bony and gnarled and rough—beautiful, but not feminine. Not in the way those early photographs are; and I thought she has been somehow conditioned by the land. This is rough country, canyon country, full of knarled growth—and look at those hands!"[163] He found the same intangible influence in her paintings: ". . . in her the sense of place is definitive of her great, artistic spirit. She perceives in the landscape of New Mexico an essence and a quality of life that enables her to express her genius." This attunement proved to Momaday that she "is a native in her soul."[164]

"Forms of the Earth at Abiquiu" is more than a commemorative poem; it is a celebration of the spiritual kinship Momaday experienced on his visits with O'Keeffe. The lines below suggest an understanding between the two artists which needs no words: "And the many smooth stones in the window, / In the flat winter light, were beautiful. / I wanted to feel the sun in the stones—/ The ashen, far-flung winter sun— / But this I did not tell you, I believe, / But I believe that after all you knew." O'Keeffe's writings reflect the same delight in the natural beauty of commonplace things which emanates from Momaday's prose and poetry. She explained the meaning of the collection of objects which Momaday celebrates in the poem and the function of those objects for her art:

I have picked flowers where I found them—have picked up sea shells and rocks and pieces of wood where there were sea shells and rocks and pieces of wood that I liked. . . . When I found the beautiful white bones on the desert I picked them up and took them home too. . . . I have used these things to say what is to me the wideness and wonder of the world as I live in it.[165]

The closing lines of "Forms of the Earth at Abiquiu" define the distinctive perception with which O'Keeffe—and Momaday—appropriate themselves to the natural world: ". . . you knew the forms of the earth at Abiquiu: / That time involves them and they bear away, / Beautiful, various, remote, / In failing light, and the coming of cold." The sensibility of both artists penetrates the surface and form of the objects and centers on the myriad forces which have shaped them. It is a vision beyond time, an awareness of infinite possibilities in the ordinary. O'Keeffe wrote:

The black rocks from the road to the Glen Canyon dam seem to have become a symbol to me—of the wideness and wonder of the sky and the world. They have lain there for a long time with the sun and the wind and the blowing sand making them into something that is precious to the eye and hand—to find with excitement, to treasure and to love.[166]

This passage is a final confirmation of how accurately Momaday has captured her sense of the landscape in "Forms of the Earth at Abiquiu."

Adventures with Billy the Kid

The original manuscript of *The Gourd Dancer* includes, as its second part, a sequence of seventeen poems and four stories collected under the title "The Strange and True Story of My Life with Billy the Kid."[167] From this material Momaday selected only one poem, "The Wound," for the final volume.

Three other pieces, "Trees and Evening Sky," "Wide Empty Landscape with a Death in the Foreground," and "He Entered upon the Afternoon of His Last Day," appeared in an anthology of contemporary American Indian poetry, the latter poem under the title "But Then and There the Sun Bore Down."[168] None of these published poems reveals its original connection with the legend of Billy the Kid. Since they were initially conceived as parts of a sequence, however, they require examination against the background of the unpublished manuscript material.

A number of stories Momaday wrote for his *Viva* columns reveal further aspects of his treatment of the legend of Billy the Kid and bear witness to its importance in Momaday's work. In superimposing his imagination on one of the classic western heroes, Momaday deals, in a sense, with the oral tradition of the American frontier in much the same way as he explores imaginatively the oral tradition of his Kiowa ancestors. "The Strange and True Story of My Life with Billy the Kid" is therefore a good example of Momaday's bicultural orientation. That it seems incongruous with the work of an "Indian" writer may be why this area of Momaday's work has, by and large, gone unnoticed.

The legend of Billy the Kid figures prominently in Momaday's childhood fantasies. In the opening story of "The Strange and True Story of My Life with Billy the Kid" he writes: "Riding is an exercise of the mind. I dreamed a good deal on the back of my horse, going out into the hills alone."[169] In his imaginative flights he experiences such familiar frontier scenes as attacks on wagon trains and rescues of innocent people from the hands of villains. Not without irony is Momaday's following statement: "More than once I came upon roving bands of hostile Indians and had, on the spur of a moment, to put down an uprising."[170] Momaday adopts here, seemingly without the least conflict of allegiance, the perspective of the American frontier hero. He goes on to say that "after a time Billy the Kid was with me on most of those adventures. . . . He rode on my right and a couple of steps behind. I watched him out of the corner of my eye, for he bore watching. We got on well together in the main, and he was a good man to have along in a fight."[171] Two other pieces, "Billy the Kid, His Rocking Horse: A Lullaby" and "He Encounters a Player at Words" deal with the legend in the form of children's rhymes.[172]

Momaday experienced the presence of Billy the Kid so vividly that he referred to the pieces he wrote about him as autobiographical. In an interview with William T. Morgan, Jr., Momaday noted:

I grew up with Billy the Kid. I lived much of my life in New Mexico, which was his part of the world, and so I had heard stories about him all my life, and he excited my imagination. I appropriated him to my experience when I was growing up. . . . So this is a group of poems that bears upon his life, and upon my life, and the way in which those things come together in my imagination.[173]

In the second story of the sequence, "The Man in Black," Momaday elaborates on the beginning of his imaginative partnership with Billy the Kid and gives a detailed portrayal of him.[174] He describes him as a man of pure instinct, devoid of thought and emotion: "If a rational thought, or a whole emotion, had ever grown up inside of him, he should have suffered a great dislocation of himself in his mind and soul."[175] The shadow of death which lies upon him is reflected in a "certain sombreness, a touch of grief" as well as in his physical appearance: his skin is colorless; his protruding teeth resemble those of a skull; his eyes are without expression.[176]

Momaday draws here the familiar picture of Billy the Kid as a ruthless killer:

. . . his instincts were nearly infallible. Nothing should ever take him by surprise—and no one, except perhaps himself. Only one principle motivated him, that of survival—his own mean and exclusive survival. For him there was no morality in the universe but that, neither choice nor question. And for that reason he was among the deadliest creatures on the face of the earth.[177]

This stereotyped image is modified considerably in Momaday's other pieces where he speculates on the "true" nature of Billy the Kid.

In an imaginative dialogue published as "Cherish the Legend of Billy the Kid," Momaday's vision of Billy the Kid as "a kind of American literary and folk phenomenon" is articulated by a fictitious character: "I am not so much interested in the facts, but in the larger, legendary matter." Against the suggestion that the man was "an unscrupulous killer, a homicidal maniac," the persona argues: "I am talking about a legend. When I mentioned Billy the Kid, you formulate an idea of William Bonney, or Henry McCarty, or whatever his real name was. That man doesn't interest me in the least. I am interested in Billy the Kid." [178]

Momaday's strategy aims at filling the spaces between historical facts with imaginative speculation. He is not concerned with how it was, but how it might have been. The image of Billy the Kid as a basically good and honest youth corrupted by evil company is as ambiguous and narrow as the image of a mindless, instinctual killer. Momaday concluded that "the truth is not necessarily to be found in either of these directions. (Nor is it necessarily to be found at all.)" [179]

The third story of "The Strange and True Story of My Life with Billy the Kid" shows Billy as a congenial character who expresses his appreciation of the company of an old man by giving him a small present. [180] Billy's positive features of courtesy and chivalry are also central to his encounter with the nun Sister Blandina Segale. According to Momaday's fourth story, the woman had learned about Billy the Kid's plan to kill four men in Trinidad, Colorado. She met him in the room of a young man belonging to Billy's gang whom she had nursed after a shooting. Billy offered her any favor in gratitude for her attention to his friend. She asked him to spare the lives of the four men, which he did graciously.

They met again two months before Billy's death when she visited him in jail. His hands and feet were chained and he was fastened to the floor to prevent a repetition of his previous escapes. Billy's words, on her arrival, were an apologetic "I wish I could place a chair for you, Sister."[181] Momaday re-created this incident in a poem entitled "He Would Place a Chair for Sister Blandina":

> They had met at Trinidad,
> The nun and the renegade;
> They had measured each other
> And exchanged confidences.
> He was simply chivalrous,
> She thought; she prudent, he thought.
> Precisely, they got on well.
> And now, in her charity,
> After years, she comes to him
> At the jail in Santa Fé.
> There is nothing in his eyes;
> He is shackled, hand and foot.
> Still, he regards her. "I wish
> I could place a chair for you,
> Sister." And she regards him.
> Later she will weep for him.[182]

"The Wound" is perhaps the most unusual poem of Momaday's Billy the Kid sequence. The published version of *The Gourd Dancer* makes no mention of its connection to the legendary figure.[183] There the piece appears simply as a poetic depiction of a landscape. The context of the original manuscript, however, indicates that the poem's persona is Billy the Kid.[184] He is portrayed as an extremely sensitive, perceptive observer of the natural world, attuned to the beauty and vitality of the landscape. The second stanza suggests a degree of tenderness and affection toward creation which stands in sharp contrast to the idea of Billy the Kid as a mindless villain.

One external clue which corroborates that the poem is indeed a highly original depiction of a southwestern landscape appears in a short essay in which Momaday relates his journey to the Kiowa Gourd Dance ceremony in Oklahoma. He wrote: "The earth is red along the way. There are escarpments like great gaping flesh wounds in the earth. Erosion is an important principle of geography here, something deep in the character of the plains."[185] In "The Wound" the land appears as an organic entity which challenges the human imagination and creates a sense of belonging based on some unconscious life principle. The poem celebrates the raw, vital force which emanates from the spectacular landscape, the fascination of which lies not only in its superficial beauty but in the implicit violent forces which created it. The desire to kiss the wound suggests an instinctual impulse to tap the "irresistible force of being" which inheres in the land and thus to draw strength from the aboriginal soil.

The death of Billy the Kid has engaged Momaday's imagination more than any other single event in the hero's life. Billy's violent end stands in a peculiar relation to his seemingly immortal existence in legend. The strength and vividness of the legend cast doubt on the reality of Billy the Kid's death. Fiction seems to override reality. One example of this phenomenon is a story related to Momaday by an old man, Charlie Powers. Momaday refers to it in one of his columns: "Charlie knew Billy the Kid, so he says, and he assured me that Billy lived to a ripe old age in Mexico, under an assumed name. Pat Garrett was Billy's true friend, it seems, and it was he who engineered the Kid's escape on that fateful night in 1882 [sic]."[186]

A similar, perhaps even more telling suggestion of doubt about Billy the Kid's death appears in another column in which Momaday wrote: "Finally, did the four men really see Billy the Kid there on the floor at their feet, or were they possibly dreaming? Could it be that they, in some extraordinary concert of mind, imagined him there, dead?—or, indeed, could it be that these men were four more or less equal figments of Billy the Kid's imagination?"[187] These questions reveal Momaday's delight in dealing with legendary material: imagination has no boundaries; everything is possible; fiction and reality become indistinguishable.

Another facet of the relation between Billy the Kid's death and his legendary dimension is the way in which the anticipation of death affects a man who is conscious of his status as a living legend. Momaday probes this issue in two poems. In "Billy the Kid at Silver City" the protagonist's awareness of his dual existence as a living person and a legendary figure is heightened by his instinctual knowledge of impending death:

> Already, in the sultry streets,
> the mean quotient of suspicion
> settles at his crooked mouth, but
> just inside himself, he perceives,
> in the still landscape of legend,
> the cold of his dark destiny;
> already, in the sultry streets,
> he resembles himself in death. [188]

Given his prospect of immortality in American folklore, the fact of physical death seems to pose no threat to him. In "He Reckons Geologic Time According to His Sign," Momaday uses the image of a fossil fish to suggest the security of Billy the Kid's place in the oral tradition of the American West: "He reckons upon time, / And time is on his side. / His legend is secure; / He bodies resistance. / The fossil is himself, / His own indifference." [189]

The theme of Billy the Kid's foreknowledge of death is further explored in "Henry McCarty Witnesses His Mother's Marriage, 1 March 1873" and "He Foresees Disaster in a Dream." [190] In "Billy the Kid, the Departure of His Soul, 13/14 July 1881," Momaday seeks to re-create the desperado's moment of death:

> There where I watch you walk
> In quiet and in dark;
> To where your time has come
>   And you grow old
> In ignorance and vain;
>
> There where I hear the shot,
> In quiet and in dark,
> I think of what you think
>   And of the cold
> That fixes you in thought;

> There where you are not, yet,
> In quiet and in dark
> I imagine you there
> And you appear
> and are indefinite. [191]

The final stanza renders Billy's death as the point of transition from physical to legendary existence. The fact that he appears "indefinite" indicates that he has left the historical dimension and entered the realm of the imagination in which his being is open to an infinite number of interpretations.

In the published poems from the Billy the Kid cycle Momaday deals with "the still landscape of legend" referred to in "Billy the Kid at Silver City." [192] "Trees and Evening Sky" must be read in this context. The poem published as "But Then and There the Sun Bore Down" was originally entitled "He Entered upon the Afternoon of His Last Day," establishing the connection with Billy the Kid. [193] His looming death is here portrayed in terms of the landscape, a technique similarly employed in "Wide Empty Landscape with a Death in the Foreground," which concludes the Billy the Kid sequence. [194]

Billy the Kid's physical disintegration is depicted as a merging with the landscape. His spirit becomes inseparable from it. Since the physical and legendary landscape are identical, Billy the Kid's death does not result in annihilation: "Death displaces him / No more than life displaced him; / He was always here." As long as the stories of Billy the Kid and the landscape to which they refer prevail, his existence remains secure. The same is true of the Indian woman whose existence Momaday sustains in his story in *The Way to Rainy Mountain*. [195] The crucial point with respect not only to this poem but to the entire sequence is this: language and the oral tradition, whether in Anglo-American or native cultures, represent a dimension of immortality which rests on the human imagination.

Afterword

Any study of a living author must, by its very nature, remain open-ended. All it can hope to establish is the intellectual, cultural, biographical and literary framework of a writer's accomplishments against which his or her future work can be measured and judged. If my research can assist in a better understanding of N. Scott Momaday's published work and in the evaluative process of his future literary production, it will have achieved its aim.

By way of conclusion I shall attempt to guess at what we may find in Momaday's yet unpublished writings. On 25 January 1983, Momaday gave a reading to the Oxford Poetry Society. Among his material were a number of pieces which suggest the direction of his work in the near future. His epitaphs and epigraphs, which are humorous commentaries on the darker side of life, introduce a lighter note into his poetry. Momaday's concern with the oral tradition takes new shape in a group of poems which emulate Indian charms. These formulas, which were traditionally used to produce specific, practical results, are based on the belief in the magical power of words. In "Rings of Bone," Momaday returns to the Kiowa Gourd Dance which was the subject of "The Eagle-Feather Fan" and "The Gourd Dancer." "The Great Fillmore Street Buffalo Drive" grew out of his experience as an urban Indian in San Francisco. It conjures up the days of the buffalo and combines past and present in a moving poetic vision.

Momaday's recent fiction suggests a growing interchange between his work as a painter and as a writer of prose. The protagonist of his novel in progress, Catlin Set, is a painter. The
first part of his name is a reference to the important nineteenth-
century artist George Catlin, while Set is the Kiowa word for
bear. He is an Indian, lives in San Francisco, and docs not
know of his native origin. He has only a vague idea that he is
something other than a twentieth-century urban American.
His perception of himself takes a dramatic turn when he receives a telegram on the occasion of the death of an ancestor,
summoning him to Oklahoma. It reads: "The old woman Kop-
mah, the grandmother, is dying. She asks for you repeatedly.
Please come." Catlin Set does not know the old woman Kop-
mah. He knows that she is not his grandmother in the literal
sense of the word. But something about the telegram compels
him, and so he makes the trip. It results in the discovery that
he has a certain cultural experience, valuable in itself, which
opens a new dimension in his perception of self.

Momaday's work as a painter has recently expanded into the
medium of watercolor. His interest in Plains Indian shields,
which were the subject of a series of paintings in recent years,
is being pursued in the compilation of a major exhibit of
Plains, Apache, and Pueblo shields, due to go on show in one
or two years. Momaday's concern with the painter George Catlin may well produce a play in the near future. Catlin (1796–
1872) was one of the first persons to realize the impending
disintegration of traditional Indian life. His extensive travels
to nearly fifty tribes in the 1830s resulted in his "Indian Gal-
lery," one of the greatest artistic records of North American
aboriginal life.

Momaday's racial experience will remain the catalyst of his
future works. They will continue to contribute an important
aspect of American culture to literature and art. During his
reading at Oxford, Momaday noted: "We have not yet begun
to tap that great literary, or literary-like resource in our past.
But when we have put together a real collection of American

Indian oral tradition, we will have to change our idea of American literature, so rich is that tradition." Momaday's work will be a crucial factor in bringing about this broader view of literature and art in America.

Abbreviations

Where no source is given for an unpublished document, the original is in private hands. For the locations of other unpublished materials the following Library of Congress abbreviations are used:

CoFS	Colorado State University, Fort Collins
CLSU	University of Southern California, Los Angeles
CSt	Stanford University, Stanford, California
CU	University of California, Berkeley
MnU	University of Minnesota, Minneapolis
NmLcU	New Mexico State University, Las Cruces
NmU	University of New Mexico, Albuquerque

Notes

Introduction

1. Herbert Mitgang quotes Ellison in "Ralph Ellison," *International Herald Tribune*, 12 March 1982, p. 16.

2. The excerpt from this anonymous review in the *Chicago Tribune Book World* is reprinted on the dustcover of the paperback edition of Momaday's *The Names: A Memoir*.

3. Margaret F. Nelson, "Ethnic Identity in the Prose Works of N. Scott Momaday" (Ph.D. diss., Oklahoma State University, 1979), p. 13.

4. Ibid., p. 34.

5. Ibid., p. 13.

6. Wallace Stegner to author, 2 May 1981 and 14 April 1984.

7. Duane Niatum, "On Stereotype," *Parnassus* 7, no. 1 (1978): 161.

8. Saul Bellow, on the occasion of a lecture at Linacre College, Oxford, in 1981, rejected the label "urban Jewish writer" with the remark, "It's the zoologist who invents the name, not the animal." James Welch, who is of Blackfeet descent, disapproved of being called an Indian poet and novelist but accepted that it may have benefited him materially; see his "Tradition and Indian Poetry," *South Dakota Review* 11, no. 3 (1973): 39–40.

9. N. Scott Momaday, interview with Charles Woodard, Stanford, 19 November 1974.

10. N. Scott Momaday, "The Native Californian: Centennial Views of the American Indian," lecture to the Friends of the Bancroft Library, Berkeley, 1975 (CU).

11. Galen Buller, "New Interpretations of Native American Literature: A Survival Technique," *American Indian Culture and Research Journal* 4, nos. 1–2 (1980): 166.

12. N. Scott Momaday, "The American Indian: A Contemporary Acknowledgement," *Intellectual Digest* 2, no. 1 (1971): 12.

13. N. Scott Momaday, "Bringing on the Indian," *New York Review of Books*, 8 April 1971, p. 39.

14. Robert F. Berkhofer, Jr., *The White Man's Indian: Images of the American Indian from Columbus to the Present*, pp. 6–9; for this brief historical overview I rely on Berkhofer's study as well as on Roy Harvey Pearce, *Savagism and Civilization: A Study of the American Mind*, and Bernard Sheehan, *Savagism and Civility: Indians and Englishmen in Colonial Virginia*.

15. Berkhofer, *The White Man's Indian*, p. 55.

16. N. Scott Momaday, "The Morality of Indian Hating," *Ramparts* 3, no. 1 (1964): 37.

17. Berkhofer, *The White Man's Indian*, p. 30.

18. N. Scott Momaday, "A First American Views His Land," *National Geographic Magazine* 150, no. 1 (1979): 13–18; N. Scott Momaday, "Native American Attitudes to the Environment," in *Seeing with a Native Eye*, ed. Walter Holden Capps, pp. 79–85; N. Scott Momaday, "Learning from the Indian," *Viva*, 9 July 1972, p. 2.

19. Momaday, "The Morality of Indian Hating," p. 40.

20. Ibid., p. 38.

21. Momaday, quoted in Myra MacPherson, "American Indian, Pulitzer Prize Winner, Tells of Violent Plight," *Denver Post*, 8 December 1969.

22. N. Scott Momaday, "The Man Made of Words," in *Indian Voices: The First Convocation of American Indian Scholars*, ed. Rupert Costo, p. 70.

23. Martha Scott Trimble, *N. Scott Momaday*, p. 5.

24. Berkhofer, *The White Man's Indian*, p. 29.

25. Momaday, "Bringing on the Indian," p. 42.

26. Murray L. Wax, *Indian Americans: Unity and Diversity*, p. 173.

27. Momaday, "The Man Made of Words," p. 55.

28. Wallace Stegner to author, 2 May 1981.

29. Alfonso Ortiz, "A Unique American Legacy," *Princeton University Library Chronicle* 30 (1969): 156–57.

30. Leslie Fiedler, *The Return of the Vanishing American*, p. 10.

Chapter 1

1. N. Scott Momaday, *The Names: A Memoir*, pp. 41–42.

2. Martha Scott Trimble, *N. Scott Momaday*, p. 10.

3. Momaday, *The Names*, p. 42. Momaday's mother is one-eighth Cherokee; thus his degree of Indian blood is a little over one-half.

4. Wilcomb E. Washburn, *The Assault on Indian Tribalism: The General Allotment Law (Dawes Act) of 1887*.

5. Marion E. Gridley, ed., *Indians of Today*, 4th ed., p. 358.

6. Dorothy Dunn, *American Indian Paintings of the Southwest and Plains Area*, pp. 356–57.

7. Dorothy Dunn, "Al Momaday: An Artist and His Family," *New Mexico Magazine* 48, nos. 1–2 (1970): 37.

8. Momaday, *The Names*, p. 38.

9. Gridley, *Indians of Today*, p. 358.

10. Momaday, *The Names*, pp. 23–25.

11. Natachee Scott Momaday to author, 6 July 1981.

12. Momaday, *The Names*, p. 55.

13. Ibid., p. 42.

14. Ibid., p. 55.

15. Ibid., pp. 38–39.

16. N. Scott Momaday, quoted in Melissa Baumann, "Native American Storyteller and Poet: English Professor Shares His Heritage," *Stanford Daily*, 14 January 1975, p. 3.

17. Momaday, *The Names*, p. 84.

18. Natachee Scott Momaday's recollections, quoted by Peter Nabokov in an unpublished manuscript.

19. N. Scott Momaday, interview with author, Tucson, December 1981.

20. N. Scott Momaday, "Growing Up at Jemez Pueblo," *Viva*, 25 June 1972, p. 2.

21. Ibid.

22. Joe S. Sando, "Jemez Pueblo," in *Southwest*, ed. Alfonso Ortiz, vol. 9 of *Handbook of North American Indians*, ed. W. C. Sturtevant, p. 418.

23. N. Scott Momaday, "Revisiting the Family Home," *Viva*, 16 July 1972, p. 2.

24. Ibid.

25. N. Scott Momaday, "The Morality of Indian Hating," *Ramparts* 3, no. 1 (1964): 40.

26. Ibid.

27. Natachee Scott Momaday to author, 6 July 1981.

28. Marion F. Love, "N. Scott Momaday," *Santa Féan*, October 1980, p. 36.

29. N. Scott Momaday, "Graduation Brings Memories," *Viva*, 10 June 1973, p. 2.

30. Love, "N. Scott Momaday," p. 37.

31. Natachee Scott Momaday to author, 6 July 1981.

32. Dustcover of the paperback edition of *The Names: A Memoir*.

33. Lee Abbott, "An Interview with N. Scott Momaday," *Puerto Del Sol* 12, no. 2 (1973): 24.

34. Ibid., p. 30.

35. Ibid., p. 24.

36. N. Scott Momaday, "A Crucial Year at Dulce, and a Boy I Shall Call David," *Viva*, 18 February 1973, p. 2.

37. N. Scott Momaday, interview with author, Tucson, December 1981.

38. Trimble, *N. Scott Momaday*, p. 11.

39. N. Scott Momaday, interview with author, Tucson, December 1981.

40. Ibid.

41. N. Scott Momaday, "Praise So Dear," *Imprint of the Stanford Libraries Associates* 1, no. 2 (1975): 8–9.

42. James D. Hart, ed., *Oxford Companion to American Literature*.

43. N. Scott Momaday, interview with the author, Tucson, December 1981.

44. Ibid.

45. Yvor Winters, "Introduction to the Early Poems of Yvor Winters, 1920–1928," in his *The Collected Poems of Yvor Winters*, p. 12.

46. Constance Lindsay Skinner's "Summer Dawn (Tem-Eyos-Kwi)" is a dramatic poem about an Indian community's invocation of and encounter with a mythical female figure. "Kan-Il-Lak the Singer—To Nak-Ku" is a lyrical exchange between two lovers, rendered in terms of the mysterious immediacy of nature and the Indian belief in witchcraft, dreams, and an animated universe. *Poetry: A Magazine of Verse* 7 (1916): 169–74.

47. Contributions to *Poetry: A Magazine of Verse* 9 (1917) included Frank S. Gordon's chantlike sequence "Along the South Star Trail, Tribal Songs from the South-west," 221–31; Alice Corbin Henderson's "Indian Songs," 235–38; Mary Austin's "Neither Spirit Nor Bird, Shoshone Love Song" and "Prayer to the Mountain Spirit, from the Navajo," 239–41; and Constance Lindsay Skinner's "Spring to the Earth-Witch Pai-iya to Swi-ya Kwenewesals" and "Chief Capilano Greets His Namesake at Dawn," 244–46.

48. Carl Sandberg, "Editorial Comment, Aboriginal Poetry, II," *Poetry: A Magazine of Verse* 9 (1917): 255.

49. Winters, "Introduction to the Early Poems," p. 12.

50. Ibid., p. 13.

51. The first group of these pieces was published in *Poetry: A Magazine of Verse* 17 (1920): 142–47.

52. Alice Corbin Henderson, "Indian Songs," *Poetry: A Magazine of Verse* 9 (1917): 235–38; Alice Corbin Henderson, "A Note on Primitive Poetry," *Poetry: A Magazine of Verse* 14 (1919): 330–35; Alice Corbin Henderson, "Poetry of the North-American Indian," review of *Path on the Rainbow: An Anthology of Songs and Chants from the Indians of North America*, ed. George Cronyn, with an introduction by Mary Austin, *Poetry: A Magazine of Verse* 14 (1919): 41–42.

53. Henderson, "Poetry of the North-American Indian," p. 42.

54. Winters, "Introduction to the Early Poems," p. 12.

55. Yvor Winters, "The Indian in English," in *Yvor Winters: Uncollected Essays and Reviews*, ed. Francis Murphy, p. 36.

56. Ibid., p. 37.

57. Yvor Winters, "Open letter to the Editor of *This Quarterly* (Fall 1926)," in *Yvor Winters: Uncollected Essays and Reviews*, ed. Francis Murphy, p. 33.

58. Winters, "The Indian in English," p. 42; the poem Winters refers to is, curiously enough, a Navajo gambling song, not a creation of a Plains tribe, as he seems to suggest. "The Magpie! The Magpie! Here underneath / In the white of his wings are the footsteps of morning. / It dawns! It dawns!" This piece was collected by Washington Matthews and is reprinted, with an explication, in A. Grove Day, *The Sky Clears*, p. 96.

59. Yvor Winters, "The Magpie's Shadow," in *The Collected Poems of Yvor Winters*, pp. 31–34.

60. Day, *The Sky Clears*, p. v.

61. N. Scott Momaday, "The Man Who Took Literature Seriously," *Viva*, 2 September 1973, p. 2.

62. Ibid.

63. N. Scott Momaday, interview with Charles Woodard, Stanford, 19 November 1974.

64. N. Scott Momaday, "The Collected Poems of N. Scott Momaday" (M.A. thesis, Stanford University, 1960), p. 2. Momaday acknowledged his debt by adding "To Faulkner" to the title of the poem. This addition was deleted in later collections.

65. Momaday, "Praise So Dear," p. 9.

66. Yvor Winters, *Forms of Discovery: Critical and Historical Essays on the Form of the Short Poem in English*, p. 289.

67. Momaday, "The Collected Poems of N. Scott Momaday," p. 3 (CSt).

68. N. Scott Momaday, "The Influence of Edmund Wilson," *Viva*, 2 July 1972, p. 2.

69. N. Scott Momaday, ed., *The Complete Poems of Frederick Goddard Tuckerman*, p. v.

70. N. Scott Momaday, interview with author, Tucson, December 1981.

71. Momaday, "The Morality of Indian Hating," pp. 29–40; "The Well," *Ramparts* 2, no. 1 (1963): 49–52.

72. Wallace Stegner to author, 10 July 1981 and 14 April 1984.

73. For a detailed discussion of the relationship between "The Well" and *House Made of Dawn* see chapter 4 below.

74. N. Scott Momaday to Whitney Blake, 21 May 1965.

75. Yvor Winters to N. Scott Momaday, 2 June 1963.

76. Winters, *Forms of Discovery*, p. 368.

77. Yvor Winters to N. Scott Momaday, 23 July 1964.

78. Yvor Winters to N. Scott Momaday, 3 November 1966.

79. For a more detailed account of this crucial experience see chapter 5 below.

80. N. Scott Momaday, interview with author, Tucson, December 1981.

81. N. Scott Momaday, *The Journey of Tai-me*. I used the proof copy in the Rare Book Collection at the Library of Congress, Washington.

82. N. Scott Momaday to Orton Loring Clark, 11 March 1965.

83. Yvor Winters to N. Scott Momaday, 8 April 1964 and 5 December 1965.

84. N. Scott Momaday to Yvor Winters, 1 November 1966.

85. Announcement in the *Emily Dickinson Bulletin* 9 (June 1969; rev. November 1969): 2.

86. N. Scott Momaday to Whitney Blake, 23 June 1966 (CU).

87. For a detailed account of the novel's genesis and the circumstances of its unexpected rise to fame see chapter 4 below.

88. N. Scott Momaday, "Driving East for Kiowa Dancing," *Viva*, 23 July 1972, p. 2.

89. N. Scott Momaday, "A Vision beyond Time and Place," *Life*, July 1971, p. 67; N. Scott Momaday, "Bringing on the Indian," *New York Review of Books*, 8 April 1971, pp. 39–42.

90. N. Scott Momaday, "An American Land Ethic," in *Ecotactics: The Sierra Club Handbook For Environmental Activists*, ed. John G. Mitchell with Constance L. Stalling, pp. 97–105.

91. N. Scott Momaday, *Colorado: Summer, Fall, Winter, Spring*.

92. Ansel Adams and Mary Austin, *Taos Pueblo*; Ansel Adams, Nancy Newhall, et al., *This Is the American Earth*.

93. David Muench, "Light Is My Constant Companion and Tool . . . ," *Arizona Highways*, August 1981, p. 23.

94. Momaday, *Colorado*, pp. 6 and 100.

95. N. Scott Momaday, manuscript of *The Gourd Dancer*.

96. N. Scott Momaday, interview with author, Tucson, December 1981.

97. N. Scott Momaday, *The Gourd Dancer*, p. 54.

98. A description of these meetings and the story of Quincy Tahoma can be found in "The Isolation of Quincy Tahoma," *Viva*, 20 August 1972, p. 2.

99. N. Scott Momaday, interview with author, Tucson, December 1981.

100. Momaday, *The Gourd Dancer*, p. 55.

101. Momaday, *The Names*, p. 93.

102. N. Scott Momaday, interview with author, Tucson, December 1981.

103. Momaday, *The Gourd Dancer*, pp. 10, 34, and 52.

104. Momaday, "Praise So Dear," p. 6; N. Scott Momaday, *The Colors of Night*.

105. Momaday, *The Names*, leaf following the dedication page, and p. 69.

106. N. Scott Momaday, "The Pear-Shaped Legend: A Figment of the American Imagination," *Stanford Magazine* 3, no. 1 (1975): 46–47.

107. N. Scott Momaday, "Plainview: 2," *Puerto Del Sol* 12, no. 2 (1973): 39.

108. "Shouting at the Machine: An Interview with N. Scott Momaday," *Persona: The University of Arizona Undergraduate Magazine of Literature and Art* (Spring 1982): 24.

109. Anon. "Unique Exhibit of Family Talent," *Four Winds* 1, no. 3 (1980): 42.

110. N. Scott Momaday, "Tsoai and the Shield Maker," *Four Winds* 1, no. 3 (1980): 34–42.

111. Yvor Winters, *Forms of Discovery*, p. 277.

112. Yvor Winters to N. Scott Momaday, 15 July 1964.

113. Review of *The Names*, by N. Scott Momaday, *Choice* 14 (May 1977): 376.

114. N. Scott Momaday, "I Am Alive," in *The World of the American Indian*, ed. Jules B. Billard, pp. 11–26.

115. N. Scott Momaday, interview with author, Tucson, December 1981.

116. Yvor Winters to N. Scott Momaday, 21 April 1965.

Chapter 2

1. N. Scott Momaday, "The Man Made of Words," in *Indian Voices: The First Convocation of American Indian Scholars*, ed. Rupert Costo, pp. 49–62.

2. N. Scott Momaday, quoted in "American Indian Literature Major Will Be Established This Fall," *Journal of Educational Change* 2, no. 7 (1971): 2.

3. N. Scott Momaday, *House Made of Dawn*, p. 59.

4. N. Scott Momaday, *The Gourd Dancer*, p. 46; Gary Witherspoon, in his study of Navajo thought, noted that "a child does not acquire human status until he or she masters the art of speaking a language. It is clear from this that the Navajo considers speech . . . not only characteristic of, but necessary to, human life." *Language and Art in the Navajo Universe*, p. 53.

5. Momaday, "The Man Made of Words," p. 49.

6. Ibid.

7. Yvor Winters described languages as "forms of being and forms of discovery" and added that "it is in our language that we live the life of human beings, and only in our language." "Forms of Discovery: A Preliminary Statement," *Southern Review* n.s. 3 (1967): 1.

8. N. Scott Momaday, interview with author, Tucson, December 1981.

9. N. Scott Momaday, *The Names: A Memoir*, p. 154.

10. Ibid., p. 13.

11. Yvor Winters to N. Scott Momaday, 21 April 1965.

12. This crucial event is described in detail in the context of the genesis of *The Way to Rainy Mountain* in chapter 5.

13. N. Scott Momaday, "Discussion: The Man Made of Words," in *Indian Voices: The First Convocation of Indian Scholars*, ed. Rupert Costo. pp. 66–67.

14. N. Scott Momaday, interview with author, Tucson, December 1981.

15. N. Scott Momaday, "A Love Affair with Emily Dickinson," *Viva*, 6 August 1972, p. 2.

16. N. Scott Momaday, interview with author, Tucson, December 1981.

17. Ibid.

18. Wallace Stevens, "Men Made out of Words," in *The Collected Poems of Wallace Stevens*, pp. 355–56.

19. Wallace Stevens, "The Idea of Order at Key West," stanza 4, lines 17ff., in *Collected Poems*, pp. 129–30.

20. Wallace Stegner to Ronald Lane Latimer, 5 November 1935 and 15 November 1935; in *Letters of Wallace Stegner*, ed. Holly Stevens, p. 293.

21. N. Scott Momaday, interview with author, Tucson, December 1981.

22. N. Scott Momaday, Untitled column, *Viva*, 30 April 1972, p. 2.

23. Momaday, *The Names*, p. 128.

24. Momaday, "The Man Made of Words," p. 55.

25. Ibid., p. 56.

26. N. Scott Momaday, interview with author, Tucson, December 1981.

27. Stevens, *Collected Poems*, p. 25.

28. N. Scott Momaday, interview with author, Tucson, December 1981.

29. Momaday, *House Made of Dawn*, pp. 86–91; Momaday "The Man Made of Words," pp. 51–52.

30. See, for example, Ernst Cassirer, *Language and Myth*, trans. Susanne K. Langer, p. 45.

31. Momaday, *House Made of Dawn*, p. 85.

32. Ibid., p. 87.

33. Ibid., p. 89.

34. Ibid., p. 89.

35. Gary Witherspoon, *Language and Art in the Navajo Universe*, p. 9.

36. Leslie A. White, "The World of the Keresan Pueblo Indians," in *Primitive Views of the World*, ed. Stanley Diamond, p. 87.

37. Witherspoon, *Language and Art in the Navajo Universe*, p. 34.

38. N. Scott Momaday, "Twenty-six Years Ago on This Day," *Viva*, 19 November 1972, p. 2.

39. Momaday, *The Names*, page following the genealogical chart.

40. N. Scott Momaday, interview with author, Tucson, December 1981.

41. N. Scott Momaday, "At Best—A Minor Tragedy?" *Viva*, 6 May 1973, p. 24.

42. Momaday, "The Man Made of Words," p. 51.

43. Ibid.

44. Ibid., p. 52.

45. N. Scott Momaday, interview with author, Tucson, December 1981.

46. Momaday, "The Man Made of Words," p. 60.

47. While there is no conclusive evidence that Momaday has first-

hand knowledge of Proust's texts, he is undoubtedly familiar with Proust's literary theories by way of Edmund Wilson's *Axel's Castle*, which deals with the French symbolists and their influence on Yeats, Eliot, and Joyce. Momaday acknowledges Wilson's influence and considers himself one of the "literary beneficiaries . . . who in one way or another remained in Wilson's debt." "The Influence of Edmund Wilson," *Viva*, 2 July 1972, p. 2.

48. Marcel Proust, *Time Regained*, trans. Andreas Mayor, p. 234.

49. Ibid., p. 233.

50. Ibid., p. 262.

51. Ibid., p. 222.

52. Ibid., p. 451; Momaday makes the same point in his column "In Praise of Books since 868," *Viva*, 8 April 1973, p. 2.

53. Proust, *Time Regained*, p. 458.

54. N. Scott Momaday, "Letters: A Window to the Past," *Viva*, 15 April 1973, p. 2.

55. See, for example, "Briefly Noted," *New Yorker*, 17 May 1969, p. 152; Wayne Gard, "Review of Books: Southwestern Chronicle," *Southwest Review* 54, no. 3 (1969): and Dudley Wynn, "Book Review: *The Way to Rainy Mountain*," *New Mexico Historical Review* 45, no. 1 (1970): 89.

56. Momaday, *The Way to Rainy Mountain*, p. 4.

57. T. E. Sawyer, "Assimilation Versus Self-Identity: A Modern Native American Perspective," in *Contemporary Native American Address*, ed. John R. Maestas, p. 203.

58. Momaday, *The Way to Rainy Mountain*, p. 4.

59. Momaday, *The Gourd Dancer*, p. 30.

60. N. Scott Momaday to Yvor Winters, 3 January 1966.

61. N. Scott Momaday, "I Am Alive," in *The World of the American Indian*, ed. Jules B. Billard, p. 14.

62. Dennis Tedlock, "Toward a Restoration of the Word in the Modern World," *Alcheringa* 2, no. 2 (1976): 128; Walter J. Ong, *The Presence of the Word: Some Prolegomena for Cultural and Religious History*, pp. 22, 34, 41, 113; Ong argued that the word in an oral culture is not primarily a record but something that happens, an event in the world of sound through which the mind is enabled to related actuality to itself (p. 22).

63. Mircea Eliade, *The Sacred and the Profane: The Nature of Religion*, p. 14.

64. Ibid., p. 68.

65. Ibid., p. 68.

66. N. Scott Momaday, quoted in Chris Tucker, "Scott Momaday, Writing Little But Writing Well," *Dallas Morning News*, 8 November 1981, p. 5G.

67. N. Scott Momaday, *Remember My Horse*.

68. Momaday, *The Gourd Dancer*, pp. 36–37.

69. N. Scott Momaday, "Figments of Sancho Panza's Imagination," *Viva*, 31 December 1972, p. 2.

70. N. Scott Momaday, commencement address, Hobart and William Smith Colleges, Geneva, New York, 1 June 1980.

71. N. Scott Momaday, "Billy Offers a Kindness to an Old Man at Glorietta," *Viva*, 9 December 1973, p. 12.

72. Momaday, *The Way to Rainy Mountain*, p. 46; the story has also been published in the *New York Times Book Review*, 4 May 1969, p. 2.

73. Momaday, "The Man Made of Words," p. 60.

74. Ibid., pp. 61–62.

75. Ibid., p. 58.

76. René Wellek and Austin Warren, *Theory of Literature*, p. 47.

77. Ong, *The Presence of the Word*, p. 73.

78. Ruth Finnegan, *Oral Poetry: Its Nature, Significance and Social Context*, p. 24; see also Jan Vansina, *Oral Tradition: A Study in Historical Methodology*, p. 53.

79. Lawrence J. Evers, "A Conversation with N. Scott Momaday," *Sun Tracks* 2, no. 2 (1976): 21.

80. Yvor Winters to N. Scott Momaday, 30 July 1964.

81. Isak Dinesen, "The Great Gesture," in her *Shadows on the Grass*, pp. 90–91.

82. Isak Dinesen, *Out of Africa*, p. 104.

83. Ibid., p. 105.

84. Momaday, "The Man Made of Words," p. 56.

85. Ibid., p. 57.

86. Isak Dinesen, *Ehrengard*, p. 5.

87. Momaday quoted Vladimir Nabokov's statement in his commencement address, "Imagine Time, Place, Presence," University of New Mexico, 18 May 1975 (NmU); see "The Pear-Shaped Legend: A Figment of the American Imagination," *Stanford Magazine* 3, no. 1 (1975): 46, for another reference to Nabokov's *Speak Memory*. The quotation is from Nabokov's *Speak Memory: An Autobiography Revisited*, p. 137. In the same work Nabokov describes the reality of his imaginative experience in a way which clearly shows that it is of the same order as Proust's and Momaday's: "I felt myself plunged abruptly into a radiant and mobile medium that was none other than the pure element of time"

(p. 21); "A sense of security, of well-being, of summer warmth pervades my memory. That robust reality makes a ghost of the present" (p. 77).
88. Momaday, "The Man Made of Words," p. 56.

Chapter 3

1. N. Scott Momaday, *Colorado: Summer, Fall, Winter, Spring*, p. 34.

2. Ibid., p. 43.

3. N. Scott Momaday, "Eve My Mother, No," *Sequoia* 5, no. 1 (1959): 37.

4. N. Scott Momaday, "The Man Made of Words," in *Indian Voices*, ed. Rupert Costo, p. 53. See also N. Scott Momaday, "A First American Views His Land," *National Geographic Magazine* 150, no. 1 (1979): 13–18.

5. N. Scott Momaday, "An Idea of the Land as Sacred," typed manuscript (CU); N. Scott Momaday, "I Am Alive," in *The World of the American Indian*, ed. Jules B. Billard, pp. 11–26; N. Scott Momaday, "An Opportunity to Speak Out," *Viva*, 3 June 1973, p. 2; N. Scott Momaday, "Singing about the Beauty of the Earth," *Viva*, 4 June 1972, p. 2; N. Scott Momaday, "Learning from the Indian," *Viva*, 9 July 1972, p. 2; N. Scott Momaday, "Native American Attitudes toward the Environment," in *Seeing with a Native Eye*, ed. Walter Holden Capps, pp. 79–85.

6. Tom Bathi, *Southwestern Indian Ceremonials*, pp. 5 and 24; Edgar L. Hewett and Bertha P. Dutton, *The Pueblo Indian World*, p. 24.

7. Vine Deloria, *God Is Red*, pp. 166–67.

8. Paula Allan, "The Sacred Hoop: A Contemporary Indian Perspective on American Indian Literature," in *Literature of the American Indians*, ed. Abraham Chapman, p. 116.

9. Momaday, "Native American Attitudes to the Environment," p. 81.

10. N. Scott Momaday, "A Vision beyond Time and Place," *Life*, July 1971, p. 67.

11. Momaday, "Native American Attitudes to the Environment," pp. 80–81.

12. Ibid., p. 80; in "A First American Views His Land," Momaday dramatizes the evolution of a moral equation between man and nature.

13. Excellent studies of this tradition are Roderick Nash, *Wilderness and the American Mind*; Stewart Udall, *The Quiet Crisis*; and Lee Clark

Mitchell, *Witnesses to a Vanishing America: The Nineteenth-Century Response*.

14. Lawrence J. Evers, "A Conversation with N. Scott Momaday," *Sun Tracks* 2, no. 2 (1976): 19.

15. Momaday, *Colorado*, p. 30.

16. N. Scott Momaday, *The Names: A Memoir*, p. 19.

17. N. Scott Momaday, "Three Personalities, One Landscape," *Viva*, 10 December 1972, p. 2.

18. For two useful summaries of the "Indian-as-ecologist" discussion and its merits and distortions see Calvin Martin, "*Epilogue*: The Indian and the Ecology Movement," in his *Keepers of the Game: Indian-Animal Relationships and the Fur Trade*, pp. 157–88; and Christopher Vecsey, "American Indian Environmental Religions," in *American Indian Environments: Ecological Issues in Native American History*, ed. Christopher Vecsey and Robert W. Venables, pp. 1–37.

19. Terry Anderson, "Momaday's *Names* Told through Childhood's Impressionistic Eyes," *Denver Post*, 16 January 1977.

20. For an interesting comparison between *House Made of Dawn* and *The Sound and the Fury* see David Robinson, "Angles of Vision in N. Scott Momaday's *House Made of Dawn*," in *Essays on Minority Cultures: Selected Proceedings of the Annual Conference on Minority Studies*, ed. George E. Carter et al., II, 129–30.

21. Frederick L. Gwynn and Joseph L. Blotner, eds., *Faulkner in the University*, p. 47.

22. Momaday, *The Names*, p. 97.

23. Cleanth Brooks, *William Faulkner: The Yoknapatawpha Country*, p. 2.

24. William Faulkner, "Big Woods," in his *Big Woods*, n. p.

25. William Faulkner, *As I Lay Dying*, p. 38.

26. William Faulkner, *Light in August*, p. 254.

27. Lewis M. Dabney, *The Indians of Yoknapatawpha Country: A Study in Literature and History*, p. 156; Momaday's hunting story in *House Made of Dawn* was published separately as "The Bear and the Colt" in *American Indian Authors*, ed. Natachee Scott Momaday, pp. 119–24.

28. Isak Dinesen, *Out of Africa*.

29. N. Scott Momaday, "The Woman Who Knew Africa," *Viva*, 18 June 1972, p. 2.

30. Lee Abbott, "An Interview with N. Scott Momaday," *Puerto Del Sol* 12, no. 2 (1973): 30.

31. Momaday, "The Woman Who Knew Africa," p. 2.

32. "Five Stanford Authors Converse," *Stanford Alumni Almanac*, October 1971, p. 5.

33. Dinesen, *Out of Africa*, pp. 22, 377, 22.

34. Momaday, "I Am Alive," p. 23.

35. Dinesen, *Out of Africa*, p. 79.

36. N. Scott Momaday, "A Special Sense of Place," *Viva*, 7 May 1972, p. 2.

37. Dinesen, *Out of Africa*, p. 356; N. Scott Momaday, *The Way to Rainy Mountain*, p. 82.

38. N. Scott Momaday, "Finding a Need for Nature," *Viva*, 13 May 1973, p. 2.

39. John Muir, *The Mountains of California* p. 2; see also pp. 3, 4, 28, and 57, and his *My Summer in the Sierra*, pp. 113, 144, and 205, for examples of luminist descriptions.

40. Nash, *Wilderness and the American Mind*, p. 123.

41. Thomas J. Lyon, *John Muir*, pp. 18–19.

42. Henry David Thoreau, "Walking," in *Excursions and Poems*, vol. 5 of *The Writings of Henry David Thoreau*, p. 207.

43. Thoreau, "Walking," pp. 216, 224, 225.

44. N. Scott Momaday, "Reflections on the First Day of Class," *Viva*, 10 September 1972, p. 2.

45. Momaday, *The Names*, p. 6.

46. Ibid., p. 4.

47. Jonathan Edwards, *Basic Writings*, ed. Ola E. Winslow, p. 250.

48. Muir, *My First Summer in the Sierra*, p. 18.

49. Momaday, *The Names*, p. 6.

50. This term is attributed to John Eliot, as cited in George H. Williams, *Wilderness and Paradise in Christian Thought* (New York, 1962), p. 102.

51. Nash, *Wilderness and the American Mind*, p. 36.

52. Edwards, *Basic Writings*, p. 250.

53. Ibid., p. 251.

54. Ralph Waldo Emerson, "Nature," in *Nature, The Conduct of Life and Other Essays*, p. 4.

55. Thoreau, as quoted in Nash, *Wilderness and the American Mind*, p. 85.

56. Henry David Thoreau, *A Week on the Concord and Merrimack Rivers*, p. 237.

57. Emerson, "Nature," p. 33.

58. Frederick Goddard Tuckerman, *The Complete Poems of Frederick Goddard Tuckerman*, ed. N. Scott Momaday p. xxv.

59. Tuckerman, *The Complete Poems*, pp. xxv–xxvi.

60. Abbott, "Interview with N. Scott Momaday," p. 30.

61. See, for example, Tuckerman's "Sonnet XVIII" (Second Series), in *The Complete Poems*, p. 27.

62. See Yi-Fu Tuan, "Geopiety: A Theme in Man's Attachment to Nature and Place," in *Geographies of the Mind: Essays in Historical Geography*, ed. David Lowenthal and Martyn J. Bowden, pp. 11–39; Lynn White, Jr., "The Historical Roots of Our Ecological Crisis," *Science* 155 (1967): 1203–07; F. S. C. Northrop, "Man's Relation to the Earth in Its Bearing on His Aesthetic, Ethical, and Legal Values," in *Man's Role in Changing the Face of the Earth*, ed. W. L. Thomas, pp. 1052–67.

63. Momaday, "A Vision beyond Time and Place," p. 67.

64. Oswald Spengler, *The Decline of the West: Form and Actuality*, trans. Charles Francis Atkinson, p. 21.

65. Oswald Spengler, *The Decline of the West: Perspectives of World-History*, trans. Charles Francis Atkinson, p. 92.

66. D. H. Lawrence, "A Propos Lady Chatterley's Lover," in *Lady Chatterley's Lover*, ed. Ronald Friedland, p. 348.

67. D. H. Lawrence, "Introduction to Studies in Classic American Literature: I. The Spirit of Place," *English Review*, November 1918, p. 323.

68. Rose Marie Burwell's "A Catalogue of D. H. Lawrence's Reading from Early Childhood," *D. H. Lawrence Review* 3 (1970): 193–330, contains no reference to Spengler.

69. D. H. Lawrence to B. W. Huebsch, 30 September 1919, in *The Collected Letters of D. H. Lawrence* ed. Harry T. Moore, I, 595–96.

70. C. G. Jung, "The Role of the Unconscious," in his *Civilizations in Transition*, vol. 10 of *The Collected Works of Carl G. Jung*, trans. R. F. C. Hull, p. 13.

71. Jung, "Mind and Earth," *Collected Works*, 10, 46.

72. Jung, "Complications of American Psychology," *Collected Works*, 10, 510.

73. Ibid., p. 511.

74. Jung, "Mind and Earth," p. 49.

75. D. H. Lawrence, *The Symbolic Meaning: The Uncollected Versions of Studies in Classic American Literature*, ed. Armin Arnold, p. 80.

76. Stanley E. Hyman argued that Williams was influenced by Lawrence's *Studies in Classic American Literature* in writing his *In the American Grain*; see *The Armed Vision: A Study in the Methods of Modern Literary Criticism*, p.96.

77. Mary Austin, *The American Rhythm: Studies and Reexpressions of Amerindian Songs*, p. 56.

78. Ibid., p. 42.

79. William Carlos Williams, *In the American Grain*, pp. 116, 213, 212, 32, and 39.

80. Ibid., pp. 137–38.

81. Waldo Frank, *The Re-Discovery of America: An Introduction to a Philosophy of American Life*, p. 219.

82. Ibid., p. 229.

83. N. Scott Momaday, "To the Singing, to the Drum," in *Ants, Indians, and Little Dinosaurs*, ed. Alan Ternes, p. 251.

84. Lawrence, *The Symbolic Meaning*, p. 16.

85. N. Scott Momaday, "The Land Inspired the Artist," review of *American Indian Painting of the Southwest and Plains Area*, by Dorothy Dunn, *New York Times Book Review*, 28 July 1968, pp. 6–7.

86. Lawrence, *The Symbolic Meaning*, p. 20.

87. Momaday, *Colorado*, p. 51.

88. See her painting "The Lawrence Tree" in Georgia O'Keeffe, *Georgia O'Keeffe*, n. p.

89. D. H. Lawrence, "Pan in America," in *Phoenix*, ed. Edward D. McDonald, p. 25.

90. N. Scott Momaday, interview with author, Tucson, December 1981; Momaday was a participant in the 1970 D. H. Lawrence Festival; see L. D. Clark, "The D. H. Lawrence Festival: Kiowa Ranch, New Mexico September 30–October 4, 1970," *D. H. Lawrence Review* 4 (1971); photographs on pp. 50 and 54 show Momaday during a panel discussion and with Emile Delavenay and David Garnett, Lawrence's publisher.

91. D. H. Lawrence, "The Princess," "The Woman Who Rode Away," and "Sun," in his *The Complete Short Stories*, II 473–512, 546–581, and 528–545; "St. Mawr," in *St. Mawr and The Man Who Died*, pp. 3–159.

92. Lawrence, "The Princess," p. 477.

93. Ibid., p. 503.

94. Ibid., p. 512.

95. Lawrence, "St. Mawr," p. 50.

96. Ibid., p. 128.

97. Ibid., p. 137.

98. Ibid., p. 139.

99. Ibid., pp. 158–59.

100. Lawrence, "Sun," p. 538.

101. Ibid., p. 545.

102. N. Scott Momaday, *House Made of Dawn*, p. 36.

103. Ibid.

104. Ibid., p. 34.

105. Ibid., p. 62.

106. Ibid., p. 68.

107. Lawrence, "The Princess," p. 496.

108. Momaday, *House Made of Dawn*, p. 70.

109. Ibid., p. 71.

Chapter 4

1. John Hohenberg, *The Pulitzer Prizes*, p. 320; Henry Raymond, "Award Surprises an Indian Author," *New York Times*, 6 May 1969, p. 35.

2. Hohenberg, *The Pulitzer Prizes*, p. 320.

3. Wallace Stegner and Richard Snowcroft, eds. *Twenty Years of Stanford Short Stories*.

4. N. Scott Momaday, "The Well," *Ramparts* 2, no. 1 (1963): 49–52.

5. Ibid., p. 49.

6. Ibid., p. 50.

7. N. Scott Momaday, *House Made of Dawn*, p. 28; all subsequent references are to the 1969 Signet edition and appear parenthetically in the text. I have chosen the Signet paperback, which is identical to the Perennial paperback, because it is more readily available than the hardcover edition.

8. Momaday, "The Well," p. 50.

9. Frances McCullough to N. Scott Momaday, 14 February 1966. All correspondence between McCullough and Momaday cited below are in CU.

10. N. Scott Momaday to Frances McCullough, 21 February 1966.

11. Frances McCullough to N. Scott Momaday, undated.

12. Frances McCullough to N. Scott Momaday, 3 November 1966.

13. Frances McCullough to N. Scott Momaday, 10 August 1966 and 22 August 1966. In an earlier version of the novel, "Three Sketches from *House Made of Dawn*," published in the *Southern Review* n.s. 2 (1966), Angela appears with her mother and her brother, the priest Fr. Bothene (Fr. Olguin in the final version). Apparently on McCullough's advice Momaday removed the character of Mrs. Bothene and abandoned the idea of a family tie between the priest and Angela. A fragment of this early draft of *House Made of Dawn* can be found in Momaday's *Viva* column, "Cryptic Tale from Past," 1 April 1973, p. 7. It contains a conversation between Fr. Raoul Bothene, "a man of the cloth" not to be trusted, Ellen Bothene, the widowed mother, and Angela, about the family's wealth and tradition.

14. Frances McCullough to N. Scott Momaday, 23 May 1967.

15. Ibid.

16. "Brief Description," attached to a letter from Frances Mc-Cullough to N. Scott Momaday, 4 December 1967.

17. N. Scott Momaday to Frances McCullough, 8 December 1967 (CU).

18. See, for example, review of *House Made of Dawn*, by N. Scott Momaday, *Amerindian* 17, no. 1 (1968): 8; John Z. Bennett, review of *House Made of Dawn*, by N. Scott Momaday, *Western American Literature* 5 (1970): 69; Sara Blackburn, "Book Marks," *Nation*, 5 August 1968, p. 91; Charles Dollen, review of *House Made of Dawn*, by N. Scott Momaday, *Best Sellers*, 15 June 1968, p. 131; Jay L. Halio, "Fantasy and Fiction," *Southern Review* n.s. 7 (1971): 635.

19. Kenneth Graham, "Wind and Shadow," *Listener*, 15 May 1969, p. 686.

20. P. L. Adams, "Short Reviews: Books," *Atlantic Monthly*, July 1968, p. 106.

21. Joseph Illick, "Looking Westward," *American West*, November 1969, pp. 50–52.

22. See, for example, Charles R. Larson's reading of *House Made of Dawn* in his *American Indian Fiction*, pp. 78ff.; and Floyd C. Watkins's "Culture Versus Anonymity in *House Made of Dawn*," in his *In Time and Place*, pp. 131ff.

23. William J. Smith, review of *House Made of Dawn*, by N. Scott Momaday, *Commonweal*, 10 September 1968, p. 636.

24. Ibid.

25. Mary Borg, "Victims," *New Statesman*, 16 May 1969, p. 696.

26. Ibid.

27. "Exhibition," *Times (London) Literary Supplement*, 28 May 1969, p. 549.

28. John Leonard, "The Pulitzer Prizes: Fail-Safe Again," *New York Times Book Review*, 14 May 1972, p. 47.

29. N. Scott Momaday, interview with students at New Mexico State University, Las Cruces, 1973 (NmLcU).

30. N. Scott Momaday, "A Pyre of Moments, Peculiarly Mine," *Viva*, 14 January 1973, p. 2; see also *The Names*, p. 119.

31. N. Scott Momaday, interview with Charles Woodard, Stanford, 20 November 1974.

32. Ibid.

33. John Adair, "The Navajo and Pueblo Veterans: A Force for Culture Change," *American Indian* 4, no. 1 (1947): 5–11; and Evon Z. Vogt, "Between Two Worlds: Case Study of the Navajo Veteran," *American Indian* 5, no. 1 (1949): 13–21.

34. N. Scott Momaday, "The Man Made of Words," in *Indian Voices*, ed. Rupert Costo, p. 55.

35. N. Scott Momaday, quoted in Margaret Cooley, "Alien in a Mass Culture," *Library Journal*, 1 June 1968, p. 2271.

36. N. Scott Momaday, "American Indians in the Conflict of Tribalism and Modern Society," lecture at Colorado State University, Fort Collins, 31 January 1971 (CoFS).

37. N. Scott Momaday, summary on the dustjacket of the first edition of *House Made of Dawn*.

38. Momaday, "American Indians in the Conflict of Tribalism and Modern Society."

39. N. Scott Momaday to Frances McCullough, 6 July 1966 (CU).

40. Tom Bathi, *Southwestern Indian Tribes*, p. 11; according to the *Handbook of the American Indian*, ed. Frederick Webb Hodge, I, 630, the name means "village of the bear."

41. For a novel depicting the generation conflict in a Pueblo community see Frank Waters, *The Man Who Killed the Deer*.

42. Robert F. Spencer et al., *The Native Americans* p. 526.

43. Thomas Weaver and Ruth H. Gartell, "The Urban Indian: Man of Two Worlds," in *Indians of Arizona: A Contemporary Perspective*, ed. Thomas Weaver, p. 81.

44. Tom Bathi, *Southwestern Indian Ceremonials*, p. 43.

45. Bertha P. Dutton, *Indians of the American Southwest*, p. 7.

46. Harold E. Driver, *Indians of North America*, p. 205.

47. Alfonso Ortiz, *The Tewa World: Space, Time, Being, and Becoming in a Pueblo Society*, p. 109; James Mooney, *The Ghost Dance Religion and the Sioux Outbreak of 1890*, p. 243.

48. Gretchen Bataille, "An Interview with N. Scott Momaday—April 16, 1977," *Iowa English Bulletin* 29, no. 1 (1979): 30; see also Momaday's personal account of a captured eagle at Jemez in *The Names*, p. 147: "In North Street, near Turquoise Kiva, there was kept a golden eagle in a cage. Always, in passing, I spoke to it; and then, for a long moment, it held me fast in its regard, which was like doom. There was much shame between us, at the wire."

49. Watkins, *In Time and Place*, p. 138.

50. Calvin Martin, *Keepers of the Game: Indian-Animal Relationships and the Fur Trade*, p. 186.

51. John Witthoft, quoted in Martin, *Keepers of the Game*, p. 115.

52. Waters, *The Man Who Killed the Deer*, p. 36; see also Barre Toelken, "Seeing with a Native Eye: How Many Sheep Will It Hold?" in *Seeing with a Native Eye: Essays on Native American Religion*, ed. Walter Holden Capps, p. 14.

53. Spencer, *The Native Americans*, p. 532.

54. Momaday indicated that Abel was born in 1920; see "American Indians in the Conflict of Tribalism and Modern Society," lecture at Colorado State University, Fort Collins, 31 January 1971.

55. Erik Erikson, *Identity: Youth and Crisis*, p. 87. The use of Erikson's work seems particularly appropriate because of his research into the problems of identity among American Indian peoples. See, for example, "Childhood in Two American Indian Tribes," in his *Childhood and Society*, pp. 99–168.

56. Erikson, *Identity*, p. 309.

57. Mircea Ediade, *The Sacred and the Profane: The Nature of Religion*, pp. 27–28.

58. Bathi, *Southwestern Indian Ceremonials*, p. 53.

59. In a letter to Yvor Winters (15 November 1966), Momaday pointed out that he had seen the ceremony "several times" and that his observations differed in some ways from those of Elsie Clew Parsons, who witnessed it in the early twenties. Momaday adopted the name "corre de gaio" from Parsons's description in her *The Pueblo of Jemez*, p. 95.

60. N. Scott Momaday, *The Names*, p. 145.

61. Alfonso Ortiz, "Ritual Drama and the Pueblo World View," in *New Perspectives on the Pueblos*, ed. Alfonso Ortiz, p. 151.

62. Lawrence J. Evers, "Words and Place: A Reading of *House Made of Dawn*," *Western American Literature* 11 (1977): 309.

63. Margot Astrov, *North American Indian Prose and Poetry*, p. 19.

64. Erikson, *Identity*, pp. 135–36.

65. For a discussion of this stereotype see Shirley H. Witt, "Listen to His Many Voices: An Introduction to the Literature of the American Indian," in *The Way*, ed. Shirley H. Witt and Stan Steiner, p. xvii.

66. Although my examination of the relationship between Abel and Angela centers on Abel's shortcomings, I am aware that Angela carries part of the responsibility for the failure of the relationship. For two excellent examinations of her role in the novel see Marion Willard Hylton, "On a Trail of Pollen: Momaday's *House Made of Dawn*," *Critique* 14 (1972): 60–69; and Harold S. McAllister, "Incarnate Grace and the Path of Salvation in *House Made of Dawn*," *South Dakota Review* 12 (1974): 115–25. The two articles are diametrically opposed in their view of Angela as a villain and a saint.

67. Frederick Hodge, ed., *Handbook of the American Indians*, II, 965.

68. Clyde Kluckhohn, *Navaho Witchcraft*, p. 109.

69. Ibid., p. 5.

70. The killing of the albino is modeled on an incident at Jemez in 1958, in which one Jemez man killed another who had threatened to "turn himself into a snake and bite." The attorney dealing with the case noted that it raised "interesting questions about the law of self-defence." See the *Albuquerque Journal*, 7 and 9 December 1958 and 21 February 1959.

71. Kluckhohn, *Navaho Witchcraft*, p. 98.

72. "Shouting at the Machine: An Interview with N. Scott Momaday," *Persona: The University of Arizona Undergraduate Magazine of Literature and Art*, Spring 1982, p. 34.

73. Evers, "Words and Place: A Reading of *House Made of Dawn*," p. 309.

74. Kluckhohn, *Navaho Witchcraft*, p. 98.

75. Momaday, quoted by Watkins, *In Time and Place*, p. 141.

76. See Charles Woodard's interview with Momaday, Stanford, 20 November 1974, in which Momaday acknowledged a Melvillean element in the albino. Alan R. Velie, who supervised Woodard's research, reiterated the connection to Melville in his article "Cain and Abel in N. Scott Momaday's *House Made of Dawn*," *Journal of the West* 17 (1978): 58–59.

77. N. Scott Momaday, interview with author, Tucson, December 1981.

78. Herman Melville, *Billy Budd, Sailor, and Other Stories* pp. 354 and 377.

79. N. Scott Momaday, interview with author, Tucson, December 1981. See also Momaday's reference to Camus in "Finding a Need for Nature," *Viva*, 13 May 1973, p. 2.

80. Albert Camus, *The Outsider*, trans. Stuart Gilbert, p. 99.

81. Ibid.

82. Eliade, *The Sacred and the Profane*, pp. 189–90.

83. Ibid., p. 189.

84. Ibid., p. 190.

85. Mircea Eliade, *Patterns in Comparative Religion*, trans. Rosemary Sheed, p. 188.

86. Ibid.

87. James Frazer, quoted by Eliade, *The Sacred and the Profane*, p. 174.

88. Eliade, *Patterns in Comparative Religion*, p. 176.

89. Eddie W. Wilson, "The Moon and the American Indian," *Western Folklore* 24, no. 2 (1965): 88.

90. Ibid., p. 91.

91. Eliade, *Patterns in Comparative Religion*, p. 428.

92. Dutton, *Indians of the American Southwest*, p. 5.

93. Edgar L. Hewett and Bertha P. Dutton, *The Pueblo Indian World*, p. 23.

94. Eliade, *Patterns in Comparative Religion*, p. 184.

95. John Skinner, "On Indian Poetry and Religion," *Little Square Review*, nos. 5–6 (1968): 10.

96. Bataille, "An Interview with N. Scott Momaday—April 16, 1977," p. 30.

97. Franchot Ballinger, "The Responsible Center: Man and Nature in Pueblo and Navaho Ritual Songs and Prayers," *American Quarterly* 30 (1978): 92.

98. Barbara Strelke, "N. Scott Momaday: Racial Memory and Individual Imagination," in *Literature of the American Indians*, ed. Abraham Chapman, p. 352.

99. Gladys A. Reichard, *Navaho Religion: A Study in Symbolism*, p. 288.

100. Paula Allan, "The Sacred Hoop: A Contemporary Indian Perspective on American Indian Literature," in *Literature of the American Indians*, ed. Abraham Chapman, p. 117.

101. Reichard, *Navaho Religion*, p. 34.

102. Ibid.

103. Ibid.

104. Bathi, *Southwestern Indian Ceremonials*, pp. 5, 16, 27, 37.

105. Hartley Burr Alexander, *The World's Rim: Great Mysteries of the North American Indians*, pp. 15 and 17.

106. The first sentence of this passage refers not to the mythical emergence of the tribe from an underground world but to its migration from the north. Momaday described a stretch of the Kiowa migration route: ". . . the highland meadows are a stairway to the plain," *The Way to Rainy Mountain* p. 7.

107. Lee Abbott, "An Interview with N. Scott Momaday," *Puerto Del Sol* 12, no. 1 (1973): 33.

108. Bataille, "An Interview with N. Scott Momaday—April 16, 1977," p. 30.

109. N. Scott Momaday, "The Morality of Indian Hating," *Ramparts* 3, no. 1 (1964): 40.

110. Richard Erdoes, *The Rain Dance People*, p. 2.

Chapter 5

1. Yvor Winters, *Forms of Discovery*, p. xix, quoted by Momaday in "The Man Who Took Literature Seriously," *Viva*, 2 September 1973, p. 2.

2. Yvor Winters, "Forms of Discovery: A Preliminary Statement," *Southern Review* n.s. 3 (1967): 4.

3. Momaday, quoted by Peter Nabokov in an unpublished biographical essay, typescript p. 7; a copy is in the possession of the author.

4. N. Scott Momaday, interview with author, Tucson, December 1981.

5. N. Scott Momaday, interview with students at New Mexico State University, Las Cruces, 1973 (NmLcU).

6. N. Scott Momaday, "The American Indian in the Conflict of Tribalism and Modern Society," lecture at Colorado State University, Fort Collins, 31 January 1971 (CoFS).

7. N. Scott Momaday, interview with students at New Mexico State University, Las Cruces, 1973; see also Lee Abbott, "An Interview with N. Scott Momaday," *Puerto Del Sol* 12, no. 2 (1973): 22.

8. Manuscript material of *The Way to Rainy Mountain*—Notes and Fragments (CU).

9. Wilbur S. Nye, *Bad Medicine and Good: Tales of the Kiowas*, p. 141.

10. Momaday, quoted by Nabokov, pp. 7 and 8.

11. For a closer discussion of this experience see chapter 2.

12. N. Scott Momaday, "The Morality of Indian Hating," *Ramparts* 3, no. 1 (1964): 33, 34, and 36; the two stories have been published as sections X and XIX of *The Way to Rainy Mountain*.

13. Yvor Winters to N. Scott Momaday, 15 July 1964.

14. Yvor Winters to N. Scott Momaday, 23 July 1964.

15. Henry Raymond, "A Novelist Fights for His People's Lore," *New York Times*, 26 July 1969, p. 22.

16. N. Scott Momaday to Yvor Winters, 3 January 1966.

17. Al Momaday to N. Scott Momaday, 19 April 1968; the letter is among N. Scott Momaday's correspondence with Gus Blaisdell (CU).

18. N. Scott Momaday, quoted by Dale Rodebaugh in "Indians Keep Identity in Cultural Migration," *San José News*, 10 March 1977.

19. James Mooney, *Calendar History of the Kiowa Indians*; Mildred Mayhall, *The Kiowas*; Alice Marriott, *The Ten Grandmothers* and *Saynday's People: The Kiowa Indians and the Stories They Told*; Wilbur Sturtevant Nye, *Carbine and Lance: The Story of Old Fort Sill* and *Bad Medicine and Good: Tales of the Kiowas*.

20. N. Scott Momaday to Whitney Blake, 5 April 1965 (CU).

21. N. Scott Momaday, *The Journey of Tai-me*; the book was handprinted at the University of California, Santa Barbara, in an edition of one hundred leather-bound copies. The type is twelve point Monotype Baskerville on handmade paper. The typography is the work of D. E. Carlsen. Interspersed with the stories are six prints by Bruce S. Mc-

Curdy which depict the plains landscape. The format of the edition is folio in sixes, unpaginated. The dedication on A2r is "To the Old Woman Ko-Sahn." I used the proof copy Momaday deposited in the Library of Congress in 1971.

22. N. Scott Momaday, "Kiowa Legends from *The Journey of Tai-me,*" *Sun Tracks* 3, no. 1 (1976): 6–8.

23. Yvor Winters to N. Scott Momaday, 21 April 1965; the "crucifixion piece" is Momaday's poem "Before an Old Painting of the Crucifixion."

24. N. Scott Momaday, "The Way to Rainy Mountain," *Reporter*, 26 January 1967, pp. 41–44; this piece, with few modifications, appears in chapter 2 of *House Made of Dawn* and as the introduction to *The Way to Rainy Mountain.*

25. Yvor Winters, letter to editors, *Reporter*, 23 February 1967, p. 8.

26. N. Scott Momaday, *The Way to Rainy Mountain*, n. p.; all subsequent references are to 1976 University of New Mexico Press edition and appear parenthetically in the text.

27. N. Scott Momaday, quoted by Ken Sekaquaptewa, "N. Scott Momaday Visits B.Y.U.," *The Eagle's Eye*, Brigham Young University, February 1975, p. 1.

28. Ibid.

29. From the 1970 Ballantine edition of *The Way to Rainy Mountain.*

30. William T. Morgan, Jr., "Landscapes: N. Scott Momaday," *Sequoia* 19, no. 2 (1975): 44.

31. Yi-Fu Tuan borrowed the term "geopiety" from J. K. Wright's "Notes on Early American Geopiety," *Human Nature in Geography* (Cambridge, Mass.: Harvard University Press, 1966), p. 251. He describes it as covering "a broad range of emotional bonds between man and his terrestrial home—reverence, piety, compassion, affection, propitiation." See "Geopiety: A Theme in Man's Attachment to Nature and to Place," in *Geographies of the Mind: Essays in Historical Geosophy*, ed. David Lowenthal and Martyn J. Bowden, p. 12.

32. Morgan, "Landscapes," p. 39; see also Momaday, *The Way to Rainy Mountain*, p. 83, and "The Man Made of Words," in *Indian Voices*, ed. Rupert Costo, p. 53.

33. N. Scott Momaday, "Native American Attitudes to the Environment," in *Seeing with a Native Eye*, ed. Walter Holden Capps, p. 81; see also Morgan, "Landscapes," p. 39.

34. Momaday, "The Man Made of Words," p. 54.

35. Wallace Stevens, "Examination of the Hero in a Time of War," stanza III, in *The Collected Poems of Wallace Stevens*, p. 274.

36. Wallace Stevens, *The Necessary Angel: Essays on Reality and the Imagination*, p. 65.

37. Momaday, "Native American Attitudes to the Environment," p. 81; Stevens, *Collected Poems*, p. 401.

38. Jan Vansina, *Oral Tradition: A Study in Historical Methodology*, p. 38.

39. Tuan, "Geopiety," p. 33.

40. Yi-Fu Tuan, "Place: An Existential Perspective," *Geographical Review* 65, no. 2 (1975): 164.

41. Stevens, *Collected Poems*, p. 413.

42. Frederick Goddard Tuckerman, *The Complete Poems of Frederick Goddard Tuckerman*, ed. N. Scott Momaday, p. 26.

43. N. Scott Momaday, "An Edition of the Complete Poems of Frederick Goddard Tuckerman," (Ph.D. diss., Stanford University 1963), p. 47.

44. Tuckerman, *Complete Poems*, p. 27.

45. Ibid.

46. Mick McAllister, "The Topography of Remembrance in *The Way to Rainy Mountain*," *Denver Quarterly* 12, no. 4 (1978): 25.

47. N. Scott Momaday to Gus Blaisdell, 10 November 1968 (CU).

48. Momaday, "Poems of Frederick Goddard Tuckerman," p. 41.

49. Ibid., p. 42.

50. H. and H. A. Frankfort, "Myth and Reality," in *The Intellectual Adventure of Ancient Man: An Essay on Speculative Thought in the Ancient Near East*, ed. H. Frankfort et al., p. 3.

51. Ibid., p. 5.

52. Robert Redfield, *The Primitive World and Its Transformation*, p. 105.

53. Ibid., p. 105; see also his "The Primitive World View," *Proceedings of the American Philosophical Society* 96, no. 1 (1952): 34.

54. Redfield, *The Primitive World and Its Transformation*, p. 106.

55. Momaday, *The Way to Rainy Mountain*—Notes and Fragments (CU).

56. Mooney, *Calendar History of the Kiowa Indians*, particularly pp. 148–49, 402, 413, and 425.

57. A version of the story about "The Udder Angry Travellers Off" can be found in John P. Harrington, *Vocabulary of the Kiowa Language*, pp. 252–53.

58. Mooney, *Calendar History of the Kiowa Indians*, pp. 154 and 287–88.

59. Ibid., p. 238.

60. Gretchen Bataille, "An Interview with N. Scott Momaday—April 16, 1977," *Iowa English Bulletin* 29, no. 1 (1979): 29.

61. Momaday, "The Morality of Indian Hating," p. 34.

62. Ibid., p. 36.

63. Mooney, *Calendar History of the Kiowa Indians*, p. 239.

64. N. Scott Momaday, interview with author, Tucson, December 1981.

65. I rely for this reading on Robert L. Berner's article "N. Scott Momaday: Beyond Rainy Mountain," *American Indian Culture and Research Journal* 3, no. 1 (1979): 60.

66. Mooney, *Calendar History of the Kiowa Indians*, p. 239.

67. For a good interpretation of the function of language in these stories see Roland Garrett, "The Notion of Language in Some Kiowa Folktales," *Indian Historian* 5, no. 2 (1972): 32–37 and 42.

68. Nye, *Bad Medicine and Good: Tales of the Kiowas*, p. ix.

69. Section XIV, 2 is a gloss of a description by Mildred Mayhall, who wrote: "At times the Plains are still and quiet; at times, sudden, violent, ominous with weather and temperature changes. Almost always the wind blows," *The Kiowas*, p. ix.

70. Among the manuscript material of *The Way to Rainy Mountain* (CU) is this excerpt from E. Douglas Branch, *The Hunting of the Buffalo*, p. 233, which may have inspired Momaday's piece: "And it is only thirty years ago that a band of Indians, in the spring, saddled their ponies and rode away—as of old, but in silence and sadness. 'Where are you bound?' some white man asked; and they answered, 'For the buffalo.' 'But there are no more.' 'No, we know it.' 'Then why are you going on such a foolish chase?' 'Oh, we always go at this time; maybe we shall find some.'"

71. Mayhall, *The Kiowas*, p. 108.

72. Mooney, *Calendar History of the Kiowa Indians*, p. 310.

73. N. Scott Momaday, "A First American Views His Land," *National Geographic Magazine* 150, no. 1 (1976): 16.

74. Ibid., p. 16.

75. See Momaday's "The Man Made of Words," pp. 51–52; his visionary experience with Ko-sahn and its impact on his perception of language has been discussed in chapter 2.

Chapter 6

1. N. Scott Momaday, *Colorado: Summer, Fall, Winter, Spring*, p. 30.

2. N. Scott Momaday to Yvor Winters, 4 January 1968.

3. Yvor Winters to N. Scott Momaday, 8 July 1966.

4. Yvor Winters to N. Scott Momaday, 30 July 1964; Isak Dinesen, *Out of Africa*; all subsequent references are to the 1972 Vintage Books edition and appear parenthetically in the text.

5. Some aspects of the common ground Momaday and Dinesen hold with regard to the man-land relationship have been examined in chapter 3.

6. N. Scott Momaday, interview with author, Tucson, December 1981; see also Frances McCullough's letter to Momaday, 12 July 1969, in which she comments on Momaday's reference to *Out of Africa*.

7. N. Scott Momaday, *The Names: A Memoir*, p. 120; all subsequent references are to the 1977 Harper edition and appear parenthetically in the text.

8. Cf. Dinesen's *Out of Africa*, p. 4.

9. Isak Dinesen, *Shadows on the Grass*, p. 144.

10. See particularly Momaday's interview with students at New Mexico State University, Las Cruces, 1973 (NmLcU).

11. Dinesen, *Shadows on the Grass*, p. 18.

12. An early example of this image appears in Momaday's *Colorado*, p. 12, where he ends his description of tribal migrations, wars, and trading expeditions: ". . . inherent in this motion, as yet indigenous, was a prophetic shadow on the grass, a wind in advance of change, change absolute and unimaginable."

13. Momaday makes the same point in an earlier passage where he writes: "I existed in that landscape at Jemez, and then my existence was indivisible with it. I placed my shadow there in the hills . . ." (p. 142); further elements of this symbolic pattern can be traced throughout *The Names*.

14. Dinesen, *Shadows on the Grass*, p. 134.

15. Ibid., p. 148.

16. Albert Camus, *The Outsider*, trans. Stuart Gilbert, p. 120; Momaday referred to this quotation in his column "Finding a Need for Nature," *Viva*, 13 May 1973, p. 2: "Camus speaks of 'the benign indifference of the universe.' It strikes me that there is a great solace in that idea, but perhaps you have to see the stars in order to believe it."

17. See particularly Faulkner's "Delta Autumn," in *Go Down, Moses*, pp. 256–57.

18. The similarities between Proust's and Momaday's notions of time and memory have been discussed in chapter 2.

19. Mick McAllister, "The Names," *Southern Review* n.s. 14 (1978): 387.

20. Joseph Campbell, *The Masks of God: Creative Mythology*, pp. 92–93.

21. James Joyce, *A Portrait of the Artist as a Young Man*, p. 167.

22. Ibid., p. 62.

23. Ibid., p. 170.

24. Ibid., p. 252.

25. N. Scott Momaday, interview with author, Tucson, December 1981.

26. N. Scott Momaday, "Tsoai and the Shield Maker," *Four Winds* 1, no. 3 (1980): 38–43.

27. N. Scott Momaday to author, 25 Aug. 1982.

28. Ibid.

29. Campbell, *The Masks of God*, p. 36.

30. N. Scott Momaday, interview with author, Tucson, December 1981.

31. N. Scott Momaday, *The Way to Rainy Mountain*, p. 4.

32. N. Scott Momaday, "A Vision beyond Time and Place," *Life*, July 1971, p. 67.

33. For this distinction I am indebted to James Olney, "Some Versions of Memory / Some Versions of Bios: The Ontology of Autobiography," in *Autobiography: Essays Theoretical and Critical*, ed. James Olney, p. 239.

34. N. Scott Momaday, "Indian Art," lecture at the Heard Museum, Phoenix, Arizona, 10 December 1972, in Rose Marie Smith, "A Critical Study of the Literature of N. Scott Momaday as Intercultural Communication," (Ph.D. diss., University of Southern California, 1975), p. 148.

35. William T. Morgan, Jr., "Landscapes: N. Scott Momaday," *Sequoia* 19, no. 2 (1975): 41.

36. Ibid., p. 49.

37. N. Scott Momaday, "The Man Made of Words," in *Indian Voices*, ed. Rupert Costo, p. 56.

38. Momaday, *The Way to Rainy Mountain*, p. 33.

39. N. Scott Momaday, interview with author, Tucson, December 1981.

40. Several of these autobiographical passages are drawn from Momaday's *Viva* columns. The opening story about the burning of Jemez day school (pp. 117–19) was published as "A Pyre of Moments, Peculiarly Mine . . ." in *Viva*, 14 January 1973, p. 2; the passage on the Navajo dog (pp. 135–36) is based on "Caveat Emptor," *Viva*, 21 October 1973, p. 6; the story of Tolo (pp. 137–42) appeared as "The Circle—A Fable of Christmas" in *Viva*, 24 December 1972, pp. 4–5;

the vignette of the old man at Jemez (pp. 148–49) was published as part of "Unholy Sights" in *Viva*, 9 September 1973, p. 7; the story of the goose hunt (p. 150) appeared in "One of the Wild, Beautiful Creatures," *Viva*, 23 September 1973, p. 13; and the story of Quincy Tahoma (pp. 150–52) is an adaptation from "The Isolation of Quincy Tahoma," *Viva*, 20 August 1972, p. 2.

41. For examinations of this inherent contradiction in Indian autobiographies see Robert Sayre, "Vision and Experience in *Black Elk Speaks*," *College English* 32 (1971): 512 and 515; and William Bloodworth, "Neihardt, Momaday, and the Art of Indian Autobiography," in *Where the West Begins*, ed. Arthur R. Huseboe and William Geyer, p. 153.

42. S. M. Barrett, ed. *Geronimo: His Own Story*, pp. 51–54.

43. I am indebted to Carter Revard's excellent article "History, Myth, and Identity among Osage and Other People," *Denver Quarterly* 14, no. 4 (1980): p. 85.

44. John G. Neihardt, *Black Elk Speaks*.

45. Ibid., p. 6.

46. Northrop Frye, *Anatomy of Criticism: Four Essays*, p. 307; Thomas Cooley, *Educated Lives: The Rise of Modern Autobiography in America*, p. x; Albert E. Stone, "Autobiography and American Culture," *American Studies: An International Newsletter* 11, no. 2 (1972): 21; Wallace Stegner argues this case in "On the Writing of History," in his *The Sound of Mountain Water*, p. 205.

47. "The Writing of Nonfiction Prose," Momaday's contributions to a discussion at the Library of Congress; published in *Teaching Creative Writing*, p. 106.

48. N. Scott Momaday, interview with author, Tucson, December 1981.

49. John Bushnell, "From American Indian to Indian American: The Changing Identity of the Hupa," *American Anthropologist* 70 (1968): 1108.

Chapter 7

1. N. Scott Momaday, interview with author, Tucson, December 1981. Most of Momaday's poems in traditional meter and rhyme were written at Stanford in 1960. Among them are the following unpublished pieces: "Passive Spirit in Retrospect," "In View of a Certainty," "Autumn Break," "Epitaph," and "The Creche," in "The Collected

Poems of N. Scott Momaday," (Master's thesis, Stanford University, 1960), pp. 5, 6, 7, 8, 10, 13 (CSt).

2. The only other pieces of a similar kind are "Eve My Mother, No," *Sequoia* 5, no. 1 (1959): 37, and the two versions of "Pit Viper," one of which was included in "The Collected Poems of N. Scott Momaday."

3. N. Scott Momaday, interview with author, Tucson, December 1981.

4. Ibid.

5. Yvor Winters, *In Defense of Reason*, p. 585.

6. Hart Crane, *The Complete Poems and Selected Letters and Prose of Hart Crane*, ed. Brom Weber, p. 45.

7. N. Scott Momaday, "Los Alamos," *New Mexico Quarterly* 29 (1959): 306.

8. Momaday explained this position: "I think the earth is yet greater than all we have devised and we can destroy ourselves, but I don't think we can destroy the earth or the wilderness. You can sometimes see grass growing up through the freeway, and that to me is evidence that nature is finally greater, and that it will pop up out of the concrete despite everything, given enough time," N. Scott Momaday, interview with author, Tucson, December 1981.

9. N. Scott Momaday, Peculiarly Mine . . . ," *Viva*, 14 January 1973, p. 2.

10. N. Scott Momaday, "Earth and I Gave You Turquoise," *New Mexico Quarterly* 29 (1959): 156; Momaday could not remember which poems he sent to Stanford, but he was almost certain that "Earth and I Gave You Turquoise" was among them; interview with author, Tucson, December 1981.

11. N. Scott Momaday, interview with author, Tucson, December 1981.

12. Ibid.

13. N. Scott Momaday to author, 18 June 1982.

14. Gladys A. Reichard, *Navaho Religion: A Study of Symbolism*, p. 209.

15. N. Scott Momaday to author, 18 June 1982; in *Colorado: Summer, Fall, Winter, Spring*, p. 110, Momaday wrote: "I am told by an old Indian that it is good for the eye to behold a sky-blue stone."

16. Momaday incorporated lines from the Night Chant, originally collected by Washington Matthew, into *House Made of Dawn*, p. 134. For another version of this prayer see *In the Trail of the Wind: American Indian Poems and Ritual Oration*, ed. John Bierhorst, p. 34; see also

"First Song of Dawn Boy," quoted in A. Grove Day, *The Sky Clears: Poetry of the American Indians*, p. 64.

17. Reichard, *Navaho Religion*, p. 291.

18. Clyde Kluckhohn and Dorothea Leighton, *The Navaho*, p. 185.

19. N. Scott Momaday to author, 18 June 1982.

20. Reichard, *Navaho Religion*, pp. 41 and 42.

21. Ibid., p. 43.

22. Kluckhohn and Leighton, *The Navaho*, p. 184.

23. Reichard, *Navaho Religion*, p. 44.

24. Kluckhohn and Leighton, *The Navaho*, p. 202. Although Kluckhohn's view is shared by other anthropologists, it is not undisputed. Reichard claims that "the Navaho delight in talking about the life, good deeds, and accomplishments of the deceased," *Navaho Religion*, p. 45.

25. N. Scott Momaday to author, 18 June 1982.

26. Adolph Bittany, quoted in Reichard, *Navaho Religion*, p. 44.

27. Yvor Winters, "The Morality of Poetry," in his *In Defense of Reason*, p. 19.

28. Ibid., p. 21.

29. Yvor Winters, "Forms of Discovery: A Preliminary Statement," *Southern Review* n.s. 3 (1967): 9; see also his *Forms of Discovery: Critical and Historical Essays on the Forms of the Short Poem in English*, p. xix.

30. Winters, "Forms of Discovery: A Preliminary Statement," p. 4.

31. Winters, *In Defense of Reason*, p. 13.

32. Winters, *Forms of Discovery*, p. 244.

33. Winters, *In Defense of Reason*, p. 9.

34. Yvor Winters, "Poetic Styles, Old and New," in *Four Poets on Poetry*, ed. Don Cameron Allen, p. 71.

35. Ibid.

36. Ibid.

37. Ibid., pp. 70–72.

38. Ibid., p. 72.

39. Winters, *Forms of Discovery*, p. 251.

40. Yvor Winters, "Problems of the Modern Critic of Literature," in his *The Function of Criticism*, p. 69.

41. Winters, *In Defense of Reason*, p. 20.

42. Ibid., p. 22–23.

43. Ibid., p. 22.

44. Ibid., p. 62.

45. Ibid., p. 64.

46. Ibid., pp. 22–23.

47. Yvor Winters, Introduction to *The Early Poems of Yvor Winters*

1920–1928, in *The Collected Poems of Yvor Winters*, ed. Donald Davie, p. 15.

48. Winters, *Forms of Discovery*, p. xvii.

49. N. Scott Momaday interview with author, Tucson, December 1981.

50. Winters, *Forms of Discovery*, p. 253.

51. Paul Valéry, *Paul Valéry: An Anthology*, selected, with an introduction by James R. Lawler, p. 269.

52. Paul Valéry, quoted in James R. Lawler, *Form and Meaning in Valéry's Le Cimetière Marin*, p. 9.

53. Valéry, *Anthology*, p. 269.

54. Ibid., p. 275.

55. Frederick Goddard Tuckerman, *The Cricket*," in *The Complete Poems of Frederick Goddard Tuckerman*, ed. N. Scott Momaday, p. 70.

56. N. Scott Momaday, Introduction to "An Edition of the Complete Poems of Frederick Goddard Tuckerman," (Ph.D. diss., Stanford University, 1963), p. 43; parts of this introduction have been published in Momaday's "The Heretical Cricket," *Southern Review* n.s. 3 (1965): 43–50.

57. N. Scott Momaday, interview with author, Tucson, December 1981.

58. Yvor Winters, "Wallace Stevens or The Hedonist's Progress," in his *In Defense of Reason*, particularly pp. 431–33 and 447–48.

59. Paul Ramsey, "Some American Poetry of 1974: Three Traditions," *Sewanee Review* 84 (1975): 354; Kathleen Weigner, "Books: Poetry as Ritual," *American Poetry Review* 6, no. 1 (1977):46; Jim Young, "Tradition and the Experimental," *Compass* 1 (1977): 106.

60. Wallace Stevens, "Sunday Morning," in *The Collected Poems of Wallace Stevens*, p. 67.

61. Ibid.

62. Ibid., p. 70.

63. N. Scott Momaday, interview with author, Tucson, December 1981.

64. David Levin, "Yvor Winters at Stanford," *Virginia Quarterly Review* 54 (1978): 478.

65. N. Scott Momaday, interview with author, Tucson, December 1981.

66. Yvor Winters, "A Fragment," in *The Collected Poems of Yvor Winters*, p. 184.

67. Yvor Winters, "A Song in Passing," in *The Collected Poems of Yvor Winters*, p. 185.

68. Yvor Winters, "To the Holy Spirit—From a Deserted Grave-

yard in the Salinas Valley," *The Collected Poems of Yvor Winters*, pp. 183–84.
   69. Ibid., p. 184.
   70. N. Scott Momaday, "A Love Affair with Emily Dickinson," *Viva*, 6 August 1972, p. 2.
   71. N. Scott Momaday, interview with author, Tucson, December 1981.
   72. Winters, *In Defense of Reason*, p. 288.
   73. Emily Dickinson, *The Complete Poems of Emily Dickinson*, ed. Thomas H. Johnson, pp. 599–600.
   74. Winters, *In Defense of Reason*, p. 294.
   75. N. Scott Momaday, Introduction to his "An Edition of the Complete Poems of Frederick Goddard Tuckerman," (Ph.D. diss., Stanford University, 1963), pp. 32–33.
   76. N. Scott Momaday, "Before an Old Painting of the Crucifixion," in his *The Gourd Dancer*, pp. 26–27.
   77. Winters, *Forms of Discovery*, p. 292.
   78. N. Scott Momaday to Yvor Winters, 18 August 1966.
   79. Ralph Waldo Emerson, "Nature," in his *Nature, The Conduct of Life, and Other Essays*, p. 4.
   80. N. Scott Momaday to Yvor Winters, 18 August 1966.
   81. N. Scott Momaday, manuscript of *The Gourd Dancer*; a copy is in possession of the author.
   82. Stevens, *The Collected Poems of Wallace Stevens*, p. 70.
   83. N. Scott Momaday, "Angle of Geese," in *The Gourd Dancer*, pp. 31–32.
   84. N. Scott Momaday to Yvor Winters, 20 November 1967.
   85. Roger Dickinson-Brown, in his article "The Art and Importance of N. Scott Momaday," *Southern Review* n.s. 14 (1978), does not recognize the specific situation of the poem as the mourning for a dead child. He takes the "dead firstborn" to mean "the Darwinian animal which we were, who is our ancestor, and who cannot be rediscovered in our language" (p. 43). His uncertainty about the actual context of the first half of the poem leads him to assume that "the mute presence" in stanza two is not "the presence of language . . . but the presence of wilderness" (p. 43). However, the context of this stanza seems to suggest that "the mute presence" is the presence of the mourners who are unable to put their feelings into words.
   86. Winters, *Forms of Discovery*, p. 290.
   87. Momaday, *House Made of Dawn*, p. 110.
   88. This reading is corroborated by another version of this scene which was published in "One of the Wild, Beautiful Creatures," *Viva*,

23 September 1973, p. 13. In this essay Momaday describes the dying bird: "There was no longer any fear in its eyes, only something like sadness and yearning, until at last the eyes curdled in death. The great shape seemed perceptibly lighter, diminished in my hold, as if the ghost given up had gone at last to take its place in that pale angle in the long distance."

89. N. Scott Momaday, "Comparatives," in his *The Gourd Dancer*, p. 13; an earlier version of the poem, "An Agony in Threes and Fours"—a reference to the syllabic meter—comprises only the first stanza of "Comparatives" and the following seven lines: "Now perceive / An agony; / It is like / Wind over waves—/ A motion, / That is all." These lines reappear in a revised form as the third stanza of the final version. In adding the second stanza and establishing the comparison between the two scenes of death, Momaday achieves much greater depth than in the early version (CU).

90. The full title of the earliest version is "The Bear (From Faulkner)," in "The Collected Poems of N. Scott Momaday," (Master's thesis, Stanford University, 1960), p. 2; for a detailed comparison of the poem with Faulkner's "The Bear" see Kenneth M. Roemer, "Bear and Elk: The Nature(s) of Contemporary Indian Poetry," *Journal of Ethnic Studies* 5, no. 2 (1977): 75.

91. N. Scott Momaday, "Pit Viper," in his *The Gourd Dancer*, p. 12.

92. Momaday, "The Collected Poems of N. Scott Momaday," p. 9.

93. Momaday, *The Gourd Dancer*, pp. 41, 25, 26, 25.

94. Ibid., p. 27.

95. This early version, which lacks the final stanza of six lines, shows some minor textual variations and includes the following six lines which have subsequently been deleted: "I am the foam at the margin of the sea. / I am the grasses that bend in the wind. / I am the peal of laughter, breaking on a silence. / I am a whale sounding. / I am a field of poppies. / I am the call of a gull far from land." The line "I am a field of Sumac and the pomme blanche" and the final stanza are the only sections which have been newly written for the published version. Manuscript of "The Delight Song of Tsoai-talee" (CU).

96. Mary Austin, *The Land of Journeys' Ending*, pp. 437–38.

97. From the Navajo Night Chant; for an adaptation of the poem see Momaday's *House Made of Dawn*, pp. 134–35.

98. Momaday, *The Gourd Dancer*, pp. 20–24.

99. N. Scott Momaday, "Reflections on the Uncertainty of Winter," *Viva*, 26 November 1972, p. 2.

100. Frank Doggett, "This Invented World: Stevens' 'Notes toward

A Supreme Fiction',," in *The Act of the Mind: Essays on the Poetry of Wallace Stevens*, ed. Roy Harvey Pearce and J. Hillis Miller, p. 16.

101. In the manuscript version of "Plainview: 4," Momaday refers to the man as "Goomdah."

102. For information on Milly Durgan see Mildred P. Mayhall, *The Kiowas*, pp. 228–29; George Hunt, "Milly Durgan," *Chronicle of Oklahoma* 15 (1937): 480–82; and Wilbur S. Nye, *Carbine and Lance: The Story of Old Fort Sill*, pp. 45–46 and 286.

103. N. Scott Momaday, manuscript of "Plainview: 4" (CU).

104. Ibid.

105. Momaday, *The Gourd Dancer*, pp. 35–37.

106. N. Scott Momaday, *The Names: A Memoir*; N. Scott Momaday, "Driving East for Kiowa Dancing," *Viva*, 23 July 1972, p. 2; N. Scott Momaday, "A Memory that Persists in the Blood," *Viva*, 22 July 1973, p. 9.

107. Momaday, "A Memory that Persists in the Blood," p. 9.

108. James Mooney, *Calendar History of the Kiowa Indians*, p. 237.

109. "Kiowa History Lives Again on Commemorative Occasion," *Kiowa County Star Review*, 25 October 1972, p. 1.

110. Dickinson, *Complete Poems* p. 118.

111. N. Scott Momaday, untitled column, *Viva*, 30 April 1972, p. 2; and "The Man Made of Words," in *Indian Voices*, ed. Rupert Costo, p. 51.

112. *Webster's New Collegiate Dictionary*, s.v. "glance."

113. N. Scott Momaday, "The the Singing, to the Drum," in *Ants, Indians, and Little Dinosaurs*, ed. Alan Ternes, pp. 250–251.

114. *Webster's New Collegiate Dictionary*, s.v. "concise."

115. Mooney, *Calendar History of the Kiowa Indians*, p. 231.

116. "A First American Views His Land," *National Geographic Magazine* 150, no. 1 (July 1976): pp. 13–18; *The Gourd Dancer* appeared on 21 July 1976; "New World" is on side b pp. 38–40.

117. Momaday, "A First American Views His Land," p. 17.

118. N. Scott Momaday, *Remember My Horse*.

119. Momaday, "A First American Views His Land," p. 18.

120. N. Scott Momaday, "So Crisply Summer," *Viva*, 8 October 1972, p. 2.

121. See, for example, the account of a Pueblo creation myth in Richard Erdoes, *The Rain Dance People*, p. 2.

122. Wallace Stevens, "Thirteen Ways of Looking at a Blackbird," in *The Collected Poems of Wallace Stevens*, p. 95; the last stanza of this poem reads: "It was evening all afternoon. / It was snowing / And it was going to snow. / The blackbird sat / In the cedar-limbs."

123. Momaday, *The Gourd Dancer*, p. 43; "The Eagle-Feather Fan" was first published as the final section of Momaday's essay "To the Singing, to the Drum," which deals with the Kiowa Gourd Dance celebration. Momaday blends expository writing on the historical and contemporary aspects of the ceremony with impressionistic passages relating to his personal experience of it. Excerpts of this essay were published in the official program, "Welcome: Kiowa Gourd Dance Ceremonials," of the 1976 celebration of the Gourd Dance at Carnegie, Oklahoma, pp. 2–3.

124. Rosalie Wax and Murray L. Wax, "The Magical World View," *Journal of the Scientific Study of Religion* 1, no. 2 (1962): 182.

125. Momaday, *Colorado*, p. 51.

126. Momaday, *The Gourd Dancer*, p. 42.

127. Ibid., pp. 44–47; "The Colors of Night" was also published separately as *The Colors of Night*.

128. N. Scott Momaday, "Imagine Time, Place, Presence," commencement address at the University of New Mexico, Albuquerque, 18 May 1975 (NmU).

129. N. Scott Momaday, interview with author, Tucson, December 1981.

130. Mooney, *Calendar History of the Kiowa Indians*, pp. 327–28; see also Mayhall, *The Kiowas*, pp. 124–25.

131. Momaday, *Remember My Horse*, side b.

132. N. Scott Momaday, untitled newspaper column, *Viva*, 30 April 1972, p. 2.

133. H. Frankfort noted that for primitive man the distinction between subjective and objective knowledge was meaningless. He added: "Meaningless, also, is our contrast between reality and appearance. Whatever is capable of affecting mind, feeling, or will has thereby established its undoubted reality." In *The Intellectual Adventures of Ancient Man: An Essay on Speculative Thought in the Ancient Near East*, ed. H. Frankfort et al., p. 11.

134. N. Scott Momaday, interview with author, Tucson, December 1981.

135. Momaday, *The Gourd Dancer*, pp. 47–50.

136. On a visit to Monument Valley with Peter Nabokov, Momaday said: "Look at them sticking up there, those horizontal bars of light behind them. A man could go crazy here. He might begin to pray to them. When I first came here I wrote about this place, and I said it was like entering the nearest corner of eternity. Somewhere between here and there time ends." Unpublished biographical essay by Peter Nabokov, p. 15.

137. Momaday wrote about this time in "A Crucial Year at Dulce, and a Boy I Shall Call David," *Viva*, 18 February 1973, p. 3.

138. The original typescript of *The Gourd Dancer* also contains a number of poems which remained unpublished, among them "Bibikhanym Mosque," "Earth under Earth," "Drawn in Lesions of Light," and "The Nickname of Nothing."

139. Momaday, *The Gourd Dancer*, p. 63; this poem was originally entitled "Krasnopresnenskaya Metro" in the manuscript version. The dedication is to Will Sutter, a cultural attaché at the U.S. embassy in Moscow.

140. Momaday, *The Gourd Dancer*, p. 54.

141. "'Arkhangelskoe' is a pre-revolutionary estate outside Moscow, and a kind of museum now, of which there are many in and about Moscow and Leningrad." N. Scott Momaday to author, 20 May 1983.

142. In the original typescript Momaday opened this final stanza with the holographic addition: "I imagine . . .".

143. Momaday, *The Gourd Dancer*, p. 55.

144. *Encyclopedia Britannica*, 1966 ed., s.v. "Hokusai."

145. Yone Noguchi, *Hokusai*, pp. 5–6; see also C. J. Holmes, *Hokusai*, pp. 14–15.

146. Noguchi, *Hokusai*, pp. 5–6.

147. Momaday's reference to "a corpulent merchant and his pillow" may have been inspired by Hokusai's drawing entitled "The Deity Hotei"; a reproduction can be found in Edward F. Strange, *Hokusai: The Old Man Mad with Painting*, n. p.

148. Momaday, *The Gourd Dancer*, p. 56.

149. Ibid., p. 53.

150. Stevens, "Thirteen Ways of Looking at a Blackbird," *The Collected Poems*, pp. 92–95.

151. Stevens, "Yellow Afternoon," in *The Collected Poems*, p. 236.

152. N. Scott Momaday, "Four Epigrams for Bobby Jack Nelson," manuscript of *The Gourd Dancer*, n. p.

153. Bobby Jack Nelson, *The Last Station*. Nelson acknowledged his admiration of Momaday's work by using the last three lines from "Headwaters" as an epigraph to his book.

154. N. Scott Momaday, interview with students at New Mexico State University, Las Cruces, 1973.

155. Momaday, *The Gourd Dancer*, p. 62.

156. N. Scott Momaday, interview with students at New Mexico State University, Las Cruces, 1973.

157. N. Scott Momaday, interview with Peter Nabokov; unpublished biographical essay by Peter Nabokov, p. 15.

158. Nabokov, unpublished biographical essay, p. 15.

159. Momaday, *The Groud Dancer*, p. 60.

160. N. Scott Momaday, interview with author, Tucson, December 1981.

161. Examples of this period are "Black Rock with Blue III" (1970; Georgia O'Keeffe Collection), and "Black Rock with Blue Sky and White Clouds" (1972; Georgia O'keeffe Collection); these paintings are reprinted in Georgia O'keeffe, *Georgia O'Keeffe*, n. p.

162. Georgia O'Keeffe, *Georgia O'Keeffe: A Portrait by Alfred Stieglitz*.

163. N. Scott Momaday, interview with author, Tucson, December 1981.

164. N. Scott Momaday, "Three Personalities, One Landscape," *Viva*, 10 December 1972, p. 2.

165. O'Keeffe, *Georgia O'Keeffe*, n. p.

166. Ibid.

167. Momaday, manuscript of *The Gourd Dancer*.

168. Duane Niatum, ed. *Carriers of the Dream Wheel: Contemporary Native American Poetry*, pp. 90, 102, 105.

169. N. Scott Momaday, "Riding Is an Exercise of the Mind," manuscript of *The Gourd Dancer*, p. 17; this story was published under the title "Growing Up at Jemez Pueblo," *Viva*, 25 June 1972, p. 2.

170. Momaday, manuscript of *The Gourd Dancer*, pp. 17–18.

171. Ibid., p. 18.

172. Momaday, manuscript of *The Gourd Dancer*, pp. 20–38.

173. William T. Morgan, Jr., "Landscapes: N. Scott Momaday," *Sequoia* 19, no. 2 (1975): 45.

174. Momaday, manuscript of *The Gourd Dancer*, pp. 23–26.

175. Ibid., p. 24.

176. Ibid., pp. 23–24.

177. Ibid., pp. 24–25.

178. N. Scott Momaday, "Cherish the Legend of Billy the Kid," *Viva*, 29 October 1972, p. 2.

179. N. Scott Momaday, "The Dying Cowboy," manuscript of *The Gourd Dancer*, p. 41; part of this story appeared as section two of "Thoughts on Jemez and Billy the Kid, *Viva*, 18 November 1973, p. 2.

180. N. Scott Momaday, "Billy Offers a Kindness to an Old Man at Glorietta," manuscript of *The Gourd Dancer*, pp. 35–37; published under the same title in *Viva*, 9 December 1973, p. 12.

181. N. Scott Momaday, "Sister of Charity and Desperado," *Viva*, 5 August 1973, p. 2.

182. N. Scott Momaday, manuscript of *The Gourd Dancer*, p. 39.

183. Momaday, *The Gourd Dancer*, p. 59.

184. Momaday, manuscript of *The Gourd Dancer*, p. 29.

185. Momaday, "To the Singing, to the Drums," p. 253.

186. N. Scott Momaday, "Indignation, Young and Old," *Viva*, 25 February 1973, p. 4; the correct date is 1881.

187. Momaday, "Thoughts on Jemez and Billy the Kid," p. 2.

188. Momaday, manuscript of *The Gourd Dancer*, p. 21; the poem was published in "The Pear-Shaped Legend: A Figment of the American Imagination," *Stanford Magazine* 3, no. 1 (1975): 47.

189. Momaday, manuscript of *The Gourd Dancer*, p. 27.

190. Ibid., pp. 22 and 46.

191. Ibid., p. 48; Momaday, "The Pear-Shaped Legend," p. 48.

192. Momaday, manuscript of *The Gourd Dancer*, p. 21.

193. Niatum, *Carriers of the Dream Wheel*, p. 105; Momaday, manuscript of *The Gourd Dancer*, p. 47.

194. Niatum, *Carriers of the Dream Wheel*, p. 102.

195. N. Scott Momaday, *The Way to Rainy Mountain*, p. 82.

Bibliography

WORKS BY N. SCOTT MOMADAY

Unpublished Materials

"The American Indian in the Conflict of Tribalism and Modern Society." Lecture at Colorado State University, Fort Collins, 31 January 1971. CoFS.

"The Collected Poems of N. Scott Momaday." Master's thesis, Stanford University, 1960. CSt.

"Commencement Address." Hobart and William Smith Colleges, Geneva, N.Y., 1 June 1980.

"Commencement Address." University of Minnesota, Minneapolis, 20 August 1971. MnU.

Correspondence with Whitney Blake, editor, Oxford University Press, New York. CU.

Correspondence with Gus Blaisdell, editor, University of New Mexico Press, Albuquerque. CU.

Correspondence with Frances McCullough, editor, Harper and Row, New York. CU.

Correspondence with Yvor Winters.

"An Edition of the Complete Poems of Frederick Goddard Tuckerman." Ph.D. diss., Stanford University, 1963. CSt.

"The Gourd Dancer." Manuscript.

"House Made of Dawn." Printer's copy of typewritten MS with Momaday's revisions. CU.

"An Idea of the Land as Sacred." CU.

"Imagine Time, Place, Presence." Commencement Address, University of New Mexico, Albuquerque, 18 May 1975. NmU.

"Indian Art." In Rose Marie Smith. "A Critical Study of the Literature

300 N. SCOTT MOMADAY

of N. Scott Momaday as Intercultural Communication," pp. 144–
65. Ph.D. diss., University of Southern California, 1975. CLSU.
Interview with students at New Mexico State University, Las Cruces,
1973. NmLcU.
Interview with author, Tucson, December 1981.
Interview with Floyd C. Watkins, Santa Fe, June 1971. Robert W.
Woodruff Library, Emory University, Atlanta, Ga.
Interview with Charles Woodard, Stanford, 19 and 20 November
1974.
"The Man Who Killed the Deer." Screenplay of novel by Frank Wa-
ters. CU.
"The Native Californian: Centennial Views of the American Indian."
Lecture to the Friends of the Bancroft Library, Berkeley, 1975. CU.
The Names: A Memoir. Printer's copy of typewritten MS. CU.
Poems published as *Angle of Geese and Other Poems* and several unpub-
lished pieces, typescripts and manuscripts. CU.
The Way to Rainy Mountain. Notes and fragments. CU.

Published Works

BOOKS

Angle of Geese and Other Poems. Boston: David R. Godine, 1974.
Colorado: Summer, Fall, Winter, Spring. New York: Rand McNally, 1973.
The Colors of Night. Arion Press Broadsides no. 3. San Francisco, 1976.
(Editor). *The Complete Poems of Frederick Goddard Tuckerman*. Foreword
by Yvor Winters. New York: Oxford University Press, 1965.
The Gourd Dancer. New York: Harper and Row, 1976.
House Made of Dawn. New York: Harper and Row, 1968. Paperback
eds.: New York: Signet, 1969; New York: Perennial, 1977; Har-
mondsworth: Penguin Books, 1973. Translations: *Dom UTKany Ze
Švitu* (Warsaw: Ksiqzkai Wiedza, 1976); *Et Hus av Demring* (Oslo:
J. W. Cappelens Forlaga·s, 1975); *Haus Aus Dämmerung* (Frankfurt
am Main: Verlag Ullstein, 1978).
The Journey of Tai-me. Santa Barbara: Privately printed, 1967.
The Names: A Memoir. New York: Harper and Row, 1976. Paperback
ed., Harper Colophon Books, 1977.
The Way to Rainy Mountain. Albuquerque: University of New Mexico
Press, 1969. Paperback ed.: New York: Ballantine, 1969; University
of New Mexico Press, 1976.

POEMS

"Angle of Geese." *New Mexico Quarterly* 38 (1968): 108.
"The Bear." *New Mexico Quarterly* 31 (1961): 46.
"Before an Old Painting of the Crucifixion." *Southern Review* n.s. 1 (1965): 421–23.
"The Burning." *Pembroke Magazine* 6 (1975): 31.
"But Then and There the Sun Bore Down." In *Carriers of the Dream Wheel*, p. 105. Ed. Duane Niatum. New York: Harper and Row, 1976.
"Buteo Regalis." *New Mexico Quarterly* 31 (1961): 31.
"The Colors of Night." *Sequoia* 19, no. 1 (1974): 22–23.
"Earth and I Gave You Turquoise." *New Mexico Quarterly* 29 (1959): 156.
"Eve My Mother, No." *Sequoia* 5, no. 1 (1959): 37.
"For the Old Man Mad for Drawing." *Pembroke Magazine* 6 (1975): 31.
"Los Alamos." *New Mexico Quarterly* 29 (1959): 37.
"New Orleans Vesper." *Sequoia* 6, no. 2 (1960): 21.
"Pit Viper." *New Mexico Quarterly* 31 (1961): 47.
"Rainy Mountain Cemetery." *New Mexico Quarterly* 38 (1968): 107.
"Simile." *Sequoia* 6, no. 1 (1960): 39.
"There, Outside, the Long Light of August. . . ." *Museum of the American Indian Newsletter* 3, no. 2 (1978).
"Trees and Evening Sky." In *Carriers of the Dream Wheel*, p. 102. Ed. Duane Niatum. New York: Harper and Row, 1976.
"Wide Empty Landscape with a Death in the Foreground." In *Carriers of the Dream Wheel*, p. 90. Ed. Duane Niatum. New York: Harper and Row, 1976.

RECORDINGS

Remember My Horse. Cambridge, Mass.: Credo Records, 1976.

SHORT PROSE, ARTICLES, AND REVIEWS

"The American Indian: A Contemporary Acknowledgement." *Intellectual Digest* 2, no. 1 (1971): 12, 14.
"An American Land Ethic." *Sierra Club Bulletin* 55, no. 2 (1970): 8–11. Reprinted in *Ecotactics: The Sierra Club Handbook for Environmental Activists*, pp. 97–105. Ed. John G. Mitchell and Constance L. Stalling. New York: Trident Press, 1970.
"Bringing on the Indian." *New York Review of Books*, 8 April 1971, pp. 39–42.

"The Circle: A Fable of Christmas." *Viva: Northern New Mexico's Sunday Magazine*, 24 December 1972, pp. 4–5.

"A First American Views His Land." *National Geographic Magazine* 105, no. 1 (1976): 13–18.

"From *The Names*." *American Poetry Review* 5, no. 6 (1976): 47.

"The Heretical Cricket." *Southern Review* n.s. 3 (1967): 43–50.

"I am Alive." In *The World of the American Indian*, pp. 11–26. Ed. Jules B. Billard. Washington: National Geographic Society, 1975.

"Kiowa Legends from *The Journey of Tai-me*." *Sun Tracks: An American Indian Literary Magazine* 3, no. 1 (1976): 6–8.

"The Land Inspired the Artist." Review of *American Indian Painting of the Southwest and Plains Area*, by Dorothy Dunn. *New York Times Book Review*, 28 July 1968, p. 6.

"The Man Made of Words." In *Indian Voices: The First Convocation of American Indian Scholars*, pp. 49–84. Ed. Rupert Costo. San Francisco: Indian Historian Press, 1970.

"The Morality of Indian Hating." *Ramparts* 3, no. 1 (1964): 29–40.

"Native American Attitudes toward the Environment." In *Seeing with a Native Eye*, pp. 79–85. Ed. Walter Holden Capps. New York: Harper and Row, 1976.

"A Note on Contemporary Native American Poetry." In *Carriers of the Dream Wheel*, pp. xix–xx. Ed. Duane Niatum. New York: Harper and Row, 1976.

"Oral Tradition and the American Indian." In *Contemporary Native American Address*, pp. 294–306. Ed. John R. Maestas. Provo, Utah: Brigham Young University Publications, 1976.

"Pamphlets and Portraits, Re-Appraisals and Reviews." *Southern Review* n.s. 3 (1967): 468–78.

"The Pear-Shaped Legend: A Figment of the American Imagination." *Stanford Magazine* 3, no. 1 (1975): 46–48.

"Praise So Dear." *Imprint of the Stanford Library Associates* 1, no. 2 (1975): 5–9.

"The Story of the Arrowmaker." *New York Times Book Review*, 4 May 1969, p. 2.

"Summary and Announcement of a Study of Anti-Romantic American Poetry." *Emily Dickinson Bulletin* 9 (June 1969; revised November 1969): 2.

"Three Sketches from *House Made of Dawn*." *Southern Review* n.s. 2 (1966): 933–45.

"To the Singing, to the Drum." *Natural History* 84, no. 2 (1975): 41–44. Reprinted in *Ants, Indians and Little Dinosaurs*, pp. 250–56. Ed. Alan Ternes. New York: Scribner's, 1975.

"Tribal Spirit." Review of *The New Indian*, by Stan Steiner. *New York Times Book Review*, 28 July 1968, p. 22.

"Tsoai and the Shield Maker." *Four Winds: The International Forum for Native American Art, Literature, and History* 1, no. 3 (1980): 38–43.

"Two Sketches from *House Made of Dawn*." *New Mexico Quarterly* 37 (1967): 101–111.

"Two Tales from *The Journey of Tai-me*." *Little Square Review* nos. 5–6 (1968): 30–31.

"A Vision beyond Time and Place." *Life*, July 1971, p. 67.

"The Way to Rainy Mountain." *Reporter*, 26 January 1967, pp. 41–43.

"The Well." *Ramparts* 2, no. 1 (1963): 49–52.

ANTHOLOGIES CONTAINING WORKS BY N. SCOTT MOMADAY

Chapman, Abraham, ed. *Literature of the American Indians: Views and Interpretations*, pp. 96–110. New York: Meridian, 1975.

Dodge, Robert K., and Joseph B. McCullough, eds. *Voices from Wah-'kon-tah*, pp. 72–77. New York: International Publishers, 1974.

Faderman, Lillian, and Barbara Bradshaw, eds. *Speaking for Ourselves: American Ethnic Writing*, pp. 472–481, 515. n.p.: Foresman, 1969.

Haslam, Gerald W., ed. *Forgotten Pages of American Literature*, pp. 58–60. Boston: Houghton, 1970.

Hobson, Geary. *The Remembered Earth: An Anthology of Contemporary Native American Literature*, pp. 162–76. 1979. Reprint. Albuquerque: University of New Mexico Press, 1981.

Lowenfels, Walter, ed. *From the Belly of the Shark*, p. 44. New York: Vintage, 1973.

Momaday, Natachee Scott, ed. *American Indian Authors*, pp. 119–31. Boston: Houghton, 1970.

Niatum, Duane, ed. *Carriers of the Dream Wheel*, pp. 85–105. New York: Harper and Row, 1976.

Turner, Frederick W. III, ed. *The Portable North American Indian Reader*, pp. 578–86. New York: Viking, 1974.

Velie, Alan R., ed. *American Indian Literature: An Anthology*, pp. 246–51, 283–86, 336–42. Norman, Okla.: University of Oklahoma Press, 1979.

Witt, Shirley H., and Stan Steiner, eds. *The Way: An Anthology of American Indian Literature*, pp. 38–39. New York: Vintage, 1972.

INTERVIEWS AND PANEL DISCUSSIONS

Abbott, Lee. "An Interview with N. Scott Momaday." *Puerto Del Sol* 12, no. 2 (1973): 21–38.

Bataille, Gretchen M. "An Interview with N. Scott Momaday—April 16, 1977." *Iowa English Bulletin* 29, no. 1 (1979): 28–32.

———. "Interview with N. Scott Momaday—April 11, 1979." *Newsletter of the Association for the Study of American Indian Literature* n.s. 4, no. 1 (1980): 1–3.

Bruchac, Joseph. "N. Scott Momaday: An Interview by Joseph Bruchac." *American Poetry Review* 13, no. 4 (1984): 13–18.

"Discussion: The Man Made of Words." In *Indian Voices: The First Convocation of American Indian Scholars*, pp. 62–84. Ed. Rupert Costo. San Francisco: Indian Historian Press, 1970).

Evers, Lawrence J. "A Conversation with N. Scott Momaday." *Sun Tracks: An American Indian Literary Magazine* 2, no. 2 (1976): 18–21.

"Five Stanford Authors Converse." *Stanford Alumni Almanac* 10, no. 1 (1971): 2–6.

Morgan, William T., Jr. "Landscapes: N. Scott Momaday." *Sequoia* 19, no. 2 (1975): 38–49.

"Shouting at the Machine: An Interview with N. Scott Momaday." *Persona: The University of Arizona Undergraduate Magazine of Literature and Art*. Spring 1984, pp. 24–44.

"The Writing of Poetry" and "The Writing of Nonfiction Prose." Momaday's contributions to the Conference on Teaching Creative Writing at the Library of Congress, Washington, 29 and 30 January 1974. In *Teaching Creative Writing*, pp. 26–64, 94–131. Washington: Government Printing Office, 1974.

WEEKLY NEWSPAPER COLUMNS FOR "VIVA: NORTHERN NEW MEXICO'S SUNDAY MAGAZINE" (16 April 1972–9 December 1973)

Untitled. *Viva*, 16 April 1972, p. 2.

"Can a Dog Be Pious?" *Viva*, 23 April 1972, p. 2.

Untitled. *Viva*, 30 April 1972, p. 2.

"A Special Sense of Place." *Viva*, 7 May 1972, p. 2.

"The Night the Stars Fell." *Viva*, 14 May 1972, p. 2.

"An Incident on the Road to Spain." *Viva*, 21 May 1972, p. 2.

"A Bridge, a Ghost, a Cowboy." *Viva*, 28 May 1972, p. 2.

"Singing About the Beauty of the Earth." *Viva*, 4 June 1972, p. 2.

"Going to the Movies." *Viva*, 11 June 1972, p. 2.

"The Woman Who Knew Africa." *Viva*, 18 June 1972, p. 2.

"Growing Up at Jemez Pueblo." *Viva*, 25 June 1972, p. 2.

"The Influence of Edmund Wilson." *Viva*, 2 July 1972, p. 2.

"Learning from the Indian." *Viva*, 9 June 1972, p. 2.

"Revisiting the Family Home." *Viva*, 16 July 1972, p. 2.
"Driving East for Kiowa Dancing." *Viva*, 23 July 1972, p. 2.
"What Will Happen to the Land?" *Viva*, 30 July 1972, p. 2.
"A Love Affair with Emily Dickinson." *Viva*, 6 August 1972, p. 2.
"Visiting the Big City." *Viva*, 13 August 1972, p. 2.
"The Isolation of Quincy Tahoma." *Viva*, 20 August, 1972, p. 2.
"Going to the Opera in the Rain." *Viva*, 27 August 1972, p. 16.
"Does One Write by Necessity . . . or by Choice?" *Viva*, 3 September 1972, p. 6.
"Reflections on the First Day of Class." *Viva*, 10 September 1972, p. 2.
"Looking at Life with Journal and Lens." *Viva*, 17 September 1972, p. 2.
"Bewitched." *Viva*, 24 September 1972, p. 2.
"Listening to Sorrow." *Viva*, 1 October 1972, p. 20.
"So Crisply Autumn." *Viva*, 8 October 1972, p. 2.
"Conscious Questioning." *Viva*, 15 October 1972, p. 2.
"Going into Navajo Land." *Viva*, 22 October 1972, p. 2.
"Cherish the Legend of Billy the Kid." *Viva*, 29 October 1972, p. 2.
"The Indians and the Dodgers." *Viva*, 5 November 1972, p. 2.
"The Persistent Life Force of Mexico." *Viva*, 12 November 1972, p. 2.
"Twenty-six Years Ago, on This Day . . ." *Viva*, 19 November 1972, p. 2.
"Reflections on the Uncertainty of Winter." *Viva*, 26 November 1972, p. 2.
"Hurrah for Sir Francis Drake—and Thanks." *Viva*, 3 December 1972, p. 2.
"Three Personalities, One Landscape." *Viva*, 10 December 1972, p. 2.
"Way Down Yonder in the Pawpaw Patch." *Viva*, 17 December 1972, p. 2.
"Approaching the Intricate Topic Obliquely." *Viva*, 24 December 1972, p. 2.
"Figments of Sancho Panza's Imagination." *Viva*, 31 December 1972, p. 2.
"The Great Wisdom of Elephant Jokes." *Viva*, 7 January 1973, p. 2.
"A Pyre of Moments, Peculiarly Mine . . ." *Viva*, 14 January 1973, p. 2.
"'I Love You and I Love Your Furry Nose.'" *Viva*, 21 January 1973, p. 2.
"Coolidge, N.M.: A State of Mind, a Point of View." *Viva*, 28 January 1973, p. 2.
"A Time to Hold All Day in Your Lungs." *Viva*, 4 January 1973, p. 2.

"A Typically Miserable Flight to an Unusually Fine Reward." *Viva*, 11 February 1973, p. 3.

"A Crucial Year at Dulce, and a Boy I Shall Call David." *Viva*, 18 February 1973, p. 3.

"Indignation, Young and Old." *Viva*, 25 February 1973, p. 3.

"Laughter Through Tears." *Viva*, 4 March 1973, p. 7.

"A Columnist Recalls." *Viva*, 11 March 1973, p. 15.

"A Few Thoughts About Buffalo." *Viva*, 18 March 1973, p. 2.

"Life in Three Wonderful Cities." *Viva*, 26 March 1973, p. 2.

"Cryptic Tales from Past." *Viva*, 1 April 1973, p. 7.

"In Praise of Books Since 868." *Viva*, 8 April 1973, p. 2.

"Letters: A Window to the Past." *Viva*, 15 April 1973, p. 2.

"About the Is-ness of It All." *Viva*, 22 April 1973, p. 2.

"A Brief Look at Three Kids." *Viva*, 29 April 1973, p. 2.

"At Best—A Minor Tragedy?" *Viva*, 6 May 1973, p. 2.

"Finding a Need for Nature." *Viva*, 13 May 1973, p. 2.

"Some Positive Signs of Spring." *Viva*, 20 May 1973, p. 11.

"A Highly Seasoned Column." *Viva*, 27 May 1973, p. 2.

"An Opportunity to Speak Out." *Viva*, 3 June 1973, p. 2.

"Graduation Brings Memories." *Viva*, 10 June 1973, p. 2.

"Day Tripping over Alaska." *Viva*, 17 June 1973, p. 8.

"That Which Glistens." *Viva*, 24 June 1973, p. 2.

"Procession of Glad People." *Viva*, 1 July 1973, p. 2.

"In the Mind's Eye." *Viva*, 15 July 1973, p. 2.

"A Memory that Persists in the Blood." *Viva*, 22 July 1973, p. 9.

"A Garment of Brightness." *Viva*, 29 July 1973, p. 2.

"Sister of Charity and Desperado." *Viva*, 5 August 1973, p. 2.

"Thoughts on Life." *Viva*, 12 August 1973, p. 8.

"The Dark Priest of Taos." *Viva*, 19 August 1973, p. 19.

"A Dialogue on the Opera." *Viva*, 26 August 1973, p. 4.

"The Man Who Took Literature Seriously." *Viva*, 2 September 1973, p. 8.

"Unholy Sights." *Viva*, 9 September 1973, p. 7.

"The Toll Road." *Viva*, 16 September 1973, p. 2.

"One of the Wild, Beautiful Creatures." *Viva*, 23 September 1973, p. 13.

"A Delicate Matter This Equation." *Viva*, 30 September 1973, p. 12.

Untitled. *Viva*, 14 October 1973, p. 2.

"Caveat Emptor." *Viva*, 21 October 1973, p. 6.

"The Gourd Dancer." *Viva*, 4 November 1973, p. 6.

"The Miraculous Comes So Close." *Viva*, 11 November 1973, p. 6.

"Thoughts on Jemez and Billy the Kid." *Viva*, 18 November 1973, p. 2.

"How It Began." *Viva*, 25 November 1973, p. 2.

"Billy Offers a Kindness to an Old Man at Glorietta." *Viva*, 9 December 1973, p. 2.

WORKS ABOUT N. SCOTT MOMADAY

Unpublished Material

Nabokov, Peter. Untitled biographical essay based on an interview with N. Scott Momaday, 1969. Original typescript in possession of Matthias Schubnell.

Published Works

CRITICAL STUDIES

Barry, Nora Baker. "The Bear's Folk Tale in *When the Legends Die* and *House Made of Dawn*." *Western American Literature* 12 (1978): 275–87.

Beidler, Peter G. "Animals and Human Development in the Contemporary American Indian Novel." *Western American Literature* 14 (1979): 133–48.

Berner, Robert L. "N. Scott Momaday: Beyond Rainy Mountain." *American Indian Culture and Research Journal* 3, no. 1 (1979): 57–67.

Billingsley, R. G. "*House Made of Dawn*: Momaday's Treatise on the Word." *Southwestern American Literature* 5 (1975): 81–87.

Bloodworth William. "Neihardt, Momaday, and the Art of Indian Autobiography." In *Where the West Begins*, pp. 152–60. Ed. Arthur R. Huseboe and William Geyer. Sioux Falls, Iowa: Center for Western Studies Press, 1978.

Brumble III, H. David. "Anthropologists, Novelists and Indian Sacred Material." *Canadian Review of American Studies* 1, no. 1 (1980): 31–48.

Buller, Galen. "New Interpretations of Native American Literature: A Survival Technique." *American Indian Culture and Research Journal* 4, nos. 1, 2 (1980): 165–77.

Cook, Elisabeth. "Propulsives in Native American Literature." *College Composition and Communication* 24 (1973): 271–74.

Davis, Jack L. "The Whorf Hypothesis and Native American Literature." *South Dakota Review* 14, no. 2 (1976): 59–72.

Dickinson-Brown, Roger. "The Art and Importance of N. Scott Momaday." *Southern Review* n.s. 14 (1978): 31–45.

Dillingham, Peter. "The Literature of the American Indian." *English Journal* 62 (1973): 37–41.

Doudoroff, Michael. "N. Scott Momaday y la novela indigenista en inglés." *Texto Crítico* 5, no. 15 (1979): 180–85.

Espey, David B. "Endings in Contemporary American Indian Fiction." *Western American Literature* 13 (1978): 133–39.

Evers, Lawrence J. "Words and Place: A Reading of *House Made of Dawn*." *Western American Literature* 11 (1977): 297–320.

Fields, Kenneth. "More Than Language Means: Review of N. Scott Momaday's *The Way to Rainy Mountain*." *Southern Review* n.s. 6 (1979): 196–204.

Garrett, Roland. "The Notion of Language in Some Kiowa Folk Tales." *Indian Historian* 5, no. 2 (1972): 32–37, 40.

Haslam, Gerald. "American Indians: Poets of the Cosmos." *Western American Literature* 5 (1970): 15–29.

Hogan, Linda. "Who Puts Together." *Denver Quarterly* 14, no. 4 (1980): 103–11.

Hylton, Marion Willard. "On the Trail of Pollen: Momaday's *House Made of Dawn*." *Critique* 14, no. 2 (1972): 60–69.

Kerr, Baine. "The Novel as Sacred Text: N. Scott Momaday's Mythmaking Ethic." *Southwest Review* 63, no. 2 (1978): 172–79.

Larson, Charles R. "Rejection: The Reluctant Return." In his *American Indian Fiction*, pp. 78–96. Albuquerque: University of New Mexico Press, 1978.

Lattin, Vernon E. "The Quest for Mythic Vision in Contemporary Native American and Chicano Fiction." *American Literature* 50 (1979): 625–40.

Lincoln, Kenneth. "Word Senders: Black Elk and N. Scott Momaday," in his *Native American Renaissance*, pp. 82–121. Berkeley: University of California Press, 1983.

McAllister, Harold S. "Be a Man, Be a Woman: Androgyny in *House Made of Dawn*." *American Indian Quarterly* 12 (1975): 14–22.

———. "Incarnate Grace and the Path of Salvation in *House Made of Dawn*." *South Dakota Review*, 12, no. 4 (1974): 115–25.

McAllister, Mick. "The Color of Meat, the Color of Bone." *Denver Quarterly* 14, no. 4 (1980): 10–18.

———. "The Topology of Remembrance in *The Way to Rainy Mountain*." *Denver Quarterly* 12, no. 4 (1978): 19–31.

McDonald, Walter R. "The Redemption Novel: Suffering and Hope in *The Assistant* and *House Made of Dawn*." *Proceedings of the Conference of College Teachers of English at Texas* 41: 55–61.

Mason, Kenneth C. "Beautyway: The Poetry of N. Scott Momaday."
South Dakota Review 18, no. 2 (1980): 61–83.

Nicholas, Charles A. "*The Way to Rainy Mountain*: N. Scott Momaday's
Hard Journey Back." *South Dakota Review* 13, no. 4 (1975): 149–58.

Oleson, Carole. "The Remembered Earth: Momaday's *House Made of
Dawn*." *South Dakota Review* 11, no. 1 (1973): 59–78.

Prampolini, Gaetano. "On N. Scott Momaday's *House Made of Dawn*."
Dismisura 9, nos. 39–50 (1980): 58–75.

Robinson, David E. "Angles of Vision in N. Scott Momaday's *House
Made of Dawn*." *Selected Proceedings of the Third Annual Conference on
Minority Studies*, pp. 129–41. Ed. George E. Carter and James R.
Parker. LaCrosse, Wis.: Institute for Minority Studies, 1976.

Roemer, Kenneth M. "Bear and Elk: The Nature(s) of Contemporary
Indian Poetry." *Journal of Ethnic Studies* 5, no. 2 (1977): 69–79.

———. "Survey Courses, Indian Literature, and *The Way to Rainy
Mountain*." *College English* 37 (1976): 619–24.

Sanders, Thomas E., and W. W. Peek, eds. "Anguish, Angry, Articulate: Current Voices in Poetry, Prose, and Protest." In their *Literature
of the American Indian*, pp. 445–51. Beverly Hills, Calif.: Glencoe
Press, 1973.

Schneider, Jack W. "The New Indian: Alienation and the Rise of the
Indian Novel." *South Dakota Review* 17, no. 4 (1979): 67–76.

Smith, Marie. "Rainy Mountain, Legends, and Students." *Arizona English Bulletin* 13 (April 1971): 41–44.

Strelke, Barbara. "N. Scott Momaday: Racial Memory and Individual
Imagination." In *Literature of the American Indians*, pp. 348–57. Ed.
Abraham Chapman. New York: Meridian, 1975.

Trimble, Martha Scott. *N. Scott Momaday*. Boise, Idaho: Boise State
College Western Writers Series, 1973.

Trimmer, Joseph F. "Native Americans and the American Mix: N. Scott
Momaday's *House Made of Dawn*." *Indiana Social Studies Quarterly* 28,
no. 2 (1975): 75–91.

Velie, Alan R. "Cain and Abel in N. Scott Momaday's *House Made of
Dawn*." *Journal of the West* 17 (April 1978): 55–62.

———. "*House Made of Dawn*: Nobody's Protest Novel." In his *Four
American Indian Literary Masters*, pp. 51–64. Norman, Okla.: University of Oklahoma Press, 1982.

———. "Post-Symbolism and Prose Poems: Momaday's Poetry." In his
Four American Indian Literary Masters, pp. 11–31. Norman, Okla:
University of Oklahoma Press, 1982.

———. "The Search for Identity: N. Scott Momaday's Autobiographical Works." In his *Four American Indian Literary Masters*, pp. 11–31. Norman, Okla.: University of Oklahoma Press, 1982.

Waniek, Marylin R. "The Power of Language in N. Scott Momaday's *House Made of Dawn*." *Minority Voices* 4, no. 1 (1982): 23–29.

Watkins, Floyd C. "Culture vs. Anonymity in *House Made of Dawn*." In his *Time and Place*, pp. 131–71. Athens: University of Georgia Press, 1977.

Winters, Yvor. *Forms of Discovery: Critical and Historical Essays on the Forms of the Short Poem in English*, pp. 289–97. Chicago: Alan Swallow, 1967.

Young, Jim. "Tradition and the Experimental." *Compass* 1 (1977): 99–107.

Zachrau, Thekla. "N. Scott Momaday: Towards an Indian Identity." *American Indian Culture and Research Journal* 3, no. 1 (1979): 39–56.

DISSERTATIONS AND THESES

Kousaleos, Peter G. "A Study of Language, Structure, and Symbolism in Jean Toomer's *Cane* and N. Scott Momaday's *House Made of Dawn*." Ph.D. Diss., Ohio University, 1973.

Ludovici, Paula. "The Struggle for an Ending: Ritual and Plot in Recent American Indian Literature." Ph.D. diss., American University, 1979.

Nelson, Margaret Faye. "Ethnic Identity in the Prose Works of N. Scott Momaday." Ph.D. diss., Oklahoma State University, 1979.

SeeKamp, Warren B. "Momaday's Pueblo Indian Triad: Heritage, the Word, and Imagination in *House Made of Dawn*." Master's thesis, University of Louisville, 1979.

Smith, Rose Marie. "A Critical Study of the Literature of N. Scott Momaday as Intercultural Communication." Ph.D. diss., University of Southern California, 1975.

Wilson, Norma Jean Clark. "The Spirit of Place in Contemporary American Indian Literature." Ph.D. diss., University of Oklahoma, 1978.

Woodard, Charles Lowell. "The Concept of the Creative Word in the Writings of N. Scott Momaday." Ph.D. diss., University of Oklahoma, 1975.

NEWSPAPER ARTICLES

"American Indian Literature Major Will Be Established This Fall." *Journal of Educational Change* 2, no. 7 (1971): 1–2.

Anderson, Terry. "Momaday's 'Names' Told through Childhood's Impressionistic Eyes." *Denver Post*, 16 January 1977, p. 23.

Baumann, Melissa. "Native American Storyteller and Poet: English Professor Shares His Experience." *Stanford Daily*, 14 January 1975, p. 3.

"Five Stanford Authors Converse." *Stanford Alumni Almanac* 10, no. 1 (1971): 2–6.

"Kiowa History Lives Again on Commemorative Occasion." *Kiowa County Star Review*, 25 October 1973, pp. 1, 10.

Leonard, John. "The Pulitzer Prizes: Fail-Safe Again." *New York Times Book Review*, 14 May 1972, p. 47.

Love, Marion F. "N. Scott Momaday." *Santa Féan*, October 1980, pp. 36–38.

MacPherson, Myra. "American Indian, Pulitzer Prize Winner, Tells of Violent Plight." *Denver Post*, 8 December 1969, p. 12.

"Pulitzer Novelist—Tribe Exploitation Decried by Kiowa." *Denver Post*, 14 January 1971, p. 21.

"Pulitzer Prize Winning Indian Addresses Grads." *Daily Times–News*, Mount Pleasant, Mich., 8 June 1970, p. 1.

Raymond, Henry. "Award Surprises an Indian Author." *New York Times*, 6 May 1969, p. 35.

————. "A Novelist Fights for His People's Lore." *New York Times*, 26 July 1969, p. 22.

Rhodes, J. L. "Momaday Gives Dramatic Reading." *State Hornet*, 17 March 1975, p. 2.

Rodebaugh, Dale. "Indians Keep Identity in Cultural Migration." *San José News*, 10 March 1976.

Sekaquaptewa, Ken. "N. Scott Momaday Visits B.Y.U." *Eagle's Eye*, Brigham Young University, February 1975, pp. 1–2.

Soceanu, Marion. "Momaday: magischer Geschichtenerzähler." *Mittelbayrische Zeitung*, 28 June 1980, p. 3.

Tucker, Chris. "Scott Momaday, Writing Little But Writing Well." *Dallas Morning News*, 8 November 1981, p. 5G.

"Unique Exhibit of Family Talent." *Four Winds*, no. 3 (1980): 42.

REVIEWS

Reviews of *Angle of Geese and Other Poems*

Bromwich, David. *New York Times Book Review*, 16 June 1974, pp. 6–7.

Choice, July 1974, p. 755.

Finlay, John. "N. Scott Momaday's *Angle of Geese.*" *Southern Review* n.s. 11 (1975): 658–61.

Gioia, Dana. "Momaday: A Cultural Vision." *Stanford Daily*, 30 April 1976, p. 5.

New Republic, 6 April 1974, p. 33.

Ramsey, Paul. "Some American Poetry of 1974: Three Traditions." *Sewanee Review* 83 (1975): 348–56.

"Reserves of Energy." *Times (London)* Literary Supplement, 30 August 1974, p. 932.

Shaw, Robert B. "Godine's Chapbooks." *Poetry* 76 (1975): 356.

Swann, Brian. "Reviewer's Corner." *Library Journal*, 1 June 1974, p. 1551.

Reviews of *The Complete Poems of Frederick Goddard Tuckerman*

American Literature, 37 (1965): 357.

Choice, November 1965, p. 584.

Eberhart, R. "Review." *New York Times Book Review*, 20 June 1965, p. 5.

Gullans, Charles. "Tuckerman's Poems Edited by Momaday." *Santa Barbara News Press*, 4 April 1965, p. 18A.

Howe, J. "Review." *New York Times Review of Books*, 25 March 1965, p. 17.

Kenny, Herbert A. "Poet Tuckerman Likely to Eclipse Cleric Uncle." *Boston Sunday Globe*, 7 March 1965, p. 30A.

"Notes on Current Books." *Virginia Quarterly* 41 (1965): lxxxv.

Times (London) Literary Supplement, 2 December 1965, p. 1102.

Reviews of *The Gourd Dancer*

Choice, November 1976, p. 1138.

Daum, Timothy. *Library Journal*, November 1976, p. 2378.

Hobson, Geary. *New Mexico Humanities Review* 2, no. 2 (1979): 59–60.

Ramsey, Paul. "Faith and Form: Some American Poetry of 1976." *Sewanee Review* 85 (1977): 532–40.

Sisco, Ellen. *School Library Journal* 23 (1976): 125.

Wiegner, Kathleen. "Books: Poetry as Ritual." *American Poetry Review* 6, no. 1 (1977): 46.

Reviews of *House Made of Dawn*

Adams, P. L. "Short Reviews: Books." *Atlantic Monthly*, July 1968, p. 106.

Amerindian 17, no. 1 (1968): 8.

Bennett, John Z. *Western American Literature* 5 (1970): 69.

Blackburn, Sara. "Book Marks." *Nation*, 5 August 1968, p. 91.

Borg, Mary. "Victims." *New Statesman*, 16 May 1969, p. 696.

Cooley, Margaret. "Alien in a Mass Culture." *Library Journal*, June 1968, p. 2270.

Dollen, Charles. *Best Sellers*, June 1968, p. 131.

Educational Leadership 31 (1974): 593.

"Exhibition." *Times (London) Literary Supplement*, 28 May 1969, p. 549.

Fleischer, Leonore. "Paperbacks: Fiction." *Publisher's Weekly*, 22 September 1969, p. 86.

Ford, Richard J. "The Indian in America's Closet." *Natural History* 79 (1970): 78–84.

"Forecasts." *Publisher's Weekly*, 1 April 1968, p. 34.

Graham, Kenneth. "Wind and Shadow." *Listener* 15 May 1969, p. 686.

Halio, Jay L. "Fantasy and Fiction." *Southern Review* n.s. 7 (1971): 635–47.

Henry, Jeanette. "Momaday's Novel Wins Pulitzer Award." *Indian Historian* 2, no. 2 (1969): 38.

Hylton, Marion Willard. "On the Trail of Pollen: Momaday's *House Made of Dawn*." *Critique* 14, no. 2 (1972): 60–69.

Illick, Joseph E. "Looking Westward." *American West*, November 1969, pp. 50–52.

New York Times Book Review, 9 August 1970, p. 27.

Observer, 25 May 1969, p. 26.

Smith, Wiliam James. *Commonweal*, 10 September 1968, p.636.

Sprague, Marshall. "Anglos and Indians." *New York Times Book Review*, 9 June 1968, p. 5.

Stevenson, Joan W. *Library Journal*, June 1968, p. 2522.

Trout, Lawana. "Paperbacks in the Classroom." *English Journal* 63 (1974): 93.

Tube, Henry. "New Novels: Freud's Boy." *Spectator*, 23 May 1969, pp. 687–88.

Village Voice, 29 January 1970, p. 8.

Woodard, Charles L. "Momaday's *House Made of Dawn*." *Explicator* 36, no. 2 (1978): 27–28.

Reviews of *The Names: A Memoir*

Abbey, Edward. "Memories of an Indian Childhood." *Harper's*, February 1977, pp. 34–35.

Adams, P. L. *Atlantic Monthly*, January 1977, p. 93.

Anderson, Terry. "Momaday's 'Names' Told through Childhood's Impressionistic Eyes." *Denver Post*, 16 January 1977, p. 23.

Choice, May 1977, p. 376.

Harper, Josie Morris. "My Name Is Tsoai-talee." *Detroit Free Press*, 20 March 1977, p. 5C.

Marken, Jack W. "Critic Calls Momaday's New Book Autobiographical." *South Dakota State University Entertainment Collegian*, 18 January 1978, p. 7.

McAllister, Mick. "The Names." *Southern Review* n.s. 14 (1978): 387–89.

McPherson, Judith. *Library Journal*, January 1977, p. 194.

Miles, Elton. *Western American Literature* 12 (1977): 86–87.

Natural History 86 (1977): 99.

Nicholls, Richard. *Best Sellers*, April 1977, p. 13.

Stegner, Wallace. *New York Times Review of Books*, 6 March 1977, pp. 6–7.

Reviews of *The Way to Rainy Mountain*

Adams, Phoebe L. "Short Reviews: Books." *Atlantic Monthly*, June 1969, p. 117.

"Books." *Amerindian* 18, no. 1 (1969): 8.

"Briefly Noted." *New Yorker*, 17 May 1969, pp. 150–52.

Dickey, Roland F. *Western Humanities Review* 24 (1970): 290–91.

Egan, Ferral. "Books in Brief." *American West*, September 1969, pp. 83–84.

Fleischer, Leonore. "Forecasts: Paperbacks." *Publisher's Weekly*, 2 February 1970, p. 91.

Fontana, B. L. *Arizona Quarterly* 25 (1969): 377.

Gard, Wayne. "Review of Books: Southwestern Chronicle." *Southwest Review* 54, no. 3 (1969): vii.

"Humanities." *Choice*, September 1969, p. 798.

Lask, Thomas. *New York Times*, 16 May 1969, p. 45.

Milton, John R. "Minorities." *Saturday Review*, 21 June 1969, p. 51.

Renner, F. G., et al. "A Roundup of Western Reading by the Old Bookaroos." *Arizona and the West* 11 (1969): 309–10.

Smith, Marie. "Rainy Mountain, Legends, and Students." *Arizona English Bulletin* 13 (1971): 41–44.

Stevenson, Joan W. *Library Journal*, 15 September 1969, p. 3079.

Taylor, J. Golden. "The Editor's Essay Review." *Western American Literature* 5 (1970): 167.

Toelken, Barre. "The Native American: A Review Article." *Western Folklore* 29 (1970): 269–70.
Wynn, Dudley. *New Mexico Historical Review* 45, no. 1 (1970): 89–90.

SELECTED LIST OF BACKGROUND MATERIAL

Adair, John. "The Navajo and Pueblo Veteran: A Force for Culture Change." *American Indian* 4, no. 1 (1947): 5–11.
Adams, Ansel, and Mary Austin. *Taos Pueblo*. San Francisco: Grabhorn Press Book, 1930. Reprint. Boston: New York Geographic Society, 1977.
———, and Nancy Newhall. *This Is the American Earth*. San Francisco: Sierra Club, 1960.
Alexander, Hartley Burr. *The World's Rim: Great Mysteries of the North American Indians*. 1953. Reprint. Lincoln: University of Nebraska Press, 1967.
Allan, Paula Gunn. "The Sacred Hoop: A Contemporary Indian Perspective on American Indian Literature." In *Literature of the American Indians*, pp. 111–35. Ed. Abraham Chapman. New York: Meridian, 1975.
Astrov, Margot. *American Indian Prose and Poetry*. 1946. Reprint. New York: Capricorn Books, 1962.
Austin, Mary. *The American Rhythm: Studies and Reëxpressions of Amerindian Songs*. 1923. Reprint. New York: Cooper Square Publishers, 1970.
———. *The Land of Journey's Ending*. London: George Allen and Unwin, 1924.
Ballinger, Franchot. "The Responsible Center: Man and Nature in Pueblo and Navaho Ritual Songs and Prayers." *American Quarterly* 30 (1978): 90–107.
Barrett, S. M., ed. *Geronimo: His Own Story*. 1970. Reprint. London: Abacus, 1974.
Bathi, Tom. *Southwestern Indian Ceremonials*. Las Vegas, Nev.: KC Publications, 1975.
———. *Southwestern Indian Tribes*. Las Vegas, Nev.: KC Publications, 1972.
Berkhofer, Robert F., Jr. *The White Man's Indian: Images of the American Indian from Columbus to the Present*. New York: Vintage, 1978.
Bierhorst, John, ed. *In the Trail of the Wind: American Indian Poems and Ritual Orations*. New York: Farrar, Straus and Giroux, 1971.
Branch, E. Douglas. *The Hunting of the Buffalo*. New York: D. Appleton and Co., 1929.

Brooks, Cleanth. *William Faulkner: The Yoknapatawpha Country.* New Haven, Conn.: Yale University Press, 1963.

Burwell, Rose Marie. "A Catalogue of D. H. Lawrence's Reading from Early Childhood." *D. H. Lawrence Review* 3 (1970): 193–330.

Bushnell, John H. "From American Indian to Indian American: The Changing Identity of the Hupa." *American Anthropologist* 70 (1968): 1108–16.

Campbell, Joseph. *The Masks of God: Creative Mythology.* 1968. Reprint. Harmondsworth: Penguin Books, 1976.

Camus, Albert. *The Outsider.* Trans. Stuart Gilbert. Harmondsworth: Penguin Books, 1961.

Cassirer, Ernst. *Language and Myth.* Trans. Susanne K. Langer. New York: Dover Publications, 1953.

Clark, L. D. "The D. H. Lawrence Festival: Kiowa Ranch, New Mexico, September 30–October 4, 1970." *D. H. Lawrence Review* 4 (1971): 44–60.

Cooley, Thomas. *Educated Lives: The Rise of Modern Autobiography in America.* Columbus: Ohio State University Press, 1976.

Crane, Hart. *The Complete Poems and Collected Letters and Prose of Hart Crane.* Ed. Brom Weber. New York: Anchor Books, 1966.

Dabney, Lewis M. *The Indians of Yoknapatawpha: A Study in Literature and History.* Baton Rouge: Louisiana State University Press, 1974.

Day, A. Grove. *The Sky Clears: Poetry of the American Indians.* 1959. Reprint. Lincoln: University of Nebraska Press, 1964.

Deloria, Vine. *God Is Red.* New York: Delta Books, 1973.

Dickinson, Emily. *The Complete Poems of Emily Dickinson.* Ed. Thomas H. Johnson. Boston: Little, Brown, and Company, 1960.

Dinesen, Isak. *Ehrengard.* London: Michael Joseph, 1963.

———. *Out of Africa.* 1937. Reprint. New York: Vintage Books, 1972.

———. *Shadows on the Grass.* 1960. Reprint. New York: Vintage Books, 1974.

Doggett, Frank. "This Invented World: Stevens' 'Notes toward a Supreme Fiction.'" In *The Act of the Mind: Essays on the Poetry of Wallace Stevens*, pp. 13–28. Ed. Roy Harvey Pearce and J. Hillis Miller. Baltimore, Md.: Johns Hopkins University Press, 1965.

Driver, Harold E. *Indians of North America.* Chicago: University of Chicago Press, 1961.

Dunn, Dorothy. *American Indian Painting of the Southwest and Plains Area.* Albuquerque: University of New Mexico Press, 1968.

Dutton, Bertha P. *Indians of the American Southwest.* Englewood Cliffs, N.J.: Prentice-Hall, 1977.

Edwards, Jonathan. *Basic Writings*. Ed. Olga E. Winslow. New York: New American Library, 1966.

Eliade, Mircea. *Patterns in Comparative Religion*. Trans. Rosemary Sheed. London: Sheed and Ward, 1958.

————. *The Sacred and the Profane: The Nature of Religion*. New York: Harper and Row, 1961.

Emerson, Ralph Waldo. *Nature, The Conduct of Life and Other Essays*. London: Dent, 1970.

Erdoes, Richard. *The Raindance People*. New York: Alfred A. Knopf, 1976.

Erikson, Erik. "Childhood in Two American Indian Tribes." In his *Childhood and Society*, pp. 99–168. 1950. Reprint. Frogmore: Paladin Granada, 1977.

————. *Identity: Youth and Crisis*. London: Faber and Faber, 1968.

Faulkner, William. *As I Lay Dying*. 1930. Reprint. Harmondsworth: Penguin Books, 1975.

————. *Big Woods*. New York: Random House, 1955.

————. *Light in August*. 1932. Reprint. Harmondsworth: Penguin Books, 1980.

Fiedler, Leslie A. *The Return of the Vanishing American*. 1968. Reprint. London: Paladin, 1972.

Finnegan, Ruth. *Oral Poetry: Its Nature, Significance and Social Context*. Cambridge: Cambridge University Press, 1977.

Frank, Waldo. *The Re-Discovery of America: An Introduction to a Philosophy of American Life*. New York: Scribner's, 1929.

Frankfort, H., and H. A. Frankfort. "Myth and Reality." In *The Intellectual Adventure of Ancient Man: An Essay on Speculative Thought in the Ancient Near East*. Ed. H. Frankfort et al. Chicago: University of Chicago Press, 1946.

Frye, Northrop. *Anatomy of Criticism: Four Essays*. Princeton, N.J.: Princeton University Press, 1971.

Gridley, Marion E., ed. *Indians of Today*. 4th ed. N.p.: J.C.F.P., 1971.

Gwynn, Frederick L., and Joseph L. Blotner, eds. *Faulkner in the University*. Charlottesville: University of Virginia Press, 1959.

Harrington, John P. *Vocabulary of the Kiowa Language*. Bureau of American Ethnology Bulletin no. 84. Washington, D.C.: Smithsonian Institution, 1928.

Hart, James D. *Oxford Companion to American Literature*. New York: Oxford University Press, 1965.

Henderson, Alice Corbin. "Editorial Comment—Aboriginal Poetry, I." *Poetry: A Magazine of Verse* 9 (1917): 256.

————. "A Note on Primitive Poetry." *Poetry: A Magazine of Verse* 14 (1919): 330–35.

————. "Poetry of the North-American Indian." Review of *Path on the Rainbow: An Anthology of Songs and Chants from the Indians of North America*, by George Cronyn. *Poetry: A Magazine of Verse* 14 (1919): 41–42.

Hewett, Edgar L., and Bertha P. Dutton. *The Pueblo Indian World*. Albuquerque: University of New Mexico Press, 1945.

Hodge, Frederick Webb, ed. *Handbook of the American Indian*. 2 vols. 1907. Reprint. New York: Roland and Littlefield, 1965.

Hohenberg, John. *The Pulitzer Prizes*. New York: Columbia University Press, 1974.

Holmes, C. J. *Hokusai*. London: Unicorn Press, 1899.

Hunt, George. "Millie Durgan." *Chronicles of Oklahoma* 15 (1937): 480–82.

Hyman, Stanley E. *The Armed Vision: A Study in the Methods of Modern Literary Criticism*. New York: Alfred A. Knopf, 1948.

Joyce, James. *A Portrait of the Artist as a Young Man*. Harmondsworth: Penguin Books, 1960.

Jung, C. G. "Complications in American Psychology." "Mind and Earth." "The Role of the Unconscious." In his *Civilization in Transition*, pp. 502–24, 29–49, 3–28. Vol. 10 of *The Collected Works of C. G. Jung*. Trans. R. F. C. Hull. Ed. Herbert Read et al. London: Routledge and Kegan Paul, 1964.

Kluckhohn, Clyde. *Navaho Witchcraft*. 1944. Reprint. Boston: Beacon Press, 1967.

————, and Dorothea Leighton. *The Navaho*. 1946. Reprint. New York: Doubleday, 1962.

Lawler, James R. *Form and Meaning in Valéry's Le Cimetière Marin*. Melbourne: Melbourne University Press, 1959.

Lawrence, D. H. *The Complete Short Stories*. Vol. 2. Harmondsworth: Penguin Books, 1976.

————. "Introduction to Studies in Classic American Literature: I. The Spirit of Place." *English Review*, November 1918, pp. 319–31.

————. *Phoenix*. Ed. Edward D. McDonald. New York: Viking Press, 1972.

————. "À Propos Lady Chatterley's Lover." In his *Lady Chatterley's Lover*. Ed. Ronald Friedland. New York: Bantam Books, 1968.

————. *The Symbolic Meaning: The Uncollected Versions of Studies in Classic American Literature*. Ed. Armin Arnold. Frontwell: Centaur Press, 1962.

————. *St. Mawr and The Man Who Died.* New York: Vintage Books, n.d.

Levin, David. "Yvor Winters at Stanford." *Virginia Quarterly Review* 54 (1978): 455–73.

Lyon, Thomas J. *John Muir.* Boise, Idaho: Boise State College Western Writers Series, 1972.

Marriott, Alice. *Saynday's People: The Kiowa Indians and the Stories They Told.* Lincoln: University of Nebraska Press, 1963.

————. *The Ten Grandmothers.* Norman: University of Oklahoma Press, 1945.

Martin, Calvin. *Keepers of the Game: Indian-Animal Relationships and the Fur Trade.* Berkeley: University of California Press, 1978.

Mayhall, Mildred P. *The Kiowas.* 2d ed. Norman: University of Oklahoma Press, 1971.

Melville, Herman. *Billy Budd, Sailor, and Other Stories.* Harmondsworth: Penguin Books, 1970.

Mitchell, Lee Clark. *Witness to a Vanishing America: The Nineteenth-Century Response.* Princeton, N.J.: Princeton University Press, 1981.

Mitgang, Herbert. "Ralph Ellison." *International Herald Tribune*, 12 March 1982, p. 16.

Mooney, James. *Calendar History of the Kiowa Indians.* 1898. Reprint. Washington, D.C.: Smithsonian Institution Press, 1979.

————. *The Ghost Dance Religion and the Sioux Outbreak of 1890.* 1896. Reprint. Chicago: University of Chicago Press, 1965.

Moore, Harry T., ed. *The Collected Letters of D. H. Lawrence.* 2 vols. London: Heinemann, 1962.

Muench, David. "Light is my Constant Companion and Tool. . . ." *Arizona Highways*, August 1981, p. 23.

Muir, John. *The Mountains of California.* London: T. Fisher Unwin, 1894.

————. *My First Summer in the Sierra.* London: Constable, 1911.

Nabokov, Vladimir. *Speak Memory: An Autobiography Revisited.* London: Weidenfels and Nicholson, 1967.

Nash, Roderick. *Wilderness and the American Mind.* Rev. Ed. New Haven, Conn.: Yale University Press, 1973.

Neihardt, John G. *Black Elk Speaks.* 1932. Reprint. New York: Pocket Books, 1972.

Nelson, Bobby Jack. *The Last Station.* Boston: Houghton Mifflin, 1972.

Niatum, Duane. "On Stereotype." *Parnassus* 7, no. 1 (1978): 160–66.

Noguchi, Yone. *Hokusai.* London: Elkin Mathews, 1925.

Northrop, F. S. C. "Man's Relation to the Earth in Its Bearing on His

Aesthetic, Ethical, and Legal Values." In *Man's Role in Changing the Face of the Earth*, pp. 1052–67. Ed. William L. Thomas, Jr. Chicago: University of Chicago Press, 1956.

Nye, Wilbur Sturtevant. *Bad Medicine and Good: Tales of the Kiowas*. Norman: University of Oklahoma Press, 1962.

———. *Carbine and Lance: The Story of Old Fort Sill*. 3d ed. Norman: University of Oklahoma Press, 1969.

O'Keeffe, Georgia. *Georgia O'Keeffe*. Harmondsworth: Penguin Books, 1976.

O'Keeffe, Georgia. *Georgia O'Keeffe: A Portrait by Alfred Stieglitz*. New York: Viking Press, 1979.

Olney, James. "Some Versions of Memory / Some Versions of Bios: The Ontology of Autobiography." In *Autobiography: Essays Theoretical and Critical*, pp. 237–67. Ed. James Olney. Princeton, N.J.: Princeton University Press, 1980.

Ong, Walter J. *The Presence of the Word: Some Prolegomena for Cultural and Religious History*. 1967. Reprint. New York: Simon and Schuster, 1970.

Ortiz, Alfonso. "Ritual Drama and the Pueblo World View." In *New Perspectives on the Pueblos*, pp. 135–61. Ed. Alfonso Ortiz. Albuquerque: University of New Mexico Press, 1972.

———. *The Tewa World: Space, Time, Being, and Becoming in a Pueblo Society*. Chicago: University of Chicago Press, 1969.

———. "A Unique Legacy." *Princeton University Library Chronicle* 30 (1969): 147–57.

Parsons, Elsie Clews. *The Pueblo of Jemez*. New Haven, Conn.: Yale University Press, 1925.

Pearce, Roy Harvey. *Savagism and Civilization: A Study of the American Mind*. Baltimore, Md.: Johns Hopkins University Press, 1965.

Proust, Marcel. *Time Regained*. Trans. Andreas Mayor. London: Chatto and Windus, 1972.

Redfield, Robert. *The Primitive World and Its Transformation*. Ithaca, N.Y.: Cornell University Press, 1953.

———. "The Primitive World View." *Proceedings of the American Philosophical Society* 96, no. 1 (1952): 30–36.

Reichard, Gladys A. *Navajo Religion: A Study in Symbolism*. 2d ed. 1950. Reprint. Princeton, N.J.: Princeton University Press, 1974.

Revard, Carter. "History, Myth, and Identity among Osage and Other People." *Denver Quarterly* 14, no. 4 (1980): 84–97.

Sandberg, Carl. "Editorial Comment—Aboriginal Poetry, II." *Poetry: A Magazine of Verse* 9 (1917), 255.

Sando, Joe S. "Jemez Pueblo." In *Southwest*, pp. 418–29. Ed. Alfonso

Ortiz. Vol. 9 of *Handbook of North American Indians*. Ed. W. C. Sturtevant. Washington: Smithsonian Institution, 1979.

Sawyer, T. E. "Assimilation Versus Self-Identity: A Modern Native American Perspective." In *Contemporary Native American Address*, pp. 197–207. Ed. John R. Maestas. Provo, Utah: Brigham Young University Publications, 1976.

Sayre, Robert. "Vision and Experience in *Black Elk Speaks*." *College English* 32 (1971): 509–35.

Sheehan, Bernard. *Savagism and Civility: Indians and Englishmen in Colonial Virginia*. Cambridge: Cambridge University Press, 1980.

Skinner, John. "On Indian Poetry and Religion." *Little Square Review*, nos. 5–6 (1968): 10–11.

Spencer, Robert F., et al. *The Native Americans*. New York: Harper and Row, 1977.

Spengler, Oswald. *The Decline of the West*. 2 vols. London: George Allen and Unwin, 1980.

Stegner, Wallace. *The Sound of Mountain Water*. New York: Doubleday, 1969.

———, and Richard Scowcroft, eds. *Twenty Years of Stanford Short Stories*. Stanford, Calif.: Stanford University Press, 1966.

Stevens, Holly, ed. *The Letters of Wallace Stevens*. London: Faber and Faber, 1966.

Stevens, Wallace. *The Collected Poems of Wallace Stevens*. London: Faber and Faber, 1945.

———. *The Necessary Angel: Essays on Reality and the Imagination*. London: Faber and Faber, 1960.

Stone, Albert E. "Autobiography and American Culture." *American Studies: An International Newsletter* 11, no. 2 (1972): 22–36.

Strange, Edward F. *Hokusai: The Old Man Mad with Painting*. London: Siecle, Hill and Co., 1906.

Tedlock, Dennis. "Toward a Restoration of the Word in the Modern World." *Alcheringa* 2, no. 2 (1976): 120–32.

Thoreau, Henry David. *Excursions and Poems*. Vol. 5 of *The Writings of Henry David Thoreau*. 1906. Reprint. New York: AMS Press, 1968.

———. *A Week on the Concord and Merrimack Rivers*. New York: Crowell, 1966.

Toelken, Barre. "Seeing with a Native Eye: How Many Sheep Will It Hold?" In *Seeing with a Native Eye: Essays on Native American Religion*, pp. 9–24. Ed. Walter Holden Capps. New York: Harper and Row, 1976.

Tuan, Yi-Fu. "Geopiety: A Theme in Man's Attachment to Nature and to Place." In *Geographies of the Mind: Essays in Historical Geosophy*. Ed.

D. Lowenthal and Martyn J. Bowden. New York: Oxford University Press, 1976, pp. 11–39.

―――. "Place: An Existential Perspective." *Geographic Review* 65, no. 2 (1975): 151–65.

Udall, Stewart. *The Quiet Crisis.* New York: Holt, Rinehart and Winston, 1963.

Valéry, Paul. *Paul Valéry: An Anthology.* Ed. James R. Lawler. London: Routledge and Kegan Paul, 1977.

Vansina, Jan. *Oral Tradition: A Study in Historical Methodology.* 1961. Reprint. Harmondsworth: Penguin Books, 1973.

Vogt, Evon Z. "Between Two Worlds: Case Study of a Navajo Veteran." *American Indian* 5, no. 1 (1949): 13–21.

Washburn, Wilcombe E. *The Assault on Indian Tribalism: The General Allotment Law (Dawes Act) of 1887.* Philadelphia: J. B. Lippincott, 1975.

Waters, Frank. *The Man Who Killed the Deer.* 1941. Reprint. New York: Pocket Books, 1975.

Watkins, Floyd C. *In Time and Place.* Athens: University of Georgia Press, 1977.

Wax, Murray L. *Indian Americans: Unity and Diversity.* Englewood Cliffs, N.J.: Prentice-Hall, 1971.

Wax, Rosalie, and Murray L. Wax. "The Magical World View." *Journal of the Scientific Study of Religion* 1, no. 2 (1962): 179–88.

Weaver, Thomas, and Ruth H. Gartell. "The Urban Indian: Man of Two Worlds." In *Indians of Arizona: A Contemporary Perspective*, pp. 72–96. Ed. Thomas Weaver. Tucson: University of Arizona Press, 1974.

Welch, James. "Tradition and Indian Poetry." *South Dakota Review* 11, no. 3 (1973): 39–40.

Wellek, René, and Austin Warren. *Theory of Literature.* New York: Harcourt, 1956.

White, Leslie A. "The World of the Keresan Pueblo Indians." In *Primitive Views of the World*, pp. 83–94. Ed. Stanley Diamond. New York: Columbia University Press, 1964.

White, Lynn, Jr. "The Historical Roots of Our Ecologic Crisis." *Science* 155 (1967): 1203–1207.

Williams, William Carlos. *In the American Grain.* 1925. Reprint. New York: New Directions, 1956.

Wilson, Eddie W. "The Moon and the American Indian." *Western Folklore* 24, no. 2 (1965): 87–100.

Wilson, Edmund. *Axel's Castle.* New York: Scribner's, 1948.

Winters, Yvor. *The Collected Poems of Yvor Winters*. Manchester: Carcanet New Press, 1978.

———. *Forms of Discovery: Critical and Historical Essays on the Forms of the Short Poem in English*. Chicago: Alan Swallow, 1967.

———. "Forms of Discovery: A Preliminary Statement." *Southern Review* n.s. 3 (1967): 1–12.

———. *The Function of Criticism*. London: Routledge and Kegan Paul, 1962.

———. *In Defence of Reason*. London: Routledge and Kegan Paul, 1960.

———. "The Indian in English." In *Yvor Winters: Uncollected Essays and Reviews*, pp. 35–43. Ed. Francis Murphy. 1973. Reprint. London: Allen Lane, 1974.

———. Letter to editors. *Reporter*, 23 February 1976, p. 8.

———. "Open Letter to the Editor of *This Quarterly*." In *Yvor Winters: Uncollected Essays and Reviews*, pp. 32–34. Ed. Francis Murphy. 1973. Reprint. London: Allen Lane, 1974.

———. "Poetic Styles, Old and New." In *Four Poets on Poetry*. Ed. Don Cameron Allen. Baltimore, Md.: Johns Hopkins University Press, 1959.

Witherspoon, Gary. *Language and Art in the Navajo Universe*. Ann Arbor: University of Michigan Press, 1970.

Witt, Shirley H. "Listen to His Many Voices: An Introduction to the Literature of the American Indian." In *The Way: An Anthology of American Indian Literature*, pp. xvii–xxix. Ed. Shirley H. Witt and Stan Steiner. New York: Vintage Books, 1972.

Index